RICHARD FINDLATER

THE PLAYER QUEENS

Taplinger Publishing Company | New York

First published in the United States in 1977 by
TAPLINGER PUBLISHING CO., INC.
New York, New York

All rights reserved. Printed in the U.S.A.
Copyright © 1976 by Richard Findlater

Library of Congress Catalog Number 76-53912
ISBN 0-8008-6324-0

CONTENTS

ILLUSTRATIONS

The author and publisher are grateful to the following sources for their kind permission to reproduce the illustrations: Dulwich College Picture Gallery for illustration number 7; Mander and Mitchenson, pictures 2, 4, 5, 9, 10, 11, 12, 13; Mansell Collection for 3 and 8; National Portrait Gallery for illustration 1; Royal Shakespeare Theatre Library for illustration 14.

INTRODUCTION

Women have served all these centuries as looking-glasses possessing the magic and delicious power of reflecting the figure of men at twice its natural size.

Virginia Woolf (1929)

Of all the arts that mankind has invented to clothe its concept of reality and to ornament its leisure moments, none is more suited to the genius of the female of the species than that of the theatre.

Rosamond Gilder (1931)

FOR NEARLY TWO THOUSAND YEARS until little more than a century ago two occupations – and two alone – were open to most Western women in search of an independent living outside the family circle, urban or agrarian serfdom, the convent or domestic service. They could try sex business or (with less certainty) show business. Or both. For both they needed no more than their bodies and their personalities as working capital. Their professional qualifications were the ability to please by making love, making money, making believe, or simply making whoopee. To the timeless tasks of entertaining, comforting, exciting, enlightening and, (with luck) exploiting men, many brought beauty, some brought artistry and a few brought genius.

The early history of Western women in the theatrical arts is necessarily sparse and sketchy, because until the Renaissance they were excluded from the performance of drama and therefore from the annals of the writing classes. Women performers do not emerge clearly from the records until around 300 BC in Roman mimes and pantomimes, and then they are seen as social pariahs, below the levol of the leading courtesans. Viewed by literary historians and moralists as crude and often porno- graphic farcical sketches, these entertainments seemed beyond the pale, in the lower depths of show business. Yet several women became rich and famous through appearing in the mimes; and others emerged as authors, directors and managers, leading their own troupes.

After the collapse of Rome women seem to have remained in the theatrical underground, largely invisible to posterity, until the Renaissance. They performed as singers, dancers, jugglers, comics, acrobats; at fairs, weddings and on the fringes of public occasions; in the castle hall, the market place, the inn yard and at the crossroads, travelling round the country with their hus- bands, lovers, fathers and brothers, troupes of all-rounders precariously selling the skills of what was later dubbed 'variety' and 'music hall'. To show business catering for the lower orders and lower appetites, they seem to have been indispensable. But they were allowed no part in the liturgical beginnings of the European drama: Eve, Mary Magdalene, the Virgin Mother and other feminine roles were played by male priests and choristers. 'Women were not allowed to speak in church even for the praiseworthy purposes of exhortation and prayer; how much less would they be tolerated as performers in its sacred mysteries.'[1] As late as the seventeenth century a woman who dared to sit in the same church pew as her husband was officially liable to penalties in the ecclesiastical courts.[2] Yet opposition to women performers was not confined to the Christian world. In Japan actresses were outlawed from 1630 until modern times, because of the moral danger they were believed to embody. In China, they were officially classed as prostitutes; and in the eighteenth century they were banned by the emperor Ch'ien Lung, a veto which endured until the first Republic sixty years ago. In the West the first actresses did not appear until some 420 years ago; and in one part of Italy – the Papal States – such anomalies were not officially sanctioned until Napoleonic times.

The arts and crafts of the singer, dancer and actress were, in fact, linked for centuries with those of the courtesan and prostitute in social function, sexist myth, religious superstition and, to some degree, through economic necessity. The history of the modern stage is, in part, a history of the attempts to dissolve those links. Yet in the more servile past many women entertainers at the foot of the ladder had to demonstrate sexual as well as theatrical skills in order to survive: even today such aptitudes, it is said, prove helpful. Those who proferred to contain their virtue within near-monogamous limits and could afford to do so were generally damned by the unco' guid as being no better than their frailer sisters, equally dangerous enemies in the showplaces of Satan, public emblems of a necessary evil. Among men the idea persisted, as it still does in many parts of the unwesternized world, that for a woman 'to show herself was to sell herself – or, at least, to put herself up for sale'.[3] In the fantasies of the male predator all actresses were cast as fair game well into the twentieth century. To many women, too, the actress seemed almost as much a traitor to their gender as the harlot, scapegoats on whom they projected their fear and envy of sex without shame. Even in a reputedly permissive society the very word 'actress' appears, from newspaper headlines, to retain a lingering redolence of sin.

Only a tiny handful of women achieved substantial success (on the male scale) in acquiring money, power and independence through the theatrical arts. In every generation (including this one) many female performers have been as overworked and underpaid as the majority of their sex. All have been governed by the rules, appetites and expectations of a male-controlled society, in which they served primarily as 'sex-objects' – objects, that is, of resentment as well as idolatry and lust. Many were (and are) treated not as artists but as things: at best, playthings. Almost without exception the best parts were written by men and many of the greatest were written *for* men (and boys), in theatres from which women performers were excluded. Generally, men have written the plays, produced and cast them, written and conducted the music, designed the scenery, built and run the theatres, and managed the actresses. The range of stage lives open to actresses has been, like the off-stage opportunities for women, far narrower than the acting repertoire of men.

Nevertheless, in Western history since the Romans it has only been in the theatre (outside a royal palace or a star courtesan's boudoir) that an exceptional woman could, until recently, hope to earn for herself as much money as an unexceptional man; to run a business as an employer of men; to enjoy through her work a measure of social and sexual independence of men. Simone de Beauvoir, who counts this history of relative freedom as no more than three centuries, wrote in *The Second Sex* that actresses, dancers and singers

have been almost the only women to maintain a concrete independence in the midst of society. Like courtesans, they spend a great deal of their time in the company of men; but making their own lives and finding the meaning of their lives in their work, they escape the yoke of men. Their great advantage is that their professional success – like that of men – contributes to their sexual valuation; in their self-realization ... they find self-fulfilment as women.[4]

Even before the era of the Hollywood dream-factory many actresses were turned into idols set high above the battle of the sexes and the squabbles of the stage: mirror-images of what women might be, or used to be, or ought to be, reflecting not only fashions in beauty, behaviour and casting but also more constant ideals and appetites. What is more, in every generation for the past three centuries the 'queens of the stage' have included not only spectacular sirens and outsize personalities but actresses of exceptional talent, even great artists.

This book is about some of the most remarkable of those women who have led the legitimate stage in Britain since 1660, when the first professional actresses appeared in London. It sketches them against the background of changing theatrical history; and behind that is the silhouette of that still-neglected field of study, the history of British women, in the shadowy perspective of the 'women's movement'. I have used contemporary evidence to outline the quality and style of these actresses' performances, the kind of theatre in which they worked, and their role in the theatrical power-game. But I have also briefly explored their private lives, in so far as they are available for scrutiny and surmise. This survey has necessarily omitted leading actresses in every century, and I make no claim that all the women of my choice are great actresses. Yet they are all of the blood royal: true player queens.

PART ONE

1 THE NEW WOMEN

O Gods: That women should so far excel
Mankind in everything, yet be so curst
To be born slaves, and live in loathed subjection.
> The Duchess of Suffolk, in
> John Banks's *The Innocent
> Usurper*: or, *The Death of the
> Lady Jane Gray* (1694)

Hang love, for I will never pine
For any man alive;
Nor shall this jolly heart of mine
The thoughts of it receive:
I will not purchase slavery
At such a dangerous rate;
But glory in my liberty
And laugh at love and fate.
> Aminta, in Aphra Behn's *The
> Forc'd Marriage* (1697)

At the new play house they are so used to be queens and princesses, and are so often in their airs-royal, forsooth!, that egad! there's no reaching one of their coppertails there without a long pole or a settlement, split me!
> Clodio, in Colley Cibber's *Love Makes a Man* (1700)

IN SHAKESPEARE'S DAY there were no actresses. They were no more missed, it seems, than were dramatic critics, agents or directors. Yet outside the theatres women enjoyed a greater equality of opportunity at work than they did in the 250 years after Shakespeare's death in 1616. Legally, women were men's chattels, deprived of rights, inferior beings. But while a woman reigned over England, and for some time afterwards, they worked as carpenters, printers, upholsterers, fishmongers, booksellers, publicans, pewterers, brewsters, butchers, shoemakers and usurers, sharing their husbands' businesses, trading on their own as widows, doing (by later standards) the impossible in many other trades. Such freedoms were doomed by 'progress'. By the end of the seventeenth century these occupations, together with all but the most menial jobs on farms and in shops and houses, were virtually monopolized by men. The advance of capitalism created differentiation of labour not only between classes but between the sexes, as a wage-earning economy pushed out domestic work based at home in the family unit.

Even before the Restoration, 'business' for a woman was increasingly restricted to the sex market. 'She could either take her wares to the exchange, protected by a marriage settlement, or she could ply her stock on the kerb with Moll Flanders.'[1] Yet in 1660 (the probable birth-year of Ms Flanders's creator, Daniel Defoe) a third trading post was suddenly opened, with results as yet neglected by historians of feminine emancipation. With the arrival on the London stage of the first inexperienced, untrained 'she-players', some seventy years after actresses had been accepted in Spain and the Netherlands, and a century after their success in France and Italy, British women built up a small enclave of potential power, wealth and independence.

The delay in the acceptance of actresses on this side of the Channel was partly due to the insular time-lag that frequently distorted Anglo-Continental cultural relations during the next three hundred years; and partly to the indigenous strength of a punitive, misogynistic Puritanism which abominated not only the public exhibition of women but the exhibitionism of the theatre itself. Playhouses existed only in London, and there they survived only by virtue of royal and aristocratic protection. When that protection was removed by the Civil War, they were suppressed. In some sections of society, and some parts of the country, moral opposition to professional play-acting persisted for over two centuries. It is not unknown today, as regional theatre activists have discovered to their cost. When Charles II authorized the employment of actresses – and he did so within a few weeks of returning from exile (on his thirtieth birthday) – it was in the name of moral reform. To tolerate boys in women's roles, the zealots argued, was to encourage homosexuality and masturbation – 'an inducement to sodomy, to self-pollution (in thought at least if not in act)': a greater sin than mere 'temptation to whoredom and adultery!'[2] The royalists seized their chance. As the King's patent stated, all the women's parts might actually be performed by women from then onwards 'so long as these recreations ... may by such reformation be esteemed not only harmless delight, but useful and instructive representations of human life, to such of our good subjects as shall resort to see the same'. The recreations did not turn out quite like that, but this was scarcely surprising.

Another explanation of this tardiness in the advent of actresses is that there seemed to be no *need* for them in the golden age of Elizabethan and Jacobean drama, or even in the silver era of the Caroline stage. Shakespeare created some of the outstanding women's roles in world drama for his fellow-actors and boy-apprentices in the all-male company that he helped to manage and to feed with plays. Within the conventions of female impersonation or, more accurately, representation, boys and men seem to have been so successful in playing Juliet, Lady Macbeth, Rosalind, Queen Margaret, Mistress Quickly – and the scores of other women and girls in that dazzling efflorescence of drama between 1570 and 1640 – that there was no overt demand by writers or playgoers for their replacement by the Real Thing.

The prime reason for the superiority of Shakespeare's women as roles for actresses is, of course, the incomparable superiority of Shakespeare himself; a secondary reason is that – unlike Ben Jonson, for instance – he apparently did not believe that men were necessarily superior to women; but there is a further, practical reason – these roles had to be boy-proof. As Juliet Dusinberre says, he wrote into the text 'a femininity which would survive the most gangling of Ganymedes'.[3] He compensated for the absence of women to look at as he compensated for the lack of scenery: by poetry. Some of his contemporaries achieved the same transcendence of their actors' gender. Indeed, 'the consciousness that they were not dealing with women actors spurred the dramatists to discover a femininity more durable than that which might be put on or taken off with a suit of clothes'.[4] They had all the more liberty to do so in being free from the obligation to suit the personality of a particular actress and to meet the expectations of the audience about what women ought, or ought not, to say and do. If there *had* been actresses in Shakespeare's company, there would certainly have been a fairer (and more economic) distribution of roles between the sexes. Never did Shakespeare, one suspects, forget his managerial responsibilities.

By the 1630's, when the vitality of the post-Shakespearian drama was diminishing, and an appetite for spectacle was fostered by Charles I and his French queen Henrietta Maria, there were probably rumbles of disaffection about the pseudo-women among courtiers who had seen and fancied French and Italian actresses. In a play of 1632 (Brome's *The Court Beggar*) somebody observed that 'women actors now grow in request'; and in *The Ball* (1639) a man says of the French stage:

> Yet the women are the best actors, they play
> Their own part, a thing much desir'd in England.

Nonetheless, they were not 'desir'd' enough by the public outside the court for any company to risk engaging them. Londoners' reaction to their first sight of actresses, only ten years earlier,– 1620 had been violent enough to deter any manager from experiment. A visiting French company which included women was 'hissed, hooted and pippin-pelted' from the stage of the Blackfriars, (and, perhaps, two other London theatres). Although this demonstration may have been prompted not only by sexism but by patriotism, it was not until after a national revolution that actresses re-appeared. Then they were warmly welcomed (with no recorded opposition in the audience) and within two years were unchallenged.

For a short period men continued to mimic women. After Samuel Pepys watched Edward Kynaston in skirts in Jonson's *The Silent Woman* in January 1661 – the month in which the diarist first saw an actress – he noted that this boy player was 'the prettiest woman in the whole house' (and, later, 'the handsomest man'). The prompter-historian John Downes recorded in his book *Roscius Anglicanus* concerning this 'complete female stage beauty' that 'it has since been disputable among the judicious, whether any woman that succeeded him so sensibly touched the audience as he'. But Kynaston seems to have been the last of the line and he rapidly reverted to characters of his own gender.

In perspective, the advent of professional women actors (and professional women dramatists, too) may be linked with larger symptoms of change such as the questioning of authority in politics and religion; experiments in sexual freedom; the stirrings of science, novel-writing and journalism; the post-war shift in class barriers, and increased social mobility; the circulation of new ideas about money, philosophy, morality and education – even the education of women. It is now claimed that the seeds of the women's movement were sowed in Shakespeare's lifetime, and that he was on their side. Juliet Dusinberre argues that 'agitation for women's rights and for changed attitudes to women . . . was a vital aspect of the society for which Shakespeare wrote'.[5] Be that as it may, by the Restoration 'the possibility that woman, although different from man, was not necessarily inferior to him and should not be subjected to him, was beginning to win a few sympathetic hearers',[6] among them Daniel Defoe ('all the world are mistaken in their practice about women', he said in 1697). By the turn of the century 'radical ideas concerning the potentialities of women' were in circulation, with 'an astonishing demonstration of equality and freedom between the sexes'.[7] The drama of the time – although lacking in feminine characters on the Shakespearian scale – reflects some of these ideas, not least in the attacks upon 'forced' marriage and, to some extent, in the pillorying of matrimony itself in many comedies, although this was largely carried out from the viewpoint of the male rake. Plays between 1660 and 1700 show women trespassing on male territory, as authors, revolutionaries, doctors, financiers and scholars; and one group of works by several hands, preoccupied with the legendary Amazons, has been described as mirroring 'the new woman's demands for greater freedom of thought and action and a nearer approach to equality with men'.[8] It was on the stage that the closest approach to equality was probably achieved – in art, if not in life. The dramatist Aphra Behn has, indeed, been acclaimed as 'the first of the modern women' and 'the pioneer of our modern womanhood'.[9] And she was not the only woman playwright, though she was by far the best. In one year (1695–6) London saw no fewer than five plays by such 'she-poets' as Catherine Trotter, Mary Manley and Mary Pix.

The admittance of women to the public stage had a more immediate cause: the break in theatrical development caused by the closure of the playhouses resulting from the Civil War. The interregnum in training dried up the supply of male girls. In a post-Restoration prologue 'to introduce the first woman that came to act on the stage' – probably, though not certainly, in *The Moor of Venice*, a free version of *Othello*, at the Vere Street Theatre on 8 December 1660 – Thomas Jordan wrote:

> Our women are so defective and so sized
> You'd think they were some of the Guard disguised;
> For to speak truth, men act, that are between
> Forty and fifty, wenches of fifteen;
> With bone so large and nerve so incompliant
> When you call Desdemona, enter Giant.

Allowing for the exaggerations of such clumsy public-relations verse, there were clearly not many Kynastons on hand.

Changes in theatrical architecture made it easier for the companies to do without male actresses. The 'public', open-air playhouses like the Globe, which could probably hold up to three thousand spectators, disappeared for ever in the 1640s. After the Restoration, drama was restricted to small indoor theatres, with an apron stage projecting deep into the audience (about seventeen feet beyond the equivalent of the proscenium). In this intimacy the inadequacies of Kynaston's less successful male sisters would have become more glaringly manifest; whereas the women – whose voices (so Glynne Wickham suggests)[10] had been thought to lack the necessary pitch or resonance for open-air performance, and were untrained in oratory (a pillar of male education) – had no difficulty in making themselves heard, as well as seen, even with the negligible store of technical expertise that is all the first actresses could have had time or opportunity to acquire.

More significantly, the restoration of the Stuarts brought to power in London an entourage of aristocrats, adventurers and their satellites who, like their royal master, had acquired in their continental exile a taste for actresses, as well as for scenery and spectacle. They expected, among other things, a good show. They demanded pretty women to look at and listen to. And their wants moulded the patterns of the new show business. This was controlled in the first decade after the Restoration by two aristocrats and friends of the King, Sir William Davenant and Thomas Killigrew, who managed to acquire a joint mono- poly of theatrical enterprise by royal patent and set up two companies – the Duke's and the King's respectively – establish- ing a dyarchy that endured for 170 years under successive heirs to their royal privilege as 'patentees'. These were the men who initiated and trained the first actresses. Both started off in converted tennis courts, in Lincoln's Inn Fields and Vere Street; but in 1663 the King's men moved into a new playhouse in Bridges Street (on part of the present site of the Theatre Royal, Drury Lane), and in 1671, after Davenant's death, the Duke's company opened a theatre in Dorset Garden.

Before the war London had supported (with a smaller population) some six to eight theatres. After the Restoration it could scarcely support two. For twelve years, indeed, only *one* contrived to stay open, when the two acting groups were combined at the King's direction into the United Company. Playgoing was no longer, as in Shakespeare's day, a genuinely popular diversion enjoyed by all classes in London (there were no theatres outside the capital). The theatre became 'a toy of the upper classes'[11] and the drama took its political colouring, its religious complexion, its moral tone and its sense of humour from the King and the cliques around him. Aristocrats like the Duke of Buckingham, Sir Charles Sedley and Sir George Etherege wrote for the stage and, like the King, recruited mistresses from it. The King himself not only ran a private playhouse but also regularly attended the public theatres – he was the first English monarch to do so. He took an intimate interest in texts and productions, sometimes lending coronation robes to help the wardrobe, sometimes vetoing a passage because of its political implications. His interest in actresses was manifest from the beginning of his reign. When the theatre was the toy of the court, who can be surprised that its women players were regarded as little more than royal playthings?

They were not *all* on the game, of course. Of some eighty actresses recorded between 1660 and 1700 by J. H. Wilson at least two dozen 'as far as we know, lived respectable lives'[12] (most of these being married women). Had there been any breath of scandal about them, it would probably have been picked up by Grub Street hacks. Perhaps even more than two dozen of these ladies were entitled to be ranked as 'respectable', in spite of traditional prejudices against women on the stage (especially those who were unmarried, beautiful and successful). But a job with one of the companies offered an attractive, *declassé* girl an unusually promising chance of acquiring a rich 'keeper' (or lover), even a husband. For a successful playwright, like John Dryden, the sexual frailty of actresses was a joke to be shared with the audience, as in his prologue to *Marriage à la Mode* (1672), describing courtiers making their last adieus in the 'tiring-room' before going off to the wars:

> The women sobbed, and swore they would be true
> And so they were, as long as ere they could;
> But powerful guinea cannot be withstood;
> And they were made of playhouse flesh and blood.

The men of the theatre, in effect, soon gave up claiming that its women were virtuous. Indeed, it was better for business to claim the reverse. Better, too, for the business of some actresses. Even for those who were not already on sale the lures were strong, especially as no work was available when the patent houses closed in the summer, and outside London there was scarcely any sustained theatrical activity.

This aura of amorality helped to darken the name of the theatre among the population at large for generations to come. But it also helped, for some years after the Restoration, to keep the playhouses open. Attendance might well have been even smaller, had men still played the women's roles. As one prologue (*c.* 1680) said:

> 'Tis seldom a new play with you prevails
> But a new woman almost never fails.
> New did I say? Nay though the town before
> Had rumpled, read and thumb'd her o'er and o'er,
> But on the stage no sooner she appears,
> But presently the sparks prick up their ears,
> And all in clusters round the scenes betake,
> Like boys about a bush to catch a snake.

Certainly the bait was used unstintingly. Not only did the authors produce a flood of new plays with fat parts for women, but they composed dozens of prologues and epilogues for actresses to deliver, and rewrote many old plays in order to enlarge the women's opportunities. (Davenant, for instance, inserted in *The Tempest* a second daughter for Prospero, a sister for Caliban and a spirit-mate for Ariel.) One of the most persistent ploys was to present actresses in men's or boy's clothes, primarily to show off their legs and thighs. Contemporary fashion already permitted almost complete exposure of their breasts. Of 375 plays first produced between 1660 and 1700, eighty-nine contained at least one breeches part; in fourteen more, women played male leads; in at least three, they played all the roles; and they were often given breeches in revivals.[13] Such appearances were, no doubt, titillating treats for men accustomed to see women in petticoats and skirts that touched the floor. J. H. Wilson claims that managers 'dressed the women as men on the slightest pretext'.[14] What is more, they were often exhibited in supposedly provocative or ambiguous sexual situations, and were sometimes required to crack dirty jokes with the audience in prologues and epilogues. Smut was no innovation. The pre-1640 drama had been thickly strewn with bawdy dialogue and violent sexual incident (or the threat of it) but the frequency of both in English playwriting over some fifty years was sharply increased by the advent of professional actresses.

Yet far more was demanded of these pioneers than to be shapely, sexy and apparently permissive. They had to tackle a formidable volume and variety of roles, with no background of professional experience. As in every generation some kinds of acting came naturally to some of the first women to wear the livery of His Majesty's Servants. 'Quickness of wit, a good sense of mimicry, an immediately engaging manner and a pert and impudent approach could do much to compensate for inexperience';[15] and these were common characteristics of the women's roles of Restoration comedy. But the demands of tragedy – deemed then, and for centuries to come, the superior art – were very different. Bosomy impudence and quick-witted charm were of little help in presenting the ranting exotic royalties of impossible villainy and virtue that peopled the world of heroic drama, a world of conventional puppets with no visible social models in Whitehall or Covent Garden. In a theatre in which mimic seduction was alternately a shared joke and a fatal crime, actresses had to encompass both comic realism and operatic idealism.

Moreover, although none of the first actresses were, as far as we know, 'ladies' – no woman of breeding and education would appear on the stage, let alone work on it for a living – they had to walk, talk, move, behave and dress *like* ladies, in an era when such distinctions were razor-sharp compared with the 1970s. They had to acquire (on stage) the deportment and elocution required of aristocrats and queens. They had to be literate enough to read, understand and memorize scores of plays (or, at least, scores of parts); few plays ran for more than four performances (sometimes never to be revived), and often the programme was changed from day to day. They had to cope with the exigencies of the public as well as the dramatists. Although the Restoration actress was closer to her audience than her successors in Regency and Victorian playhouses three or four times the size of Lincoln's Inn Fields and the first Drury Lane – working, as she did, on an apron stage jutting forward into the pit, with spectators on three sides – the audience that she had to deal with was casual, busy, restless and noisy, ranging 'from chronic inattention to near-pandemonium'.[16] All around her courtiers gossiped, got drunk, picked up whores, and started fights with each other. Some fops thought it smart to ignore or interrupt the players, who as a result had to stress and project their performances (with persistent button-holing of the public, in comedy at least) in ways that might seem to contemporary eyes a little overdone.

Actresses frequently had to control the audience backstage as well. It was hard to enjoy much privacy when any rake or fop could bribe his way into a dressing-room before and after a play; and when the personal affairs of many favourites were public property (or at least common gossip), often ventilated – or fantasized – in scurrilous and sometimes obscene lampoons. It was 'as hard a matter for a pretty woman to keep herself honest [chaste] in a theatre, as 'tis for an apothecary to keep his treacle from the flies in hot weather; for every libertine in the audience will be buzzing about her honey-pot'.[17] This back-stage scrabbling for sex was worlds away from the cool irony of the she-gallants on stage, routing their suitors with shafts of wit; or from the bantering assumption of feminine supremacy in a prologue like this (to *Amphitryon*, in 1690, delivered by Anne Bracegirdle):

> Our sex, you know, was after yours designed;
> The last perfection of the maker's mind;
> Heaven drew out the gold for us, and left your dross behind.
> Recant betimes, 'tis prudence to submit
> Our sex is still your overmatch, in wit.
> We never fail, with new, successful arts,
> To make fine fools of you, and all your parts.

With the spectacle before them of the 'vizard-masks' (whores) in the audience and the bedraggled, diseased 'punks' or 'fire-ships' in the streets outside (including ex-actresses abandoned by their 'keepers'), the women in the King's and Duke's Companies needed no further reminders of the dangers of their trade. They were sex-symbols in a man's world; and many of those men were violent, lawless, upper-class hooligans, to whom all women outside their own class (and many inside it) were made for whoring.

The financial rewards of acting, moreover, were not glittering prizes. A girl might start at ten or fifteen shillings a week, and rise to no more than thirty shillings – all that Katherine Corey was paid after a career of over thirty years (she claimed to be the first actress to appear, in 1660). Players were often paid late, and only when the theatre was open, which amounted to little more than seven months in a year; and actresses had to buy their own shoes, stockings, gloves and scarves. Even the leading ladies received no more than fifty shillings per working week, i.e. about £75 to £85 per annum. Although this could scarcely be called miserable, it was below the level of the men's salaries. Yet even the middle range of pay – say, £45 to £55 per annum – compared well with the average earnings of shop-keepers and tradesmen (£45) and farmers (£42 to £55) as estimated in 1696, for these were *men*. How else could a woman on her own earn as much as a farmer, except as a courtesan? There were, moreover, compensations and fringe benefits. As liveried servants of His Majesty actresses could run up bills in a way that would have been impossible outside the Lord Chamberlain's protection. (The first issue to women of the royal livery – four yards of bastard scarlet cloth and a quarter-yard of velvet – was recorded in 1666.) They could borrow the smarter gowns from the wardrobe for special social occasions. They could, with luck and judgement, enjoy continuity of employment: a twenty-year career was not exceptional, and Frances Knight kept going for forty-three years. And, of course, if a woman captured the right kind of 'keeper' she might (if she played her sex right) give up the stage and settle down in comfort, even luxury.

Nell Gwyn, Elizabeth Barry and their sister-players had, moreover, one great asset. Many of the characters they played in comedy took their tone from a world in which women 'had achieved, by means of sexual freedom, a degree of equality which was not to be repeated until the 1920s'.[18] What Dryden called 'the chase of wit kept up on both sides and swiftly managed', that characterized the best comedy of the age, mirrored a limited kind of women's liberation. Though only affecting a feminine elite, its membership was not rigidly restricted by caste and property qualifications; and the image of liberation, however partial and temporary it may have been, was created with their help. The sense of outrage that they provoked – and for which they have often, until comparatively recent times, been too glibly blamed – did not derive entirely from the sexual content of the plays, the bawdiness of the language or the 'viciousness' of their private lives. Something of the revulsion inspired by Restoration drama in later generations came from a reaction against the audacious independence maintained by many of the women characters in it; their strange lack of maidenly self-subordination; their frankness about the demands of husbands, lovers, brothers and fathers; their scepticism about marriage and masculine honour and morality; their claim to talk on equal terms. The traditional English horror of vulgarity, bad taste, showing off and making scenes (especially sexual ones) was intensified by the culture shock of discovering (in contemporary terms) that this *Playboy* world of the Restoration stage secreted something of a *Spare Rib*.

2 FOUR PIONEERS

Our Lady of Laughter, invoked in no psalter,
Adored of no faithful that cringe and that palter,
Praise be with thee yet from a hag-ridden age.
Our Lady of Pity thou wast; and to thee
All England, whose sons are the sons of the sea,
Gives thanks, and will hear not if history snarls.
When the name of the friend of her sailors is spoken:
And thy lover she cannot but love – by the token
That thy name was the last on the lips of King Charles.

Swinburne (1897)

Cunt! whose strong charms the world bewitches,
The joy of Kings! The beggar's riches!
The courtier's business! statesman's leisure!
The tired tinker's ease and pleasure . . .

Lord Buckhurst, 'Another letter
from Lord Buckhurst to Mr
Etherege', in The Poems of Sir
George Etherege

WILDBLOOD: Then what is a gentleman to hope from you?
JACINTHA: To be admitted to pass my time with, while a better
comes: to be the lowest step in my staircase, for a knight to
mount upon him, and a lord upon him, and a marquis upon him,
and a duke upon him, till I get as high as I can climb.

Jacintha (created by Nell Gwyn,
1668), in Dryden's An Evening's
Love

THE FIRST ENGLISHWOMAN to make acting respectable, and the
first to be buried in Westminster Abbey (if not unquestionably

the very first professional woman player, whose identity cannot now be proved) may justly be claimed as the first of the player queens. Mary Saunderson (c. 1637–1712) – better known as Mrs Betterton – held the stage for over thirty years, and was for nearly fifty years the consort of the greatest actor of his time, Thomas Betterton. Her fame, like her Abbey interment, depended to some degree on glory by association; but that she earned full honours as an artist on her own account we may be as reasonably sure as of any stage reputations in the era before press reviewers and professional critics. All we know of her family background is that her widowed mother lived in Cripplegate. When we first hear of her in 1661 she was about twenty-four and made her stage debut, with the seven other women of the Duke of York's Company, at the opening of the theatre in Lincoln's Inn Fields. She appeared as Ianthe, the near-operatic heroine of *The Siege of Rhodes,* a heroic drama with music by the manager of the company, Sir William Davenant: she lived with three other actresses in Sir William's house beside the theatre he owned, and it seems probable that he trained her for the stage. Within a year she fell in love with the leading man, Thomas Betterton, to whose Hamlet she played Ophelia. They married on Christmas Eve 1662, and lived, as far as we know, happily ever after (well into the next century, at least). Shortly before their marriage Samuel Pepys described 'Infallible Tom' as 'a very sober, serious man, and studious, and humble, following of his studies: and is rich already with what he gets and saves'. The highest salaries that Thomas and Mary Betterton earned seem to have been £5 and £2.50 a week respectively, but they acquired a house in Russell Street and a farm in Berkshire and lived in notoriously tranquil domesticity. That Mary was 'a woman of an unblemished and sober life' seems to have been accepted as axiomatic, even in the bitchy backstage world of the first English actresses. Devoted to her husband during their theatrical partnership as leaders of the stage for three decades, and in a retirement which preceded his own by over ten years, 'she appeared rather a prudent and constant than a fond and passionate wife'.[1] Yet after his death in 1710 she had a mental breakdown and followed him into his Abbey grave in 1712.

In a society where matrimonial fidelity seemed good for little more than a joke, Mary Betterton demonstrated that not all actresses were whores or even easy game. The penalty for that virtue is a lack of information about her art as well as her life. Yet it is clear that her range was wide, encompassing farce and opera, tragedy and comedy. We know of sixty roles that she played (many more are unrecorded); and the known twenty-five that she originated – her husband's total was 130 – included women as various as Elvira in Dryden's *The Spanish Friar,* Jocasta in his *Oedipus,* Bellinda in Etherege's *The Man of Mode,* and Andromache in Troy dramas by both Dryden and John Banks. Her voice was admired by Pepys for its sweetness. That her diction, as well as her virtue, set an example is suggested by her selection to coach the future Queen Anne in at least one role for Court theatricals (services rewarded after Betterton's death by a royal pension).

It was in Shakespeare (and *The Duchess of Malfi*) that Mrs Betterton shone at her brightest. She was the first woman to play Ophelia, Juliet, Lady Macbeth, Queen Katherine in *Henry VIII,* and probably Cordelia, Miranda, Beatrice, Viola and Isabella as well. Although that perceptive author-actor Colley Cibber did not see her until near the end of her career in the 1680s, he wrote in his *Apology* that 'she was so great a mistress of nature that even Mrs Barry, who acted the Lady Macbeth after her, could not in that part, with all her superior strength and melody of voice, throw out those quick and careless strokes of terror from the disorder of a guilty mind, which the other gave us with a facility in her manner that rendered them at once tremendous and delightful.' It seems clear that Mrs Betterton was no operatic bawler, stiffened by tragic protocol, but an artist of poetic naturalism. 'Time could not impair her skill', Cibber went on, 'though he brought her person to decay. She was to the last the admiration of all true judges of nature and lovers of Shakespeare, in whose plays she chiefly excelled, and without a rival.' Were it not for Mary Betterton and her husband, Shakespeare might have disappeared from the view of an age that considered him, even in an edited condition, something of a barbarian.

'Having, by nature, all the accomplishments required to make a perfect actress', wrote her husband's biographer, 'she added to them the distinguishing characteristic of a virtuous life.'[2]

Beyond such encomia, and the facts of her repertoire, there is scanty evidence for Mary Betterton's supremacy as an actress. She seems to have lost much of her original power and box-office appeal by her late forties, because her beauty had faded and her figure thickened. That so little should be known is sad and, one suspects, unfair: a major artist may well have been neglected by history. But history *has* perforce neglected Mrs Betterton, and we must pass on to a very different kind of woman, on whom the limelight has never ceased to shine. . . .

By far the most famous of Restoration actresses – and, indeed, perhaps the best known English actress of the last three hundred years among the general public – is Nell Gwyn. This chestnut-haired Cockney trollop has inspired more books, plays, films and legends than any other woman performer in the British 'straight' theatre. Yet her theatrical career lasted for no more than seven years; she retired from the stage at twenty, and she died at thirty-seven. We have no exact record of all the parts she played, and little evidence of what she did in any of those that are recorded. Of the eighteen roles about which we are fairly certain, none was in a play by Shakespeare or any other work that held the stage much beyond the Restoration era. Nell's wealth and notoriety in her brief lifetime and her persistent posthumous celebrity stem not so much from her theatrical as from her sexual and social performance.

The most popular of all royal 'doxies', Ellen or Eleanor Gwyn (or Gwynn) was born on 2 February 1650 into an English republic, a year after Charles I's head was chopped off. 'Sweet Nell of Old Drury', as she was tagged in Victorian times, deserved at least part of that name not only because she acted in the first theatre in Drury Lane (or just off it), but also because she was born and brought up very near it – probably in Coal Yard, an alley from Drury Lane to Holborn which has long since been swept away. She was brought up in squalor and poverty. Her father is said to have been a Welsh soldier turned fruit-seller, but he died in Nell's infancy, before her paternity was credited to 'a battalion of soldiers'. Her mother – 'Old Mistress Gwyn', as she became known to the town – was probably a prostitute and later perhaps a brothel-keeper in a small way. Nell's elder sister, Rose, was also probably on the game, at least until her marriage, and perhaps afterwards (her husband was reputed to be a highwayman). Nell herself, after hawking fish and vegetables in the streets around Drury Lane, was recruited when she was about thirteen for one of London's better-known brothels, run by Madam Ross in Lewknor Lane (now Macklin Street). This establishment flourished a few yards away from the Theatre Royal, which was opened by Thomas Killigrew and the King's Company in May 1663 in Bridges Street (not until after Nell's death did it begin to be known as Drury Lane Theatre). As Nell herself put it, 'I was brought up in a bawdy house to fill strong waters to the gentlemen', and it seems improbable that her duties ended there.

Nell Gwyn probably entered the playhouse as one of three girls who paraded around the pit selling 'China' oranges at sixpence each (twice the price outside). They were hired by Mary Meggs ('Orange Moll'), who not surprisingly found the concession a profitable one and ran it for nearly thirty years. She evidently looked in her 'orange-wenches' not only for a pretty face and a provocative figure but also a quick wit and ready tongue, capable of returning at speed the bawdy banter that the courtiers liked to hear both on and off the stage. This was useful experience for Nell; but she must have had some private coaching before she made her Drury Lane debut at fourteen – significantly, as a courtesan. Indeed, she must have been taught to read, for she is unlikely to have picked up any education at home or in Madam Ross's establishment. Among the leading ladies of the Restoration stage she seems to have been, if not unique, distinctive in her unconcealed working-class background and her partial illiteracy (she never learned to write). Perhaps (as contemporary gossip suggested) a wealthy lover, said to be a City merchant, paid for her early tuition. Perhaps she was helped by her sister Rose, who seems to have had connections with the King's Company. But Nell's likeliest sponsor and mentor was Charles Hart, leading actor of the Company and her first influential lover; a man who (in the role of Alexander the Great) was said to display so imperial a mien that he could 'teach any king on earth how to comport himself', and who had begun his training at the old Blackfriars as a girl-player.

In any event, 'Nelle' – as Killigrew noted her in the cast

list for his own play *Thomaso* – was already, at fourteen, a
Drury Lane personality before she set foot on the stage. In
this debut she played a 'courtesan of the first rank', Pauline,
whose arrival was preluded by eulogies of her sexual appetite.
Whereas her sister and fellow-whore, Saretta, was a 'dull sufferer
only, no acting party in the bed', according to one Spanish
cavalier, Pauline's lover boasted that 'a squirrel in a cage, a dog
with a bottle at his tail, will lie still as soon as Pauline.' Although
the part was small, Nell – or, as she was also known, Nelly and
Mistress Ellen – seems to have proved herself an apt learner,
as well as a tease, and Killigrew urgently needed new feminine
talent. Within the next six months she was probably cast in a
series of minor roles. Then in May 1665 the Plague closed the
theatre for a year. This was a time of obvious hardship for the
players of both companies. For Nell Gwyn, it was almost
certainly a year of much-needed training. She began to attract
attention as a performer soon after the King's Company
reopened the Theatre Royal in 1666. Her roles included another
of those ambiguous sexual situations dear to the hearts of
Beaumont and Fletcher, and also to Restoration audiences.
As Celia, the apparently low-born heroine of *The Humorous
Lieutenant,* she had to resist the determined advances of the
King of Syria, Antigonus, whose lust was undeterred (indeed,
whetted) by the fact that she was his son's beloved mistress.
In her spirited self-defence, Nell had to speak lines which were,
before very long, to be charged with ironic echoes. When
Antigonus (ineffectively disguised) offers jewels in the King's
name, she asks, 'What must my beauty do for these?'

> ANTIGONUS: Sweet lady
> You cannot be so hard of understanding,
> When a king's favour shines upon you gloriously
> And speaks his love in these—
> CELIA: Oh, then, love's the matter:
> Sir reverend, love! Now I begin to feel ye!
> And I should be the king's whore; a brave title!
> And go as glorious as the sun; oh, brave still!
> The chief commandress of his concubines
> Hurried from place to place to meet his pleasures . . .
> But when the good old sponge had suck'd my youth dry,

And left some of his royal aches in my bones;
When time shall tell me I have plough'd my life up
And cast long furrows in my face to sink me –
ANTIGONUS: You must not think so, lady.
CELIA: Then can these, sir,
    These precious things, the price of youth and beauty,
    This shop here of sin-offerings, set me off again?
    Can it restore me chaste, young, innocent?
    Purge me to what I was? add to my memory
    An honest and a noble fame? The king's device!
    And lights an everlasting torch to shame me . . .

In this role Pepys noticed her for the first time. Praising her as 'a most pretty woman' he recorded that she did this 'great part . . . pretty well'. It gave her a chance to show her talent for teasing, railing, insulting, independent repartee: a girl who could stand up to men – and put them down.

In the following month Nell scored her first big success, in Dryden's comedy *Secret Love*: or, *The Maiden Queen*, a play which he may have written with her in mind and view. She played Florimel, a 'mad girl' – i.e. a wilful, rebellious daughter, one of the 'liberated' kind – who conducts a witty war of words with her lover, Celadon (played by Hart), helping to establish a tradition that ran through to Millamant and Mirabell, with Beatrice and Benedick as its distant begetters. 'Impudent, brazen and devastating in her mimicry',[3] Nell carried off the verbal fencing with infectious gusto; railing against marriage and constancy ('the pleasure on't is past, when we have once learnt it'), she is secretly in love with Celadon, and skilfully draws him into her power. When Celadon asserts 'I am madder than thou art,' Florimel retorts, 'The devil you are! I'll tope with you, I'll sing with you, I'll dance with you, I'll swagger with you'; and Nell's swagger when she donned breeches and wooed women (together with her dancing of a jig) was the talk of the town. Looking at herself in a mirror, she said cheerfully, 'If I should be mistaken for some courtier now, where's the difference?' Pepys was swept off his feet by it all: he returned to see Nell play the role at least five times. 'So great a performance of a comical part was never, I believe, in the world before as Nell do this, both as a mad girl, then most and best of all when she comes in like a young gallant; and hath the motions and courage of a spark the most that ever I saw any man have . . . I never can hope ever to see the like done again, by man or woman.'

The theatre tried to show the like done again by casting her repeatedly as mad girls and in breeches parts: in James Howard's farce *All Mistaken,* for instance (which has been described as 'a weak and crude imitation of *Secret Love*'). As a female rake, Mirida, who boasted that she had betrayed five men, she was pursued by a thin suitor and a fat one, presented the fat one with a purge to slim him (a scene which was crudely exploited for stock lavatorial effects) and was given such auto-biographical, image-projecting lines as 'I'd have a dance if I had nothing but my smock on'. Nell was already famous for her jigs. A more successful version of the Florimel-Celadon double-act was provided by Dryden in *An Evening's Love* (with two songs and a jig), a play that Pepys (unaccountably) found 'very smutty' and that the Revd. Jeremy Collier singled out for its licentiousness in his later diatribe against the drama.

Nell also appeared as an angel (named Angelo) disguised as a page in breeches in *The Virgin Martyr* (by Massinger and Dekker). At the end of the play the martyr, Dorothea, led a procession of four Christian victims, under the guidance of Angelo, now revealed in 'his' true role and wearing the correct celestial attire (apparently a somewhat diaphanous robe). Pepys was very moved by this scene, especially Nell's Angel, when he watched it from the pit – so 'ravished', indeed, that it 'did wrap up my soul so that it made me really sick' and reminded him of when he was in love with his wife. But upon going backstage a day or two later and seeing the procession dispersing behind the scenes, he was somewhat taken aback by the speed with which the Angel and the chief martyr slid into sexy banter with the cluster of men who were waiting to greet them, and who, no doubt, savoured it all the more because of the piquant contrast between the actresses and their roles.

Pepys was not, indeed, an uncritical fan of 'little Nelly'. 'It is a miracle to me', he noted sadly on one occasion, 'to think how ill she do any serious part, just like a fool or a changeling.' It seems likely that sometimes she was really 'sending up' such parts; and her very presence in them must have seemed (at least to some members of the audience) a telling commentary on their moral pretensions. Comedy alone made her acting reputation. She herself shared with the audience the joke of her ineptitude outside it. In a Dryden epilogue (to *Tyrannic Love*) she said:

> I die
> Out of my calling, in a tragedy;

and in another epilogue (to *The Duke of Lerma*) she declared:

> I know you in your hearts
> Hate serious plays, as I hate serious parts.

In spite of that, Killigrew continued to cast her in them; and the contrast between her personality and her part was demonstrated to Nell's greatest advantage in what turned out to be the peak of her acting career: Dryden's *Tyrannic Love*: or, *The Royal Martyr*, a play about St Catherine of Alexandria. This was written to honour Catherine of Braganza, Charles II's queen, who had been painted as the saint some years earlier, and was now rumoured to be pregnant. Nell played a noble and royal virgin, Valeria, who kills herself because of her unrequited love for a character played by Charles Hart (by then no longer Nell's off-stage lover). At the sombre close, the 'corpse' of Valeria sat up smartly on her bier and harangued one of the bearers with mock indignation:

> Hold, are you mad? You damn'd confounded dog!
> I am to rise, and speak the epilogue.

Nell then stood up, advanced down the stage, and – with the broad, engulfing, sexy grin that was one of her trademarks – she said:

> I come, kind gentlemen, strange news to tell ye,
> I am the ghost of your poor departed Nelly.
> Sweet ladies, be not frighted, I'll be civil,
> I'm what I was, a little harmless devil.

She was, she announced, playing all her 'tricks' in hell; and threw out a poutingly erotic challenge.

> Gallants, look to 't, you say there are no sprites
> But I'll come dance about your bed at nights,

> And faith you'll be in a sweet kind of taking,
> When I surprise you between sleep and waking.

Invoking her reputation with an irresistible comic flourish she declared:

> O poet, damned dull poet, who could prove
> So senseless to make Nelly die for love!

And she finished her epilogue with these lines:

> But farewell, gentlemen, make haste to me,
> I'm sure e'er long to have your company.
> As for my epitaph when I am gone,
> I'll trust no poet, but will write my own.
> Here Nelly lies, who, though she lived a slattern,
> Yet died a princess, acting in St Catharin.

Then curtsying and winking at the audience, she stepped back to the pall-bearers, lay mock-gracefully down, and was carried off stage to loud and prolonged applause. This epilogue brought the house down; and it seems to have produced more enduring results. Sitting in the audience was the King. Not long afterwards – perhaps, so the old story goes, that same night – he sent for Nelly; and a liaison began that ended only with his death. Within two months she was pregnant. A year earlier Pepys had recorded her as, to his regret, linked with Charles's intimate circle, but it seems probable that a permanent relationship did not begin till 1669, and that it was, ironically enough, a play written for his wife that prompted the King to take his most celebrated mistress.

Charles the Third – as he was said to have dubbed himself jocularly, in succession to Nell's former lovers Charles Hart and Charles Sackville (later Earl of Dorset) – set Nell up in a house in Lincoln's Inn Fields, where their first child, Charles, was born in May 1670. Later he moved her to a grander establishment in Pall Mall, where her garden abutted on the King's, on ground now covered by Marlborough House. In December that year – partly, perhaps, as a gesture of independence, intended to put pressure on the King, whose attention had already strayed to other ladies – she returned to the Drury Lane stage, to play the romantic lead, Almahide, in Dryden's *The Conquest of Granada*, Charles Hart appeared as her stage lover (for the last time). When the play's short run ended, Nell Gwyn left the stage for ever. She was not quite twenty-one.

From then on Nell lived in conspicuously high style. She had a French coach with six horses and her initials on the panels; a sedan chair covered in leather studded with gold nails; at least eight servants in her Pall Mall mansion; a country home – Burford Hall, near Windsor; and some land in Bestwood Park, Nottinghamshire. Her extravagance was a byword. She spent over £1100 on a silver bedstead with the King's head on it. She bought for £4250 a fifty-pearl necklace which Prince Rupert had given to Margaret Hughes, his mistress and Nell's former colleague. She is said to have lost £5000 in one sitting at basset (a kind of faro). But she never lacked for money, at least while Charles was alive. He is said to have settled £4000 per annum on her initially, increasing this in 1675 to £5000 per annum, and he also paid off many debts as they arose. According to the Duke of Buckingham, he spent some £60,000 on Nell in the first four years of their relationship, and her allowances were increased for her two children by Charles. Although she herself took no title, unlike several mistresses of the King, her eldest son was created Earl of Burford at the age of six. At fourteen he became Duke of St Albans (*and* Registrar of the High Court of Chancery *and* Master Falconer of England). Her second son, James, died in 1680 at the age of nine, but Charles established a line that survives today.

Nell made – and kept – friends in high places. They included Dryden; the Earl of Dorset; George Villiers, Duke of Buckingham; Sir Robert Howard; and the Earl of Rochester. (Both the latter two aristocrats, on separate occasions, acted as her trustee in matters of business.) Yet in spite of her sudden translation to high society Nell Gwyn never attempted to play the great lady: she knew better than to risk such miscasting. She stayed, in her own view, at the centre of a comedy which she was determined to enjoy; and the fact that she remained gleefully true to her Cockney self was surely one reason why she kept the friendship of Restoration wits, the love of the King, and a high degree of public favour. One of the most familiar (and better attested) stories in the Gwyn canon illustrates her quality of outspoken honesty and humour. When she was driving through Oxford in 1681, a time of anti-Catholic demonstrations in the streets, a mob mistook her ornate coach for that of Nell's hated French rival, Louise de Keroualle, Duchess of Portsmouth. But Nell avoided trouble by putting her head out of the window and shouting, 'Pray, good people, be civil. I am the *Protestant* whore' – a line accompanied, no doubt, by her radiant smile at its highest voltage. She also won popularity by her generosity, enshrined in the old (and entirely false) tale that she persuaded the king to establish the Royal Hospital in Chelsea. Nell Gwyn certainly gave publicly to a number of charities in her lifetime and at her death left money to liberate poor debtors from prison and to clothe the needy in winter. She is said to have helped not only Thomas Otway, who tutored her eldest son for a while, but also Samuel (*Hudibras*) Butler and the dramatist Nathaniel Lee. When Lord Dorset described her to the Duke of Buckingham as 'the best woman in the world', he was surely not merely flattering the bearer (Nell) or making courtiers' phrases. Nor did she forget or disown her family. After her mother's death, caused, it was said, by falling drunk into a ditch in Chelsea) Nell paid for a handsome memorial in St Martin-in-the-Fields. She also persuaded the King to give her sister Rose a pension of £100 per annum, and to double this after her first husband's death.

However diverse her early sexual experiences may have been in and around Drury Lane, it seems likely that Nell had been faithful to one lover at a time – at least, since her first success in the theatre; and that although she might jokingly describe herself as a whore, the number of her lovers was small before she met the King. Apart from Hart and the Earl of Dorset they may have included the Earl of Rochester; but, as Graham Greene says, there is 'little real evidence' for the story,[4] and none at all for his authorship of verse-lampoons against her. Nell was almost certainly faithful to the King (or we should have heard about it); and although he took other mistresses, he kept his regard for her, not least because she could always make him laugh.

On Charles's deathbed in 1685 he is said to have charged his brother and heir, James, with one duty: 'Don't let poor Nelly starve.' In fact, she shared his last thoughts with her hated rival, Louise de Keroualle, Louise's son (the Duke of Richmond) and other royal bastards. But although she had, inevitably, to cut her conspicuous consumption, royal patronage kept the wolf a long way from Nell's door. James II granted her £1500 per annum, with additional subsidies for her ducal son, and paid off some of her bills. By the time Nell died she was said to be worth £100,000 – £2000 in revenue and the rest in jewels and plate, the fruits of royal friendship. In current terms, she was probably not far from being a millionairess.

There were, perhaps, other inheritances. If Clifford Bax was right (although in matters of detail he was frequently wrong) Charles passed on to 'poor Nelly' a venereal disease, and it was this that killed her off nearly fifty years before the Catholic whore, the Duchess of Portsmouth. Whatever the medical cause, she made a premature exit. In her first big success as Florimel she had said, 'I am resolved to grow fat and look young till forty, and then slip out of the world with the first wrinkle, and the reputation of five and twenty.' Nell slipped out a little earlier than that. She was thirty-seven when she died on 14 November 1687, less than three years after Charles, and sixteen years after her last stage appearance.

What did Nell Gwyn bring to the stage? First of all, consider her looks. Here the evidence of pamphlets and books, though incomplete, may be a more reliable aid than the prints and portraits showing Mistress Ellen after she had given up the theatre, which preserve little more than a fixed and rather sullen image, conveying nothing of the 'sprightliness', 'low of spirits' and smiling impishness of the essential Nell. She was 'below middle size', with a trim figure; unusually small feet; chestnut hair and eyebrows (or were the latter, as Dryden suggests, merely 'brown'?); an oval face; turned-up nose; hazel eyes; a provocatively pouting mouth with a 'full nether-lip'; a dimpling smile and a hearty, infectious laugh that, in seizing her whole face, convulsed entire audiences. Long after she had given up the stage, people could see and hear Nell in the audience, enjoying herself at the play.

Even before she was picked up by the King, 'the darling strumpet of the crowd' (as a satirist called her) enjoyed unusual news-value within the playgoing world. The authors of prologues and epilogues helped her to sell the image of herself to the audience. From puberty, if not before, she learned to please

men, flatter them, lead on, and deflate them: to treat life not
as a rape to be suffered, but a joke to be shared. Sometimes
the joke was bad. Often it was dirty. The important thing was
to make the best of it. She could laugh at herself, at her own
notoriety and at the sexuality on which it depended.

The personality that Nell Gwyn projected was, in the words
of her best biographer to date, 'coarse, friendly, extravagant,
generous, giddy, loyal, greedy, humorous, ambitious'.[5] It was
also distinguished by courage, outgoing energy and a no-
nonsense realism akin to the scepticism of her royal lover.
She won from both the court and the mob a kind of classless
affection and allegiance gained by few of her successors in the
'straight' theatre. Reacting against the persistently saccharine
prettification of her life, some writers have presented her as a
tart on the make, selling her sex to the highest bidder and, by a
fluke, catching the highest of all. Allowing for the fulsome
overstatement demanded by the genre, it seems likely that
Aphra Behn's dedication to Nell of *The Feigned Courtesan*
expresses a measure of truth when it says: 'You never appear
but you gladden the hearts of all who have the happy privilege
to see you, as if you were made on purpose to put the whole
world in a good humour.'

Nell Gwyn was the first woman star of the British theatre,
in any meaningful sense: she was the pioneer of the personality
cult, the first bright shiner. Her talents were closer (in twentieth-
century terms) to music hall and revue than to the 'legitimate'
stage; and the royal apotheosis of her brief career had little to
do with the advancement of theatrical art. She may be seen less
as a player queen than a pearly queen. More than any other
actress, perhaps, she helped to give a bad name to her newly-
established profession, confirming for millions of the godly
their views on the sinfulness of the stage. Yet Nell Gwyn's
career signalled for women a new approach not only to successful sexual marketing but also to a new degree of freedom,
prosperity, and near-equality. For some three hundred years the
image of this Drury Lane trollop has stood in the underground
halls of national fame as a statue of liberty-taking (of the
diabolical kind), with fingers beckoning invitingly to a declara-
tion of independence, a wage of one's own, and a share in the
kingdom of men.

In the more specialized gallery of popular moral stereotypes as preserved by theatrical historians, where Nell Gwyn (frail but golden-hearted) and Mary Betterton (the constant wife) have shone for generations among the goodies, Elizabeth Barry (c. 1658–1713) has been pilloried as a heartless enchantress, greedy Jezebel and destroyer of men. Yet she was apparently the greatest actress of her time, surpassing even (except in *Macbeth*) the doyenne of the previous generation, Mrs Betterton. Mrs Barry – she never married; the 'Mrs' was a conventional courtesy title – was on the stage for thirty-seven years and 'created' characters in some 112 plays. She appeared as heroic virgins, witches and adulterous wives; satanic empresses from Asia and lecherous beldams from the salons of Restoration London; Alcmena, Boadicea, Anne Boleyn, Elizabeth I and royalty from all sorts of places, including Arragon, Scythia, Bayonne, and Persia. Among her more enduring original roles were Monimia in Otway's *The Orphan* and Belvidera in *Venice Preserv'd*; Lady Brute in Vanbrugh's *The Provok'd Wife* and Clarissa in *The Confederacy*; Calista in Rowe's *The Fair Penitent* and Arpasia in *Tamerlane*; Zara in Congreve's *The Mourning Bride*, Mrs Frail in *Love for Love*, Mrs Marwood in *The Way of the World*; and Isabella in Southerne's *The Fatal Marriage*. 'I made the play for her part', Southerne wrote in his introduction to the last work, 'and her part has made the play for me.' The same might be said of Otway's works, which he wrote for her, and of other plays on which she set her stamp as surely as Thomas Betterton moulded stage tradition in his roles. A remarkably high number of them formed the basis of the English actress's repertoire for the next 170 years; and a few survive, vigorously, today.

Mrs Barry's family background is, not surprisingly, obscure. One of her many enemies (Robert Gould) fantasized about it in the following terms:

> Her mother was a common strumpet known,
> Her father half the rabble of the town . . .
> At twelve, she'd freely in coition join
> And far surpass'd the honours of her line.

The more probable story (though, no doubt, her own) is that she was the daughter of a barrister whose fortunes were ruined by raising a regiment for the King in the Civil War, and that Lady Davenant (a family friend) educated her and gave her the entrée to society. Elizabeth Barry certainly *did* become 'mistress of that behaviour which sets off the well-bred gentlewoman'. And she was undoubtedly helped in her social training by John Wilmot, Earl of Rochester, whose mistress she became about the age of sixteen or seventeen.

By that time she had already tried to make a career on the stage – and failed. In spite of Davenant's supposedly parental concern, he despaired of teaching her to be an actress (as he had taught Mary Betterton), and she was dismissed from the Duke's Company. According to a hack-historian.

several persons of wit and quality being at the play, and observing how ill she performed, positively gave their opinion she never would be capable of any part of acting. But the Earl of Rochester, to show them he had a judgement superior, entered into a wager, that by proper instruction, in less than six months he would engage she should be the finest player on the stage.

He is said to have chosen one role – Isabella, the captive Hungarian queen in Orrery's *Mustapha* – and to have taught his beautiful Galatea to incarnate a character, 'perfectly changing herself, as it were, into the person, not merely by the proper stress or sounding of the voice, but feeling really, and being in the humour, the person she represented, was supposed to be in.' Rochester superintended her in 'near' thirty rehearsals and 'about twelve dress rehearsals, a quite unprecedented display of preparation, and 'took such extraordinary pains with her, as not to omit the least look or motion'. He coached the page who carried her train, to give the fullest possible stage value to her inborn dignity, for she had that kind of natural regality of mien that makes up, in many aspiring player queens, for the authority of the artist. And he is said to have won his wager, so far, at least, as winning her a place in the Duke's Company was concerned. Perhaps the story *is* true; but there is no record of Mrs Barry's appearance in *Mustapha* (first performed in 1675). She did make her debut that year as Draxilla in *Alcibiades,* Thomas Otway's first play, a role 'so inconsiderable that it is amazing that she should have won any kind of recognition.'[6] Perhaps, as J.H. Wilson suggests, it was after this debut that she was taken in hand by Rochester, who was Otway's patron for a time and helped to get *Alcibiades* staged.

She played at least eighteen parts – three of them in works by Otway – before she achieved her first big success: Monimia in Otway's *The Orphan,* in February 1680. Two years later she created Belvidera in the same author's *Venice Preserv'd.* It was Otway, rather than Rochester, who was the making of Elizabeth Barry; yet she gave him little return off the stage. He was passionately in love with her, but it was Rochester who fathered her child. Through seven years of theatrical partnership, the dramatist's love was tormentingly unrequited. As Otway wrote to her in the first of six published letters: 'Since the first day I saw you I have hardly enjoyed one hour of perfect quiet; I loved you early, and no sooner had I beheld that soft bewitching face of yours, but I felt in my heart the very foundation of all my peace give way. . . .' Although he swore when she 'became another's' that he would 'recover his liberty', he was free only in the daytime. At night, he wrote, 'every treacherous thought rose up, and took your part, nor left me till they had thrown me on my bed, and opened those sluices of tears that were to run till morning. This has been for some years my best condition.'

Allowing for the idiom of the period, there was a sizeable element of self-dramatizing fantasy in Otway's version of Mrs Barry's conduct. She seems to have been guilty of little more than callousness and boredom. But she does appear to have found close emotional relationships with men hard to sustain, for she treated Rochester badly, too, during their affair. At first the arch-cynic wrote to her with apparently profound feeling, using such phrases as 'Nothing can ever be so dear to me as you are', and 'I do you justice in loving you as no woman was ever loved before'. But he became disillusioned with her, as with so much else, and they separated shortly after Elizabeth Barry gave birth to a daughter. Rochester died two years later – 'of old age at thirty-three'[7] – bequeathing an annuity to their child, Betty, just as Elizabeth began her reign as the queen of the stage.

In her lifetime Elizabeth Barry was publicly credited not only with many lovers (including Sir George Etherege, who was said to have sired a daughter by her) but with an inexhaustible sexual lust. 'Nature made her for the delight of mankind; and till Nature began to decay in her, all the town shared her beauty.' And yet, her enemies complained indignantly, she wanted to be *paid* for it. 'Should you lie with her all night she would not know you next morning', said one bitchy gossip, 'unless you had another five pounds at her service.' Something of the ferocity of the contemporary barrage against her seems to derive from a resentful male suspicion that she didn't *like* men; partly from the fact that she didn't – for all her lickerish renown – let every suitor bed her; and partly because she is thought to have overcharged those who did. After all, she was only an actress.

> So insolent! There never was a dowd
> So very basely born, so very proud:
> Yet covetous: she'll prostitute with any
> Rather than waive the getting of a penny.

One of Mrs Barry's crimes – as seen by actors and dramatists – was, one suspects, 'unwomanly' pride. She wanted recognition as an artist, with parity in work. Although she was known or believed to enjoy sex (unlike Mary Betterton), she expected to receive respect as an actress. It is surely not accidental that her most successful roles include such vigorous protests about male domination as this one made by Calista:

> Through every state of life the slaves of man!
> In all the dear delightful days of youth
> A rigid father dictates to our wills
> And deals out pleasure with a scanty hand.
> To his, the tyrant husband's reign succeeds;
> Proud with opinion of superior reason
> He holds domestic business and devotion
> All that we are capable to know, and shuts us,
> Like cloistered idiots, from the world's acquaintance
> And all the joys of freedom. Wherefore are we
> Born with high souls, but to assert ourselves,
> Shake off this vile obedience they exact,
> And claim an equal empire of the world?

Whatever the vagaries of Mrs Barry's private life, her views

on sexual equality, and her employment as a convenient scapegoat for sexual guilt, anger, fear, and frustration, she was
certainly not only a 'jilt' (as Etherege called her) but also a
woman of independent mettle. This was shown when she helped
to lead the players' rebellion in 1695 and to organize a new
company at Lincoln's Inn Fields, in which she and Anne Bracegirdle were equal sharers with the men (a step forward, indeed,
in the emancipation of women, though not one that set an
effective precedent). That she was a fighter is suggested by the
story about how, having quarrelled off stage with a fellow
actress (Mrs Boutell) about the on-stage use of a scarf in
The Rival Queens, which called for one queen to stab the other,
Mrs Barry did so with such zest that the blunted dagger pierced
right through Mrs Boutell's stays, drew blood and went down
in backstage history. Having achieved fame in her early
twenties, she was unchallenged for years as leading lady of the
United Company. Indeed, she was so popular with the public
that although her salary was half Betterton's, he complained
(in 1694) that she made more money in a year than he did
because of the earnings from her annual benefit performance.
Mrs Barry was, in fact, the begetter of the benefit system, which
endured for over two hundred years as a supplement (however
uncertain and inequitable) to theatrical wages and salaries.
About 1686 she was allowed, as a special managerial concession, to keep the gross box-office takings of a performance 'in
consideration of the extraordinary applause' that followed it
(there is no record of the play concerned); and for some years
this concession seems to have been renewed as a unique privilege, although the house 'charges' (i.e. the daily overheads) were
probably deducted, for Mrs Barry later secured a guaranteed
profit of £70 minimum. She knew her value – and fought for it.

Although she was at last obliged to leave juvenile roles to
younger players, Mrs Barry seems to have demonstrated greater
tenacity and creative vitality than Mrs Betterton, preserving
her beauty and her figure for a longer period, and she continued
to originate characters until close to her retirement at the age of
fifty-two; she died three years later, on 7 November 1713.

What was Elizabeth Barry's secret? Dark-haired and blue-
eyed, she was not, it seems, a conventional beauty. Anthony

Aston insisted that she was 'indifferently plump', with a lop-sided mouth. Nor, he said, could she sing or dance even a simple country dance. His possibly partial evidence is corroborated by a character in *A Comparison Between Two Stages,* who says, 'I do think that person the finest woman in the world upon the stage, and the ugliest woman off it.'[8] Clearly she could *assume* beauty, and she brought on stage a magnetic field of intense sexuality (energized, no doubt, by the legends of her sexual appetite). She was also, no less clearly, an accomplished technician with an artist's conscience. She was praised for being 'judicious' in her work, and – in common with Betterton – for consulting the author, showing a concern for textual values that was evidently noteworthy in this period.

Mrs Barry could unleash electrifying anger, in such curses as Calista's 'Dishonour blast thee, base, unmannered slave!' And she could do so from a great altitude: as Congreve described Zara in *The Mourning Bride,* she looked 'Born to excel, and to command'. She came on so regally as Queen Elizabeth in *The Unhappy Favourite* that the reigning Queen gave her the dress she had worn at her wedding and the mantle she had worn at her coronation. Mrs Barry could reinforce this 'natural' majesty of manner with a royal voice, 'full, clear and strong, so that no violence of passion could be too much for her' (Cibber), and there was certainly a good deal of violence in the rant she had to deliver. As Roxana, for instance, in *The Rival Queens:*

> eternal discord
> Fury, revenge, disdain and indignation
> Tear my swollen breast: make way for fire and tempest;
> My brain is burst, debate and reason quenched,
> The storm is up, and my hot bleeding heart
> Splits with the rack.

Mrs Barry, however, never lost command of the verse or the character (rudimentary though it often was). From being 'impetuous and terrible' she could 'subside into the most affecting melody and softness' and 'pour out the sentiment with an enchanting harmony', moving swiftly from bombast to lyrical pathos and back again with no clashing of gears. This mastery of vocal control and operatic power was especially useful in

Dryden's heroic dramas: most serviceably of all, he said, as Cassandra in his *Cleomenes.* 'Mrs Barry, always excellent, has in this tragedy excelled herself, and gained a reputation beyond any woman I ever saw in the theatre.' Her facial control was also notable for flexibility and range. According to Anthony Aston, 'her face somewhat preceded her action, as the latter did her words.'

Mrs Barry scored in comedy, too – 'alert, easy and genteel', said Aston – and was apparently never reluctant to play unsympathetic roles, such as Mrs Frail and Mrs Marwood. But she was most admired for her command of pathos, as in the first big successes written for her by Otway, *The Orphan* and *Venice Preserv'd.* As Colley Cibber put it, 'in the art of exciting pity she had a power beyond all the actresses I have yet seen, or what your imagination may conceive.' One of Mrs Barry's treasured and memorable effects was the heartfelt sadness with which, in *The Orphan,* she said farewell to her star-crossed lover: 'Ah, poor Castalio!' – three words at which she always used to weep, herself, profusely. As 'the mistress of tears', she made London weep, too. And like all front-rank players, 'she . . . always enters into her part and is the person she represents', as Betterton's biographer said. She could turn dross into gold: 'her acting has given success to such plays, as to read would turn a man's stomach.' And, like all great player queens, she could keep that gold glowing in men's minds and hearts long after the original act of alchemy, long after she had gone to her grave in Acton.

Elizabeth Barry was one of a triumvirate of players who dominated the London stage at the end of the seventeenth century – 'the three Bs', as they were dubbed, because the other two favourites were Thomas Betterton and Anne Bracegirdle. Mrs Bracegirdle, as she was always known, links the Restoration era with the age of Garrick; for although she retired three years before Mrs Barry, her senior, she lived on until 1748, leaving an enduring legend with a slender basis of recorded fact. Her reputation as the 'Diana of the stage' reflects, with all its ambiguities, revealing changes in the status of actresses, and suggests that she was one of the earliest stage models for a perenially popular incarnation of male fantasies.

Anne Bracegirdle was probably born in Wolverhampton, and her father Justinian was said (by some) to be a country gentleman and (by others) to be a coach-builder or inn-keeper in Northampton. Because of a collapse in the family fortunes she was brought up in London by the Bettertons, friends of her father. Her childhood seems to have been protected and unexploited. Unlike Nell Gwyn, she did not have to work for a living or offer herself for sale. At the age of about six she appeared as a boy page, Cordelio, in Otway's *The Orphan*; yet this seems to have been an isolated experiment, and she did not make her professional debut until eight years later, tutored, no doubt, by her virtual foster-parents, and encouraged (so the story goes) by Elizabeth Barry.

According to the records of Westminster Abbey, where she was buried, Anne Bracegirdle was born in 1663. It seems improbable on every count, however, that her debut (in 1688) should have been delayed until she was twenty-five, and that she should not have made her name – as Araminta, the heroine of Congreve's *The Old Bachelor*, in 1693 – until she was thirty. If she was then between eighteen and twenty, the amorous devotional cult that she inspired in her audience is more readily accountable. So, too, is the patronage of Mrs Barry, who is unlikely to have encouraged a rival only five years her junior. A further disproof of the Abbey birth-date is Colley Cibber's comment that in 1690 Mrs Bracegirdle was 'but just blooming to her maturity; her reputation as an actress gradually rising with that of her person', which scarcely suggests a young woman of twenty-seven.

During her nineteen years on the stage – some twelve of them as a reigning queen – she appeared in only minor Shakespearean roles, as then viewed (Desdemona, Ophelia, Lady Anne and Mrs Ford); but she created roles in plays by some forty authors, including Victoria in Southerne's *The Fatal Marriage*, Selima in Rowe's *Tamerlane*, Lavinia in the same author's *The Fair Penitent*, and Samantha in his *Ulysses*. Mrs Bracegirdle won her ascendancy not through Shakespeare or contemporary tragedy, heroic or sentimental, but in such roles by Vanbrugh as Flippanta in *The Confederacy* and Bellinda in *The Provok'd Wife*, and above all, in Congreve. She created the heroine in each of Congreve's five plays, culminating in Millamant; and as the author is generally believed to have been not only her admirer but her lover, it seems all the more probable that the genesis of this witty, warm-hearted, role-playing, sparring partner – 'an affected coquette who was also a woman of sense with a capacity for genuine affection' – was, in the words of a modern Congreve scholar, 'a perfect example of collaboration'.[9]

Mrs Bracegirdle's supremacy was gained in comedy, helped by the projection of her personality and her virtue. She excelled – as her foster-mother, Mrs Betterton, had done – in the portrayal of good women, but gave a strong sexual charge to the exhibition of chastity and constancy: not least because she remained unmarried, and because her reputation for inviolability gave an especial piquancy to her delivery of prologues and epilogues spiced with *double entendre* and near-obscenities. (She was the leading server of these savories, with over thirty to her credit.) Her publicized chastity had a curiosity value; or, to put it in loftier terms, she reigned as a Virgin Queen who enjoyed a dirty joke.

The spell that she cast upon her admirers did not, it seems, depend upon any formal perfection of feature. Cibber, who was one of them, said she had 'no greater claim to beauty than what the most desirable brunette might pretend to'; but he extolled the 'glow of health, and cheerfulness' that she exuded, so that 'on the stage few spectators that were not past it, could behold her without desire.' According to Anthony Aston, she was 'of a lovely height, with dark-brown hair and eyebrows, black sparkling eyes, and a fresh blushy complexion; and, whenever she exerted herself, had an involuntary flushing in her breast, neck and face, having continually a cheerful aspect, and a fine set of even white teeth.' Cibber was in no doubt of a more cogent reason for her fame than her beauty:

> Never any woman was in such general favour of
> her spectators, which, to the last scene of her dramatic
> life, she maintained, by not being unguarded in her
> private character. This discretion contributed, not a
> little, to make her the *cara*, the darling of the theatre.
> For it will be no extravagant thing to say, scarce an
> audience saw her, that were less than half of them
> lovers, without a suspected favourite among them. . . .[10]

Among the best-known stories of her virtue (told years later by Horace Walpole) was that when Lord Burlington sent her a present of fine china she told the servant who brought it that there had been a mistake and that it was meant for Lady Burlington, to whom he must carry it back. Unlike Nell Gwyn and Elizabeth Barry she was known to be unapproachable (at least by conventional routes). She was a Madonna-figure, the kind of pseudo-nun who in some men provokes an especial erotic fervour and whose image recurs frequently among twentieth-century idols of the Western stage and screen.

When she left the theatre in 1707 she was, Cibber said, 'in the height of her favour with the public' (which accords better with an age of thirty-four than forty-four). She spent over forty years in retirement. But how could an unmarried woman of impeccable virtue and no private income live at leisure on her own in London, without employment, for so long? Could Mrs Bracegirdle have survived solely on the savings from her salary, her benefits and the gifts that were lavished on her by her idolaters? That she could is not beyond the bounds of belief, especially if the scale of tribute may be measured by the story that Dorset, Devonshire, Halifax and other peers, after discussing her unique virtue, collected eight hundred guineas and presented them to her as a tribute to her private life. Yet it is not surprising that some incredulity was displayed in Mrs Bracegirdle's heyday about the immaculacy of her morality. This was ventilated in *A Comparison between the Two Stages*:

RAMBLE: And Mrs Bracegirdle . . .

CRITIC: Is a haughty conceited woman, that has got more money by dissembling her lewdness, than others by professing it.

SULLEN: But does that romantic virgin still keep up her great reputation?

CRITIC: D'ye mean her reputation for acting?

SULLEN: I mean her reputation for not acting; you understand me—

CRITIC: I do; but if I were to be sav'd for believing that single article, I could not do it; 'tis all, all a juggle, 'tis legerdemain; the best on't it, she falls into good hands, and the secrecy of the intrigue secures her . . .[11]

Even though her name was commonly bracketed with Congreve's there was little open scandal. 'It was known that Mrs Bracegirdle was Congreve's neighbour, assumed that she was his mistress, and hinted that she might have been his wife by a private marriage.' But there were no salacious details in the satires. 'In the main, the distaste for publicity of both Congreve and Mrs Bracegirdle was respected.'[12] After he fell in love with Henrietta, Duchess of Marlborough, he remained on terms of friendship with Mrs Bracegirdle, and left her £200 in his will, while bequeathing a reputed £10,000 to the Duchess, an action for which he has often understandably been attacked – notably by Dr Johnson and Macaulay, although the latter loftily dismissed Mrs Bracegirdle as 'a cold, vain, interested coquette'. Congreve's successor as her lover seems to have been Robert Leke, the third Earl of Scarsdale, who left her £1000 in 1708; but this affair (if such it was) was conducted with the 'discretion' that Cibber praised and that distinguished the actress's life. No other names have been associated with hers as 'keepers', although many tried to 'thaw her ice', as Macaulay put it.

The significant thing about 'Bracey', as her less awestruck friends and contemporaries called her, was neither the number of her lovers nor the magnetism of her stage presence, but the fact that she enjoyed so full a measure of social respect (whatever the scattered sneers on the sidelines). Within fifty years of the first whorish generation of women players a professional actress with no husband or family could maintain a private life and retire into it, with virtually unchallenged status and apparent independence.

3 MOSTLY GEORGIAN

The life of youth and beauty is too short for the bringing of an actress to her perfection.

Colley Cibber (1740)

A rape in tragedy is a panegyric upon the sex.

John Dennis (1721)

Take my word, coquetry has governed the world from the beginning, and will do so to the end o't.

Maria in Cibber's *The Non-Juror* (1717)

BY THE TIME the Bettertons, Elizabeth Barry and Anne Bracegirdle had left the London stage it had already begun to change. *Not* in the legal monopoly of the 'patentees' at Drury Lane and Lincoln's Inn Fields (Covent Garden, from 1732) over performances of the drama. This crippling privilege was confirmed by the Licensing Act of 1737, although from 1720 it was extended to the Haymarket during the summer, when the patent houses closed, and summer seasons of non-'legitimate' entertainments later flourished at several suburban theatres, led by Sadler's Wells (from 1740). *Not* in theatrical architecture: the Restoration intimacy between actress and audience persisted for the next sixty years after 'the three Bs', though both Lane and Garden later mushroomed into outsize showplaces in which the forestage receded and the player became increasingly remote from the audience. *Not*, by and large, in the disregard of realism or unity of effect in scenery and costume: in tragedy a leading actress still had to wear feathers, gloves, veil and train as emblems of authority; an incantatory, musical declamation was *de rigueur*; and concessions to human variables of place and period were little more than perfunctory 'classic 'or oriental' additions to contemporary dress. Audiences were, moreover, still often noisy, brutal and quick to take offence if the players seemed to show signs of insubordination. 'They come to a new play', said Colley Cibber, 'like hounds to a carcass and are all in full cry, sometimes for an hour together before the curtain rises.' Until well on in the century its privileged members insisted on their right to sit on the stage; so that Juliet in the Capulet tomb might be surrounded (as Susannah Cibber was) by a dense crowd of not entirely rapt spectators; and a Cordelia might (like Peg Woffington) be suddenly obliged to fend off the roving hands of an amorous neighbour while listening to her royal father.

The changes could be seen elsewhere. As the theatre moved away from its earlier dependence on the Court after the departure of the Stuarts, winning a wider public and (from the 1720s) a new prosperity, the shape of the programme altered. The drama of the spoken word, with its accompanying prologues and epilogues, was no longer the only accepted entertainment of the evening. Pantomimes, musical farces and ballad operas, which all gave new opportunities of employment to women performers, became increasingly important in theatre budgets. London, moreover, lost its monopoly of playhouses. City after city built its own, led in 1705 by Bath, which was followed in 1729 by Bristol. By 1785, when theatre law was changed, there were nearly thirty provincial playhouses. Actresses were seen in many parts of the country, either *in situ* or on tour, and many were trained outside London. In mid-century over forty companies of strollers were at work.

The expansion of the stage took place in spite of rising opposition to its morality and, in particular, to the morality of its actresses. This opposition was fuelled by the Methodist revival. Yet the moral temperature of the drama had already been readjusted. A reaction against Restoration bawdiness, cynicism and realism set in after the death of Charles II, and was reflected in the Revd. Jeremy Collier's obsessional but influential diatribe of 1697–8, *A Short View of the Immorality and Profaneness of the English Stage*. The reforming movement gathered strength during the reign of Queen Anne, with help from the ladies of the London audience and some royal encouragement. As the joking frankness of *The Country Wife* gave way to the sentimental politeness of *The Conscious Lovers,* authors of comedies were increasingly inclined to romanticize sexual politics and extol the virtues of conjugal fidelity. Adultery was permitted only in tragedies, as a cause of suicide, murder and general ruin. Authors became more circumspect in their language and their plots to the point of absurdity, not only about love and marriage but about religion and politics, after official censorship had been legally imposed by the Licensing Act of 1737 – a measure designed to protect the Government from personal attacks by political satirists but presented by Prime Minister Robert Walpole as a safeguard of public decency and national morality. The theatre became – like its audience – more committed to the defence of the social status quo; and that, of course, included the legal subjugation of women to their superiors. The male belief that this was a fact of nature seems to have been less often questioned than in the previous century. That a woman could charm, or cry, or sleep her way to equality, even mastery, was for long the conventional wisdom, illustrated not only in the drama, but, it was said, in the lives of actresses.

The repertoire of the century did, indeed, include an armoury of comedy parts, in which women conquered men with the traditional battery of feminine power, and a formidable company of women in tragedy who held sway not only over masculine hearts but entire empires, relying on more lethal weapons than killing glances and irresistible sighs. Theatrical history could provide a more selective list of conquests – notably, those in which actresses slept their way into royal and aristocratic patronage. The most celebrated of these relationships was the brief affair between George IV, when Prince of Wales, and Mary 'Perdita' Robinson (who left the stage at twenty-two after little more than three years on the stage); and the virtual marriage of Dorothy Jordan to the Prince's brother William, later William IV. Mrs Jordan bore the Duke of Clarence ten children; helped him to maintain their household by continuing to act throughout the country; led a domestic life (between engagements) of settled domesticity and conjugal fidelity; but was suddenly dropped by the Duke after twenty years when he was required to make a more suitable alliance. Less eminent players often had less stable relationships: that was an occupational risk of their profession. Male seduction was, as one social historian puts it, 'a sport that was tacitly approved, even admired – a sport that kept rich and leisured gentlemen amused and exercised out of the fox-hunting season'.[1] Actresses were sporting types believed to be daughters of the game. That was one salient reason why young men of fashion went to the theatre.

The perils and promiscuities of backstage life have often been over-emphasized in romantic biographies, novels and plays. Many women worked hard at their jobs in the theatre and pursued quiet, domestic lives outside it. As actresses, singers and dancers many enjoyed professional prestige and bargaining power in an expanding market. The top rewards steadily increased: from Mary Betterton's fifty shillings a week to Sarah Siddons's fifty pounds a performance. Yet theatrical management remained, for many years to come, a male prerogative. And married actresses had, legally, no right to their salaries and benefits, which belonged to their husbands. They enjoyed greater freedom and earned more money than any other women; but they were still second-class citizens. It is not surprising, then, that from the 1720s until mid-Victorian times most of the significant new roles available to British actresses were portraits of second-class citizens. Their status was often camouflaged by sentimentality, melodrama and didactic cant, but their place in the sexual hierarchy was fixed and they were firmly tethered to it. What is more, they were second-class parts. That is one supplementary reason why leading actresses and their managers returned continually to the pre-1720 repertoire: to Otway, Dryden, Congreve, Rowe, Southerne and, above all, Shakespeare. He emerged from the worst Restoration mutilations (though still heavily scarred) to win a new popularity among the players and their audiences. In the growing recognition of his towering theatrical genius there was a particular relish for his women.

Some Restoration comedies, too, still supplied a popular ingredient of the repertoire for much of the century. Even though bowdlerized and rewritten, they retained a flavour of freedom in their characters for which there was no real match in contemporary playwriting. Restoration tragedy had a somewhat shorter life; but leading ladies of the stage still appeared as some of the less bathetic royal roarers whose imperial ambitions may have reflected hungers for parity, even dominion, if not in the green rooms then in the antechambers of the feminine Id. Rowe's Artemisa in *The Ambitious Stepmother*, created by Mrs Barry, had a 'more than manly strength of soul', and aspired to supreme power:

> There is not, must not be, a bound for greatness;
> Power gives a sanction, and makes all things just.

Later lady monarchs were set to hunger less for power than for sympathy. They sought to demonstrate not so much their manly strength as their feminine weakness.

> What is a crown, compared with what I feel?
> Can crowns allay extremity of woe!

A Distressed Female was essential to nearly all tragedies. Aggressive Females, of the kind that Mrs Barry played, were felt increasingly to be in bad taste, and the belligerence of heroines like Calista was somewhat tamed and tranquillized in the bid to melt British hearts which was conceived as the main purpose of the theatre.

Whatever the restrictions of public taste and the debilities of the contemporary drama, this was a century distinguished by its acting; and a score of women were among the most distinctive performers – as disdainful beauties, flirtatious romps, country hoydens, comic termagants, sexy chambermaids, fashionable aristocrats, elderly grotesques, virginal misses, classical clothes-horses and (in tragedy) the victims of rape, murder, war, revenge, parental cruelty and male cruelty of every kind (with protracted death-scenes as the *bonnes bouches* of an uplifting evening at the theatre). Among those who made a special mark on their time were Mary Porter (who died in 1765), a pupil of Betterton who, in spite of 'a plain person and a bad voice', was a leading tragedienne for over forty years; Mary Ann Yates (1728–87), another tragedy queen of unparalleled majesty and poignant tenderness (but with little between these poles); George Anne Bellamy (c. 1727–1788), who in her youthful beauty scored a star's success – notably as Garrick's Juliet and in off-stage amours – but had little professional stamina or artistic integrity; Frances Abington (1737–1815), a

Cockney flower-seller – 'Nosegay Fan' – who became a leader of fashion and a top favourite in comedy in a career which lasted forty-four years; and Dorothy Jordan (1761–1816), at whose private life we have already glanced, a popular actress-of-all-work for many years, excelling in hoydens, romps and breeches parts. But with one chapter at my disposal I have selected no more than five 'queens of the stage' from the lost kingdoms of the eighteenth century; and our survey opens with Anne Oldfield.

When Anne Oldfield began her stage career in the last year of the seventeenth century at Drury Lane, Mrs Barry and Mrs Bracegirdle were still perched at the top of the theatrical tree in Lincoln's Inn Fields. Like them she had lost her father in infancy (many eminent actresses until modern times have been brought up by their mothers, or as orphans), and she had an early grounding in the lessons of poverty and the precariousness of feminine freedom.

Born in 1683, Anne Oldfield was the daughter and granddaughter of London vintners, who ran a Pall Mall tavern called the 'George'. Her spendthrift father failed as a publican, sold the 'George' to his brother, bought his way into the Horse Guards as a private, and died prematurely and penniless. His widow found employment as a dressmaker and worked for a time as a servant to Christopher Rich, the patentee of Drury Lane, a connection that may well have helped the start of her daughter's career. Anne earned her keep with a sempstress in King Street, around the corner from the 'George'. She had little time or opportunity for schooling, but she was taught to read at home and developed a taste for the theatre by studying plays as she sewed. Before she was fifteen she was serving in another family pub nearby, the 'Mitre' in St James's Market, managed by her aunt. Here, too, she browsed over plays in print; and the story goes that she was overheard by George Farquhar reading aloud from a Beaumont and Fletcher comedy, *The Scornful Lady,* in which she later played. Farquhar was so impressed by her beauty and her potential talent that he urged her to go on the stage, and also to be his mistress. Then in his early twenties, he had recently made a hit with his first play, *Love in a Bottle.* To promote the young barmaid's fortunes (and his own interest) he enlisted a man of greater pull in the theatre – John Vanbrugh, whose authorship of *The Relapse* and *The Provok'd Wife* had won him recognition as the leading dramatist of the day. Vanbrugh, too, was seduced. With characteristic shrewdness Anne played hard to get, but, as she told Chetwood, the Drury Lane prompter, 'I longed to be at it and only wanted a little decent entreaty.' This soon followed. Vanbrugh persisted, introduced her to Christopher Rich, and that hard-headed, skinflint manager engaged her at fifteen shillings a week. She was sixteen.

Anne Oldfield began without a jot of stage experience, and at first it showed. She had a fresh girlish beauty and sexual magnetism; a good figure, especially in breeches – 'tallish', with a graceful carriage; large, 'speaking' eyes; a keen intelligence; and – off-stage, at least – the self-possession and strong character that a shrewd London working girl needed to survive. She also had an artist's sensibility, not yet awakened, but later revealed not only in her career but also in her collections of paintings, sculpture and jewellery. Yet she was 'almost a mute and unheeded' until Vanbrugh gave her a chance by casting her as the lead (a breeches part, Alinda) in his revision of Fletcher's romantic comedy *The Pilgrim*. In this role she made no impression upon Cibber. He thought she had 'little more than her person' to qualify her for the stage. For one thing, her 'extraordinary diffidence' kept her 'too despondingly down to a formal, plain, (not to say) flat manner of speaking'. This 'flatness' may have been due not only to anxiety and inexperience, but also to her determination to 'talk proper', with the right accent. Yet, for all Cibber's criticism, she does not seem to have let Vanbrugh down: Chetwood, indeed, says she 'charmed' the play into a run. She appeared in Vanbrugh's next play, *The False Friend* (1702), an unsuccessful translation from the French which provided her with the first recorded opportunity to speak an epilogue, and her salary was increased to a pound a week after the Duke of Bedford ('one of her warmest admirers')[2] commended her cause to Rich. Later the Duke is said to have offered her £600 a year for life to be his mistress, a proposal which Mrs Oldfield declined. In spite of the improbability of this figure, it provides a revealing glimpse of the value she set upon herself and upon her virtue. But she remained in obscurity for the first four years of her career – partly because the senior ladies of the company held firmly on to the best acting opportunities. (By the 'possession of parts' convention they shared leading roles, and continued to play them till dismissal, retirement or death gave younger actresses a chance.)

This was an invaluable period of self-education for Anne Oldfield, so privately pursued that Cibber, for one, was 'amazed' by her progress. In the summer of 1703 he played opposite her in Bath in the presence of Queen Anne (who had succeeded to the throne the previous year). The piece was a Restoration potboiler, John Crowne's *Sir Courtly Nice,* and Mrs Oldfield was Leonora, the only role she had managed to grab in the 'female scramble' for the inheritance of Mrs Verbruggen's parts when this actress fell fatally ill. In rehearsal she seemed as humdrum as Cibber had expected; but in performance she dropped the mask and took him by surprise. She was, after all, a real actress, not just a pretty face. 'So forward, so sudden a step into nature I had never seen', Cibber wrote, 'and what made her performance more valuable was that I knew it all proceeded from her own understanding, untaught and unassisted by any one more experienced actor.' The diffidence and the flatness had vanished. So impressed was he by this transformation that he pulled out of a drawer a half-finished play, *The Careless Husband,* and completed it with Anne Oldfield in mind : he had stopped in despair after Act Two, as no actress was fit for the leading role but Mrs Bracegirdle and she worked for the rival company. When it was staged at Drury Lane in the following season, Mrs Oldfield made her reputation as Lady Betty Modish – a proud, capricious, vain, witty and extravagantly fashionable society beauty, revelling in her power over men, but finally humbled into an admission of love and the revelation of a heart of gold. From then onwards Mrs Oldfield's progress was unchecked.

Two years later she attained the heights of £4 a week in salary when Vanbrugh engaged her for the theatre he had built in the Haymarket. His company was recruited from both the patent houses, and Anne found herself acting with 'the three Bs' from Lincoln's Inn Fields – Thomas Betterton, Elizabeth Barry and Anne Bracegirdle. This was a turning-point in her career; 'not only had she the force of example and the spur of competition [especially from Mrs Bracegirdle], but the addition of their repertory of plays added to her scope.'[3] Always eager to learn and to develop, Mrs Oldfield stretched and enlarged her technique in such roles as Celia in *Volpone*, the Silent Woman, Monimia in *The Orphan*, Imoinda in *Oronooko* and Ismena in an adaptation of Racine's *Phèdre*. Within a year Mrs Bracegirdle retired from the stage (prompted, it was rumoured, by the strength of the newcomer's challenge), and Mrs Oldfield had no rival.

Perhaps, as her most recent biographer Robert Gore-Browne has suggested, the sudden flowering of Anne Oldfield in 1703 was caused (or at any rate energized) by a love affair that started in Bath that year. Sir Arthur Maynwaring was an aristocratic *flâneur* and man-about-town fifteen years her senior, a valued member of the Kit-Kat Club with Addison, Congreve, Vanbrugh and Steele (who dedicated the first volume of the *Tatler* to him), an MP and opera buff. He translated Cicero and Ovid, wrote prologues and epilogues and fancied himself as a connoisseur of acting. The stimulating influence of his theatrical coaching, cultivated taste and artistic experience, and, not least, his wide range of social acquaintance, may well have helped an uneducated London barmaid to become the glass of fashion and the mould of form.

Anne and Sir Arthur lived together in apparently unbroken domesticity for nine years, and their relationship – from which a son was born in 1705 – seems to have been generally accepted as a *de facto* marriage, free from scandal, 'far more constant than millions in the conjugal noose'.[4] It was not established, however, without stormy scenes. According to his biographer, 'his friends of both sexes blamed him often for this intrigue, and some of them of the highest rank have had such quarrels with him on this head, that even Mrs Oldfield herself has frequently represented to him that it was for his honour and interest to break it off.'[5] But the more she pleaded against her own interest, the stronger their liaison became.

The candour and confidence of Anne Oldfield's behaviour was illustrated after Maynwaring's death in 1712, when rumours spread that it was due to venereal disease. Anne scotched the story firmly. She had her lover's body dissected by two surgeons, in the presence of two physicians and an apothecary, who pronounced that there was no trace of VD and that death was caused by tuberculosis. Soon there were more rumours (harder to disprove) about Sir Arthur's successors in Mrs Oldfield's affections. But if we are to believe the testimony of her dresser, ex-actress Margaret Saunders (no better witness is available), there was only one man in Mrs Oldfield's life after Sir Arthur: Colonel (later Brigadier) Charles Churchill, the illegitimate son of General Charles Churchill, the Duke of Marlborough's brother. They met in 1718, but Churchill had to woo her for four years (so the legend goes) before she finally capitulated and agreed to live with him. The Colonel was a close friend of the Prime Minister, Sir Robert Walpole, through whose influence he was MP for Castle Rising for thirty years, and an intimate of the Prince of Wales (later George II), who made him a groom of the Bedchamber. The fact that Marlborough's nephew was born on the wrong side of the blanket and was living in sin with the queen of the stage was not held against him in these aristocratic circles. Mrs Oldfield was given entrée to the Prince's mini-court, and (as a Victorian chronicler, Dr Doran, put it) 'kept sisterhood with duchesses. She was to be seen on the terrace at Windsor, walking with the consorts of dukes, and with countesses, and wives of English barons, and the whole gay group might be heard calling one another by their Christian names.'[6] Mrs Oldfield was heard less often addressing her fellow actors on the same terms. Indeed, in her later years she seldom spoke to them at all. With unprecedented pomp and circumstance she went to the theatre every evening in a chair escorted by two footmen. Anne Bracegirdle recalled to Horace Walpole in her old age, 'I remember at the playhouse they used to call: Mrs Oldfield's chair! Mrs Barry's clogs! and Mrs Bracegirdle's pattens!'

The intimacy of Mrs Oldfield's connection with duchesses and countesses has, no doubt, been exaggerated – in the first place by Mrs Oldfield herself. But it seems likely that long before she met Colonel Churchill she acted the woman of breeding, taste and wit so consummately well on the stage, and off the stage dressed with such elegance and style, that she could not only pass as one of her high-society models – and, indeed, surpass some of them – but also earn their respect and their temporary forgetfulness that she wasn't *really* their equal.

Cibber said that 'women of the best rank might have borrowed some part of her behaviour without the least diminution of their sense of dignity'; and this professional and extravagant 'gentility', for which she was so often praised, contributed largely to the reputation of Drury Lane Theatre as 'the school of politeness' (even though this term was scarcely justified by the backstage behaviour of some of its pupils and masters). The ex-barmaid of the 'Mitre' not only mirrored 'women of the best rank', but was a model for them. She set fashions that they followed.

It was not because of her social expertise alone, however, that Anne Oldfield was buried in Westminster Abbey. One of the decisive elements in her success was the steely will and stubborn independence that she concealed behind the elegance and beauty of her public personality. Christopher Rich and his committee of 'patentees' discovered these qualities to their cost in 1709 when, after the restriction of the legitimate drama to Drury Lane (the Haymarket having returned for a time to opera), they attempted to make cuts in their actors' pay and privileges. This economy drive came to a stop when they tried to cheat Mrs Oldfield by levying an additional charge on the box-office receipts of her benefit, amounting to some £70. The next day she complained to the Lord Chamberlain, pointing out that she had returned to Drury Lane at his command, with her colleagues, on the promise that her salary and terms would be the same as those at the Haymarket, where the benefit charges were £40. Her swift action brought to a head the accumulated resentments and grievances of the company, and the Chamberlain warned Rich to mend his ways. To challenge the patentees with their monopoly control was an act of calculated courage: that it should take a woman to do so is a significant pointer, and the challenge is not devalued by the fact that Anne could enjoy, through her lover Maynwaring, a degree of political influence as well as financial security denied to other players.

Rich avoided repayment of the disputed sum, and took reprisals against Mrs Oldfield and others by allocating them inferior parts, but the Lord Chamberlain finally issued an Order for Silence and took away his licence, having meanwhile permitted the Haymarket to be reopened for plays. Anne agreed to combine with Cibber and Robert Wilks in management there on sharing terms – another milestone, this, in the advance of the English actress – but a fourth prospective partner, Thomas Doggett, objected: not to her merit, as Cibber puts it, but to the fact that 'our affairs could never be upon a secure foundation if there was more than one sex admitted to the management of them.' Instead Doggett proposed that Mrs Oldfield should have *carte blanche* on terms; and this was gracefully accepted by the lady 'rather as a favour than a disobligation', for she asked, and got, £200 per annum, with a benefit free of all charges, on a thirteen-year contract. This contract was maintained when the actors moved back in the following year to Drury Lane, where Mrs Oldfield remained for the rest of her career till it was cut short by illness at the age of forty-seven.

Anne Oldfield created sixty-five characters, and appeared in dozens of roles from the repertoire of the previous half-century. In all of them she exercised a personal authority that never faltered – partly through her voice, cajoling and creamy in comedy, passionately clear and bold in tragedy, always sweet, strong and musical; her eyes, which as Calista, 'piercing' and 'flaming', could make the prompter 'shrink with awe', and in comedy, first half-closed with private amusement, could then open to share with the audience the essential joke not only of the line but the life she played; and her combination of majestic manner with commonsense mind. She wore well: according to Cibber 'her figure was always improving to her thirty-sixth year.' More important, she was not satisfied to rest on her laurels. 'Her excellence in acting was never at a stand,' he says, and her success as Lady Townly at forty-five was 'a proof that she was still able to do more, if more could have been done for her.' Unlike nearly all her colleagues (Cibber declares), she was ready to take instruction, to the last. 'It was a hard matter to give her any hint that she was not able to take or improve.' She believed in working at a character, not just dressing up for it.

Some of the dramatists who wrote with Anne Oldfield in mind may well have been influenced by her distinctive off-stage personality and conversation. Notably, many of the sentiments expressed by Lady Betty Modish in *The Careless Husband* were originally Mrs Oldfield's own, said Cibber, 'only dressed with a little more care than when they negligently fell from her lively humour'. Among such examples of 'Oldfieldismos' (as Pope disapprovingly called it) were, perhaps, the following:

Sincerity in love is as much out of fashion as sweet snuff; nobody takes it now.

I can't see a woman of spirit has any business in the world but to dress and make the men like her.

I could no more choose a man by my eye than a shoe; one must draw 'em on a little to see if they are right to one's foot.

Will anything a man *says* make a woman less agreeable? Will his talking spoil one's complexion, or put one's hair out of order? And for reputation, look you, my dear, take it for a rule, that as amongst the lower rank of people, no woman wants beauty that has fortune; so amongst people of fortune, no woman wants virtue that has beauty; but an estate and beauty joined are of an unlimited, nay, a power pontifical, make one not only absolute, but infallible. A fine woman's never in the wrong ...

Prithee tell me, you are often advising me to it, are there those real comfortable advantages to marriage, that our old aunts and grandmothers would persuade us of? ... Can there be the same dear, full delight in giving ease, as pain? O, my dear, the thought of parting with one's power is insupportable!

Although this tone of voice may well have been close to her own, in the three years after the success of *The Careless Husband* Anne Oldfield scored a number of hits with very different parts, old and new. Among the roles she took over were Elvira in *The Spanish Friar*, Celia in *Volpone,* Lady Lurewell in *The Constant Couple* and Nell Gwyn's old part of Florimel in *The Comical Lovers* (Cibber's compound of *Secret Love* and *Marriage à la Mode*). The most important new plays were by her friend George Farquhar. In the first production of *The Recruiting Officer* she was Silvia, that enchanting Shrewsbury tomboy, loving daughter and open-hearted (but virginal) mistress, who stands out among eighteenth-century heroines (and Mrs Oldfield's roles) as an enemy of sham, affectation and false prudery.

I need no salts for my stomach, no hartshorn for my head, nor wash for my complexion; I can gallop all the morning after the hunting horn, and all the evening after a fiddle. In short, I can do everything with my father, but drink, and shoot flying; and I am sure, I can do everything my mother could, were I put to the trial.

As her lover Captain Plume says, 'There's something in that girl more than woman'; and Silvia ('I am heartily tired of my sex') shows her manly side when, in order to keep an eye on Plume, she dresses up as a fellow-officer. 'I take a bold step, a rakish toss, a smart cock, and an impudent air, to be the principal ingredients in the composition of a captain,' says Silvia, swaggeringly suiting her action to her words; and Anne Oldfield in breeches made her the talk of the town.

It seems not too far-fetched to speculate that Anne may have influenced the colouring of her next Farquhar part – in *The Beaux' Stratagem* – as Mrs Sullen, the sardonic, frustrated, flirtatious wife of a boorish squire, hiding a warm and generous heart behind her sharp word and amorous plots: a role midway between Restoration and 'sentimental' comedy. Mrs Sullen's view of life and leisure is poles apart from Silvia's: 'Country pleasures! Racks and torments! Dost think, child, that my limbs were made for leaping of ditches, and clambering over stiles?' Farquhar, who died during the run of the play, gave his ex-barmaid friend the chance for witty banter in the Restoration tradition, as in the scene where she is comparing notes with her sister on the progress of their affairs.

DORINDA: My lover was upon his knees to me.
MRS S: And mine was upon his tiptoes to me.
DORINDA: Mine vowed to die for me.
MRS S: Mine swore to die with me.
DORINDA: Mine spoke the softest moving things.
MRS S: Mine had his moving things too.

In the same play, however, Anne Oldfield broke through this mannered elegance with bitter protests about the condition of women ('in England, a country where women are its glory, must women be abused? Where women rule, must women be enslaved?'); and with sober moralizing upon the divorce laws:

Law! what law can search into the remote abyss of nature? What evidence can prove the unacountable disaffections of wedlock? Can a jury sum up the endless aversions that are rooted in our souls, or can a bench give judgment upon antipathies? . . . No, no, sister; Nature is the first lawgiver; and when age has set tempers opposite, not all the golden links of wedlock, nor iron manacles of law, can keep 'em fast.

It is tempting to suppose that this, too, reflected the views of the actress, as well as the character, especially in the light of the speech that Nicholas Rowe wrote for her in *Jane Shore*:

> Mark by what partial justice we are judged;
> Such is the fate unhappy women find,
> And such the curse entailed upon our kind.
> That man, the lawless libertine, may rove
> Free and unquestioned through the wilds of love.
> While woman, sense and nature's easy fool,
> If poor weak woman swerve from virtue's rule,
> If strongly charmed, she leave the thorny way,
> And in the softer paths of pleasure stray:
> Ruin ensues, reproach and endless shame,
> And one false step entirely damns her fame.
> In vain with tears the loss she may deplore,
> In vain look back to what she was before,
> She sets, like stars that fall, to rise no more.

Early in her career Anne Oldfield had a strong aversion to tragedy. 'I hate to have a page dragging my tail about,' she said. 'Why do they not give Mrs Porter those parts? She can put on a better tragedy face than I can.' Not until she played in Lee's *Mithridates* in 1708 did she seem 'reconciled to tragedy'; but from then on she shone in it. Nicholas Rowe wrote for her two historical 'she-tragedies' of unrelieved gloom in which she achieved a triumph, and which dominated the tragic repertoire of the following century – *Jane Shore* and *Lady Jane Gray*. In the former play she delivered the powerfully plaintive protest against man's inhumanity to woman, quoted above, which may be set beside Calista's speech in the same author's *The Fair Penitent*. It was not until 1722 (at thirty-nine) that she appeared in any of Shakespeare's plays – as Margaret in *Henry VI, Part 2* – but this mutilated version by Ambrose Philips retained no more than some thirty lines from the original. Her only other

Shakespearean role was as Katherine in *Henry V*, revised by Aaron Hill, with the comedy scissored out and a new sub-plot inserted.

In her early forties, Anne Oldfield began to suffer severely from cancer. Every now and again she collapsed on stage, and performances had to be cancelled. The first time this happened was in 1727, with *The Careless Husband*. Showing little sign of her disease, she struggled on until the spring of 1730. In what was to be her final season she acted in twenty-eight plays. Her last new role was as a tragedy queen: Sophonisba, Queen of Carthage, in James Thomson's first play; and her exertions in it were believed backstage at Drury Lane to have precipitated her death. Her final appearance was as Lady Brute in *The Provok'd Wife* on 30 April. Two months later she made her will, leaving £5000 to one illegitimate son, Arthur Maynwaring, and her new house and its valuable contents to the other, Charles Churchill. Learning from the doctors that she would never act again, she showed her professional pride for the last time by informing the Drury Lane management that she could accept no further instalments of her salary. (She was then earning twelve guineas a week, with £100 per annum as a dress allowance and about £100 in benefit takings – some three times as much as Mrs Betterton or Mrs Barry.)

Anne Oldfield died at her house in Lower Grosvenor Street on 22 October. On her instructions her faithful dresser, Margaret Saunders, ensured that she looked her best in death, as she had always done in life: she wore a linen shift (instead of the statutory woollen shroud), a cap and ruffles of the best Brussels lace, new white kid gloves, and a redeeming touch of rouge. Pope later imagined her saying:

> 'Odious! In woollen! 'twould a saint provoke!'
> (Were the last words that poor Narcissa spoke).
> 'No, let a charming chintz and Brussels lace
> Wrap my cold limbs and shade my lifeless face;
> One would not, sure, be frightful when one's dead,
> And Betty, give this cheek a little red.'

To the last, Whig influence served her well. Charles Churchill enlisted the support of Robert Walpole and Lord Hervey; a delegation went to the Dean of Westminster Abbey; and four days later 'the box's charmer and the pit's delight' lay in state in the Jerusalem Chamber on a velvet-draped bier, past which her last audience slowly filed. That night she was carried into the Abbey, with two peers among the pall-bearers and young Arthur Maynwaring as the chief mourner. After a service read by the Senior Prebendary she was buried near Congreve, who had died a few months earlier. The honours paid to Anne Oldfield, although she had publicly brought up bastards by two successive partners, shone out in striking contrast – which Voltaire pointed out in a bitter poem – to the shameful treatment that same year in Paris of her French contemporary, the great Adrienne Lecouvreur, whose body was refused Christian burial and was hastily buried in quicklime at midnight by the torches of two street porters on a patch of wasteland, with no sign of any kind to mark the place. 'For two generations after her death she remained the standard of comparison by which the merits of comedy and tragedy queens were tried.'[7] She became immortalized in stage legend (frequently as 'Nance' Oldfield, a name apparently never used in her lifetime). And two centuries after her birth she was reincarnated on the stage by one of her greatest successors, Ellen Terry.

With Catherine Clive, at whose benefit performance Anne Oldfield made her last appearance, we enter the era of David Garrick, the great actor-manager who remade the fortunes of Drury Lane and raised to new heights the standards of acting, design, production and management in the British theatre. Not the least of Garrick's problems was to keep the peace among the leading actresses in his company, to hold them away from each other's throats and from his own, while checking the wilder absurdities of the 'possession of parts' system, by which they demanded to go on playing roles long after they had outlived them. Among the most explosive, the most beloved and the most expert of these prima donnas was Kitty Clive.

Born in 1711 in London as Catherine Raftor, she was unmistakably Irish in her personality. Her father is said to have been a Kilkenny-born barrister turned soldier in the French army after the Battle of the Boyne. He had married a daughter of a London merchant, but not, apparently, with profitable results, for Catherine became the main support of her father and his large family. Chetwood, ex-prompter and stage historian, offers the romantic explanation, of a kind familiar in theatrical genealogy, that Mr Raftor lost his Irish estates through loyalty to James II, but fails to explain how he also lost the 'handsome fortune' acquired in marriage. No evidence survives about Catherine's childhood or adolescence; nor, more surprisingly, does any scandal. She told Chetwood that she was stage-struck at twelve, and used to 'tag around' with a friend after Robert Wilks, the leading actor of the day, whenever they saw him in the street. It seems clear that she started work very young – we first hear of her in service, scrubbing the steps of a Houndsditch house – but in spite of her early poverty she apparently kept to the paths of virtue, and stayed on them throughout her life. Her marriage in 1732/3 to George Clive – brother to one judge, nephew of another, but himself a non-practising barrister – ended rapidly in a separation by mutual consent; and thereafter her name was not connected with any man's in contemporary gossip. She lived most of her life with her brother Jemmy, an ugly, awkward and unsuccessful actor but an entertaining companion (he must have been, to have amused Horace Walpole for years).

Kitty Clive was, and remained, a loner: partly because she had a fierce sense of her own independence and merit; and partly because she was plain. It was not her beauty that started her off in the theatre, out of the blue, but her singing voice. It was as a singer that she joined the Drury Lane musical establishment when she was sixteen or seventeen around 1728. Her appearances in the legitimate repertoire were at first limited to singing and dancing between the acts or, at best, in the musical scenes that featured largely in *Macbeth*. According to Dr Burney, her voice caught the attention of Handel, and she sang in a number of his oratorios, although, said the Doctor, her voice was quite unfitted for sacred music – or, indeed, for music of any *serious* kind: it was 'intolerable when she meant it to be fine'.[8] Her first recorded appearance was as Bianca in *Othello*, on 12 October 1728. She achieved her first notable success three years later as Nell, the leading *soubrette* in Charles Coffey's ballad-opera *The Devil to Pay*, where her 'boisterous vivacity' made her 'a prime favourite of the public'. Long before Garrick took over Drury Lane in 1747 Catherine Clive was established as London's leading comedienne, in the lighter part of the comic repertoire, a supremacy she kept for nearly forty years. She left the stage suddenly at the age of fifty-eight, with a final performance of two of her biggest roles – Flora, the lady's maid in *The Wonder*, and Mrs Riot in Garrick's *Lethe*. Horace Walpole, one of her closest friends, had given her a house near to his own in Strawberry Hill, and there she retired with her brother Jemmy, to enjoy in relative prosperity the next seventeen years. When she died at seventy-five (6 December 1785), Walpole put on an urn in his garden the following inscription as her memorial:

> Ye smiles and jests still hover round;
> This is mirth's consecrated ground.
> Here lived the laughter loving dame,
> A matchless actress, Clive her name.
> The comic muse with her retired,
> And shed a tear when she expired.

Kitty Clive acted in nearly two hundred plays, although her basic repertoire consisted of little more than a dozen parts. They included Mrs Heidelberg, the vulgar *nouvelle riche* grotesque in *The Clandestine Marriage*; Biddy Tipkin, the romanticizing dreamer of *The Tender Husband*; Miss Prue, the teenage hoyden of *Love for Love* (which she insisted on playing into her forties); Lady Bab, the maid in Garrick's *High Life Below Stairs*; Phillis, the maid in Steele's *The Conscious Lovers*; and Catherine in *Catherine and Petruchio*, the abbreviated travesty that Garrick made of *The Taming of the Shrew*. As Mrs Riot in *Lethe*, she played a lady of fashion, but a totally unconvincing one – that was her appeal. So popular was she in this role (known as 'The Fine Lady') that with Woodward as 'The Fine Gentleman' she was translated into Bow porcelain figurines (now rare collector's pieces). Mrs Clive specialized in 'country girls, romps, hoydens and dowdies, superannuated beauties, viragoes and humourists', throwing in for good measure songs and imitations (she was known for mimicking female opera singers). Best of all were her chambermaids, the lynchpins of Old Comedy. To these bustling, pert, plotting, coolly cynical, outspoken intriguers her temperament was most conspicuously suited. She played them with an intense and infectious relish that kept the audience in smiles and laughter. Churchill wrote in *The Rosciad*:

> Easy, as if at home, the stage she trod
> Nor sought the critic's praise, nor feared his rod.
> Original in spirit and in ease,
> She pleased by hiding all attempts to please.

In characters higher up the social scale, especially those who talked in blank verse, she lost this relaxed authority. She longed to play serious parts, if only to outdo Garrick, which was her dearest wish. Watching him from the wings one night playing Lear, she was so moved (and so furious at being so) that 'she sobbed one minute and abused him the next', hurrying off with the cry, 'Damn him! I believe he could act a gridiron.' But she had to recognize (after an abortive attempt at Zara) that she would never be accepted as a tragedy queen. She was mediocre as Ophelia ('very unequal to herself', as Henry Fielding put it); a disaster as Cordelia; and as Portia she played the court scene for laughs, imitating legal luminaries of the day. (She is said to have attempted Shylock, too, with a heavy Jewish accent.)

Off the stage Clive was, in Tate Wilkinson's words, 'a mixture of combustibles: she was passionate, cross, vulgar, yet sensible'.[9] Sharply malicious, she was also the soul of generosity; a jealous colleague, but a steadfast friend; pettily vain, but unquenchably courageous, with 'a prodigious fund of natural spirit and humour'. On the debit side, the bad temper of this 'fierce Amazonian dame' made the whole green-room dread the signs of her displeasure. She did battle with Shuter, Woodward, Susannah Cibber, Peg Woffington and of course Garrick, and her scraps were usually loudly publicized. On arriving at a rehearsal of *The Merchant* and being told that Foote was to play Shylock, she cried: 'What, *you*: *you* play Shylock to my Portia! Oh, then I'm off' – and off she went. 'She instantly quitted the theatre, and the play was obliged to be changed.'[10] As she grew older, stouter, redder in the face and visibly incompatible with some of her early successes, her sense of grievances, both real and imaginary, grew more intense. On the credit side the Pivey – as she called herself to Garrick – was a dedicated professional who put her work first and fought bravely for its proper recognition and remuneration. 'Conscious of the scrupulous fashion in which she did her duty to the public, she claimed that the same regard should be paid to her by her employers. . . .'[11] (Where else outside the theatre was it possible, until the twentieth century, for a woman to make such a claim?) She was not always 'agin' the management, though. In 1733, for instance, she sided with the patentees of Drury Lane when most of her colleagues deserted with Theophilus Cibber; obstinately refused to let them down or to skimp any labours in their service; and even offered to act for nothing – or so it was asserted by Henry Fielding, in the preface to *The Intriguing Chambermaid*, in which she starred. Her role, said Fielding, writing while the dispute was still in train, 'is so full of honour, that had it been in higher life, it would have given you the reputation of the greatest heroine of the age.' How Kitty Clive must have laughed at that eulogy, but how proud she must have been, too. Her sense of humour, however, fell into abeyance when she felt that her rights were challenged – as when in 1736 Susannah Cibber tried to grab her role of Polly in *The Beggar's Opera* and, some years later, to take over Estifania in *Rule a Wife*. Mrs Cibber was better suited to both parts, but they were in Mrs Clive's 'possession', and she was a tigress in defence of her territory. When part of her salary was stopped because she missed a performance, having been delayed in the country, she wrote to Garrick: 'I believe you will not find any part of the English laws that will support this sort of treatment of an actress, who has a right from her character and service on the stage to expect some kind of respect.'[12] Characteristically, when she was attacked for refusing to act in 1743 (because the managers were proposing lower terms) she issued a twenty-two-page pamphlet. This was written, perhaps, with the help of Fielding or another friend, as her own spelling and grammar were eccentric, but she had a natural talent for writing, and was the author of several minor farces. She said:

As to my performances, the audiences are the only and proper judges; but I may *venture* to affirm that my labour and application have been greater than any other performer on the stage. I have not

only acted in almost all the plays, but in farces and musical entertainments; and very frequently two parts in a night, even to the
prejudice of my health.

Mrs Clive had a passion for addressing the public in print, for
lobbying allies in every quarter, and for challenging the authori-
ties. 'I know it is in vain to expostulate with people in power,'
she wrote in 1768, but in fact she had been sporadically
expostulating with them for nearly fifty years. She put a high
value on herself; but she was right to do so. Her letters to
Garrick show that she was an acutely perceptive and warm-
hearted observer of his work, an artist who could appreciate
(for all her flaring jealousy) true greatness.

Kitty Clive herself was an unmatchable original. She was
the queen of romps, the empress of *soubrettes*, the eighteenth-
century incarnation of Nell Gwyn without the frankly whorish
eroticism. She lacked beauty in face and figure; but she had an
abundance of comic energy and intelligence, with the skill to
channel and project it, galvanizing trifles, for a moment, into
the semblance of art. 'Nothing, though ever so barren, even
though it exceeds the limits of nature, can be flat in her hands,'
wrote Fielding.[13] She was, said Tate Wilkinson, 'a diamond of
the first water', with so much 'natural genius'[14] that her
deficiencies in youth, glamour and education mattered not at
all. Oliver Goldsmith said she had 'more true humour than any
actor or actress upon the English or any other stage I have
seen'.[15] Dr Johnson – who sought her out to sit by, in company,
because 'she always understands what you say' – declared that
'What Clive did best, she did better than Garrick' (although he
admitted that she could 'not do half so many things well').
Thomas Wilkes acclaimed her as 'the Garrick of the ladies'.
After her retirement Garrick himself, overlooking all the
trouble she had caused him, described her as 'that truly great
comedian' – and this was not one of his diplomatic managerial
encomia but a private note on the back of one of her letters to
him, letters in which a touch of her quality still lingers.

No matter how the public might idolize a Bracegirdle or a
Clive, neither could hope to match the honour and glory of a
tragedy queen. Comedy was critically devalued for generations
as the inferior theatrical form, lacking in that projection of

high-minded solemnity which many English people (especially English intellectuals) have always tended to regard as the pinnacle of theatrical achievement – indeed, the justification of theatrical activity. Of all the tragedy queens between Mrs Barry and Mrs Siddons the outstanding monarch was Mrs Pritchard. Born in the same year as Kitty Clive, who was among her closest friends, she was a versatile player who succeeded in comedy, too (unlike Mrs Siddons); and she may be rated, in the range and power of her characterization, as a more considerable artist than either Anne Bracegirdle or Anne Oldfield. If they have had a better press and a richer posthumous literature it is partly because they had beauty, wit and influential friends; and because their lives excited public interest. By comparison, Mrs Pritchard's life remained severely private, domestic and respectable; and she was both plain and reticent. She is remembered by Dr Johnson's scornful dismissal of her as a vulgar idiot till she appeared on the stage, with a 'common' accent (she called for her 'gownd', he said) and 'quite mechanical' playing; 'it is wonderful how little mind she had.' And the tale has persisted that all she had read of *Macbeth* was her own part. Perhaps; but it should be recalled that these stories emanate from Mrs Siddons, who found it difficult to believe that anybody could have played Lady Macbeth with any degree of success before she did. Fanny Burney took the opposite view to Dr Johnson: 'dear Pritchard's person came against her perpetually – but what a *mind* she had!'[16] On closer scrutiny of Hannah Pritchard, as far as this is remotely possible today – nobody has ever written a book about *her* – a somewhat different picture emerges.

Hannah Vaughan gave her birthdate as 1711, but nothing else is known of her life until her twenties except that she began her acting career at the very bottom of the ladder, in the booths of Bartholomew Fair and Southwark Fair, where her father probably acted. Here, if she was to survive long enough to earn her few shillings, an actress had to learn instant audience-control in the simplified, summary versions of popular farces, comedies and tragedies that were staged for the London holiday crowds. She may have appeared at the theatre in Goodman's Fields (which opened in 1729) in Banks's *Virtue Betrayed*; but it was through Theophilus Cibber that she embarked on a career in the 'legitimate' drama, when he leased the Haymarket in 1733. After that season she went to Drury Lane as a 'general utility' player in small parts. She married an equally obscure actor, William Pritchard, who later became treasurer of Drury Lane under Garrick; and as she appears to have been not only a plain woman but a virtuous one, rapid progress in her career may have seemed improbable. She was ill-educated (if, indeed, she had any education at all), and never achieved the social transformation (and self-liberation) contrived by Mrs Bracegirdle and Mrs Oldfield.

Within two years, however, Mrs Pritchard made a hit as Rosalind. For the first time in her career, she got a prolonged round of applause, early on, with her delivery of the line, 'Take the cork out of thy mouth, that I may drink thy tidings'; and this encouragement (according to John Hill) 'gave a new spirit to all the rest; she was applauded throughout, and ever after . . . otherwise, perhaps, the best actress of the British stage would have perished in oblivion.'[17] Hannah Pritchard emerged from obscurity to become one of the leading talents at Drury Lane. For a time she was restricted to comedy. She scored in such roles as Doll Common, Mrs Sullen, Lady Brute, Estifania, Mrs Oakley (in *The Jealous Wife*) and, above all, Rosalind and Beatrice. Although she appeared somewhat out of her social class in the aristocratic line, she shone in Shakespeare; and in her time she was saluted (and painted) as the comic Muse. However unsuitable her very bulky figure came to seem in a role, it 'was impossible to hear her speak and not forget the disadvantage',[18] even as Rosalind and Millamant – impossible, that is, in a generation of listeners to whom stage illusion mattered less than words and music. Before long she showed her mastery in tragedy, too. She became prosperous; brought up a large family; and was widely respected in the profession.

In her prime Mrs Pritchard was noted for her naturalness (if not naturalism) in tragedy as well as comedy. As Mrs Beverley in *The Gamester,* she did not appear to be conscious of the audience before her. 'She seemed to be a gentlewoman in domestic life, walking about in her own parlour, in the deepest distress, and overwhelmed with misery.'[19] Or, as John Hill testified in another role, 'When she represents the wife of Theseus, she is the wife of Theseus, and nothing of herself appears, but all the character.'[20] In her greatest role, 'Lady Macbeth, not the actress, seemed to appear before us. . . .'[21] This identification with the character's emotions at the cost of theatrical etiquette led Mrs Pritchard to a demonstrative sorrow that offended some connoisseurs. Garrick, for instance, disliked her 'blubbering of the grief' as Volumnia; and one author, Delap, complained that she 'spoilt his Hecuba with sobbing so much . . . she was really so moved, that she fell in fits behind the scenes.'[22]

In her concern for truth Mrs Pritchard never forgot, however, the need to be *heard*. According to Genest, 'however voluble in enunciation her part might require her to be, yet by her exact articulation not a syllable was lost.'[23] Her vocal delivery was 'ever varied and ever just'. And she could move swiftly from one muse to another; Gibbon commented in his journal on the 'surprising versatility of Mrs Pritchard's talents, who rehearsed, almost at the same time, the part of a furious queen in the green-room and that of a coquette on the stage; and passed several times from one to the other with the utmost ease and happiness.'[24]

In tragedy, one of her definitive roles was that of Gertrude: of her closet-scene in *Hamlet* Dr Doran wrote, 'its unequalled excellence remains a tradition of the stage.'[25] When Hamlet asked her if she could not see the Ghost, 'she turned her head slowly round . . . with a certain glare in her eyes, which looked everywhere and saw nothing,' as she said, 'nothing at all: yet all that's here I see.' According to a critic in 1772, writing after her retirement, this gave 'an expression and horror to the whole not to be described.'[26] As Lady Macbeth, among her most memorable moments were those when she snatched the daggers from her husband ('a picture of the most consummate intrepidity in mischief'); when they whispered together – softly, chillingly and audibly ('You heard what they spoke, but you learned more from the agitation of mind displayed in their action and deportment'[27]); and, of course, the sleep-walking scene, where her acting resembled 'those sudden flashes of lightning which more accurately discover the horrors of the surrounding darkness'[28] (a description by Tom Davies that anticipates Hazlitt's words on Kean). Lord Harcourt, an admirer of Mrs Siddons in the role, said that she nevertheless lacked in general 'the unequalled compass and melody of Mrs Pritchard', and in this scene 'there was not the horror in the sigh, nor the sleepiness in the tone, nor the articulation in the voice.'[29]

In her later years Garrick clearly found her not only unattractive and boring but even repellent: in a hysterical letter to his brother George (written, perhaps, when he was drunk) the year before she retired, he registered disgust at the thought of playing opposite her in *The Jealous Husband*. 'I have not played Oakley these three years – sick – sick – sick – and Mrs Pritchard will make me sicker – great bubbies, nodding head and no teeth.'[30] But beside that sad and sudden moment of candour about her old age (for so it must be reckoned) should be set the tribute of Charles Churchill:

> When love, hate, jealousy, despair and rage,
> With wildest tumults in her breast engage,
> Still equal to herself is Zara seen,
> Her passions are the passions of a queen.

Mrs Piozzi (formerly Mrs Thrale), though a close friend and fervent admirer of Mrs Siddons, noted in her diary:

Mrs Pritchard was *incomparable,* her merit overbore the want of figure, her intelligence pervaded every sense – she was the most refined coquet of quality in Cibber's Lady Betty, the most cunning and vulgar jade that Ben Jonson could invent, in Doll Common; the loftiest Roman matron that Shakespeare could conceive, in Coriolanus's mother – the tenderest, the most *instinctively* tender parent that Voltaire or his translator Hill could give us in Merope; the softest and most subdued penitent that Rowe could exhibit in Jane Shore.

Compared in 'versatility of genius' with Mrs Pritchard, said Hester Piozzi, Mrs Siddons was 'limited and confined'.[31] Charles Dibdin declared that Mrs Pritchard was 'everywhere great, everywhere impressive and everywhere feminine'.[32] She gave her farewell performance – as Lady Macbeth, with Garrick – on 24 April 1768. Within four months she was dead. Four years later a marble tablet was erected to Hannah Pritchard's memory in Westminster Abbey, next to Shakespeare in Poets' Corner. The epitaph, written by the Poet Laureate, William Whitehead, included these lines:

> Her comic vein had ev'ry charm to please,
> 'Twas Nature's dictates breath'd with Nature's ease;
> E'en when her pow'rs sustained the tragic load,
> Full, clear and just, th' harmonious accents flow'd;
> And the big passions of her feeling heart
> Burst freely forth, and sham'd the mimic art.

Yet there is little sign of these passions on the walls of the Garrick Club, where in Zoffany's famous painting she faces Garrick for ever, holding two daggers in her right hand, as Lady Macbeth. Somehow, in spite of the marble tablet and the pictures, Mrs Pritchard disappeared from the stage of memory at her death, while dozens of lesser talents linger, more vividly, on.

To many playgoers in Mrs Pritchard's heyday her greatest rival in tragedy seemed to be Susannah Cibber ('the greatest female plague belonging to my house,' said David Garrick). Born about 1715 in King Street, Covent Garden, she was the daughter of a Roman Catholic upholsterer, Thomas Arne, who was wealthy enough to send at least one son to Eton. Her background was more prosperous and settled than that of many actresses with shadowy pretensions to greater gentility and lost parental fortunes. Family influence put her on the stage. Susannah's elder brother Thomas, who later achieved fame as one of the leading English composers of the century, had a driving passion for music. Having discovered that his sister had an unusually sweet singing voice, he coached her for a theatrical debut in opera (Lampe's *Amelia*) at the Haymarket in 1732. In the following spring she attracted attention at Lincoln's Inn Fields in her brother's second opera, *Rosamond* (adapted from Addison); and, having made a success with one particular song, she was asked to sing it between the acts of several plays that year. She also appeared, a few weeks after *Rosamond*, in Thomas Arne's third opera (he was only twenty-three) at the Haymarket — *The Opera of Operas*; or *Tom Thumb the Great*. (He wrote fourteen further works in the next forty years; but is best known today for his arrangement of 'God Save the King', of which she gave the first public rendering at Drury Lane in 1745.) *Rosamond* led to the engagement of both Arnes by Drury Lane; but she seems to have been among the artists seceding in May from the Lane with Theophilus Cibber. She joined his company at the Haymarket; and she married him the following April. It proved to be the biggest mistake of Susannah's life.

Colley Cibber had opposed the match with his son 'because she had no fortune'; but as the marriage seemed to be much happier than he expected, he decided to train his new daughter-in-law for the stage. When the rebel players returned to Drury Lane Susannah Cibber came with them, almost certainly as a singer, but as she flowered under the old actor's tuition the Cibbers planned to launch her as an actress under the most favourable auspices they could contrive. They persuaded a dramatist and critic, Aaron Hill, to give Susannah the leading role in *Zara*, his adaptation of Voltaire's Parisian hit *Zaire*. John Rich had refused *Zara* in 1733. The Drury Lane manager accepted it, but kept on postponing its production. This was not accomplished until May 1735, and then it was given by a largely amateur cast in a hall in Villiers Street. It was a family occasion: Colley wrote a prologue; Theophilus played Nerestan; Susannah's brother wrote the music; and the author's nephew, Mr Hill, played Osman. He was a disaster, but Mrs Cibber was a triumphant success. Although her biographer is carrying partisanship too far when he says that 'her superiority over every other performer in that line was, from that period, scarcely disputed,'[33] she arrived overnight at the top of her new profession. Her salary was doubled that season, from £100 to £200; her benefit brought in over £100; and she stepped into a line of front-rank parts – all on the strength of her first appearance in a straight play. Having allowed for the exceptional intensive training and family kudos, it must be admitted that Susannah Cibber justified the nepotism with a rare talent and intelligence, supported by a will of steel.

During the next two years Susannah appeared as Belvidera, Monimia, Isabella (in *Measure for Measure*), Dryden's Cleopatra, the Lady in Milton's *Comus* (for which her brother wrote the music), Cassandra in James Thomson's *Agamemnon*, Amanda in *The Relapse*, Mrs Loveit in *The Man of Mode*, and Indiana in Steele's *The Conscious Lovers*. In 1738 she requested the Drury Lane management to pay her no less than the senior actress in the company and to allocate her the first benefit – in other words, to let her ignore the hierarchical ladder and be officially recognized as the leading player, although she was probably the least experienced in the theatre. When her demand was, not surprisingly, refused, she left Drury Lane, and did not return for eight years. Mrs Cibber's curious behaviour was not entirely due to vanity and ambition: she needed the money, because Mr Cibber was spending it all. The marriage idyll had quickly ended – almost as quickly as the lives of their two children, who died in infancy. The loving husband of 1734 had by 1737 shown himself to be a cruel pig. Theophilus 'collected almost all the money his wife made at the theatre; he stripped her of her clothes and even of her linen; he paid his creditors with free tickets to her benefit plays; he had himself "colorably" arrested, so that he could seize the rest of her personal effects and sell them to raise money.'[34] He went further. As Susannah was his only capital, he put her in mortgage by encouraging a younger and wealthier gentleman-friend, William Sloper, from whom he borrowed money, to borrow Mrs Cibber, too, turning a blind eye to the ensuing affair.

In the summer of 1738 Theophilus had to make a hurried trip to France to escape from his creditors, and Susannah went off to live with Mr Sloper at a house in Burnham, Bucks. After her husband's return she continued to see her lover, until the desperate Mr Cibber, having failed to regain his conjugal rights (and his wife's earning power) by persuasion, abducted her from the Burnham house with the help of two armed 'heavies'. He set her up in the care of a Drury Lane candle-snuffer, Mr Stint, at a tavern not far from the theatre: but she was rescued by her brother Thomas, at the head of a mob of a hundred (or so Stint claimed). Perceiving that no money was to be got from Susannah or Mr Sloper by his previous tactics, Theophilus sued his friend for assaulting, ravishing and carnally knowing his wife. That December Mrs Cibber's adultery was proved in court, but so was Mr Cibber's connivance in it. Instead of the £5000 he had sought in damages the special jury awarded him £10. This *cause célèbre* would seem to have ruined the reputations of both the Cibbers; yet the seedy affair was not over. Theophilus was determined to get his own back on Susannah, who early the next year gave birth to a daughter clearly fathered by Mr Sloper. She lived in hiding from her husband, but he discovered her rooms in Kennington Lane, forced his way in and seized all her remaining valuables, those possessions (and gifts from Mr Sloper) left from his earlier raids on her property – property to which, by law, he was entitled. Some weeks later he brought *another* action against Sloper, for double the original stake, to compensate him for his wife's loss of earnings. This time the jury took a more favourable view of the plaintiff and his marital grievance, and awarded him £500.

For the next two years Susannah Cibber disappeared from view: her spectacularly promising career seemed to have come to a stop as sudden as its start. She was, no doubt, living in seclusion with William Sloper, bringing up their daughter and recovering from Theophilus. If she had wanted to start acting again, her husband would have made her life impossible. She was still his legal chattel, 'and he was in no way disposed to permit her to exercise her talents for her own advantage.' When she did emerge in December 1741 it was in the relative safety of the Dublin stage. She repeated some of her London successes in a short season for which she was paid £300, £100 more than she had earned in salary at Drury Lane three years earlier. In that same month she also appeared in the first performance of *The Messiah,* under Handel's personal tuition. (At one performance an Irish cleric, Dr Delany, was so moved that, holding out his arms towards her, he shouted: 'Woman! Thy sins be forgiven thee!') Dr Burney said of her delivery of 'Return, Lord God of Hosts': 'though her voice was but a thread, and her knowledge of music very inconsiderable, yet from her intelligence of the words, and native feeling, she sang this admirable supplication in a more touching manner than the finest opera singers I ever heard attempt it.'[35] Handel, a personal friend, who wrote several songs for her, is said to have composed Micah in *Samson* and Daniel in *Belshazzar* with her in mind.

Six months later Susannah Cibber returned to England. Theophilus had at last, it seems, agreed that she should be free to earn her living and spend it as she pleased. From now on she lived openly with Sloper. Their daughter was brought up as Miss Cibber. Even in that broad-minded era, when gossip about the mistresses of kings and statesmen was an essential element in the nation's small talk, it was something of an achievement for a woman 'living in sin' to preserve both public respect and freedom of action. As a devout Catholic, she could not have married again, even if Theophilus had been prepared for a divorce; and after he was drowned in the Irish Sea in 1758, on his way to act in Dublin, she still refused to become Mrs Sloper. Or did Mr Sloper now draw the line at marriage? In any event, he remained her 'protector' until her death, and acknowledged Miss Cibber as his daughter. By and large, it seems to have been accepted that Mrs Cibber was more sinned against than sinning, was both naturally pious and monogamous, and was – perhaps most to the point – so successful and prosperous in her public life that private irregularities were generally condoned in those sectors of society where actresses were not already anathema.

In September 1742 Susannah Cibber resumed her stage career in England at Covent Garden, as Desdemona to Quin's Othello. The family scandal had created an unusual appetite for the tragedy, and when Mrs Cibber affirmed her character's innocence with passionate intensity, in what seemed to be a cry from the heart, the house rose to her – and the play was stopped by prolonged applause. Without further demonstrations she took her place at the top of her profession and remained at Covent Garden for two seasons. Proud, restless, impatient and – like Kitty Clive – a stickler for her rights, she was a skilfully harassing haggler, so much so that John Rich – Christopher's son and heir in management – sent her to Paris to negotiate terms with some French dancers. She found it hard for some years to take root with one management. During the next decade she oscillated between the two patent theatres, with two seasons at neither house. In 1753, however, she settled at Drury Lane under Garrick to become one of his biggest box-office attractions and his most infuriatingly intransigent artist; and there she stayed with 'frequent interruptions of ill health' (many of them genuine) and several premature announcements of her death, until she actually died on 5 January 1766. When Garrick heard the news, he exclaimed, 'Then Tragedy is dead'; but added swiftly, 'on one side'. She was buried in the cloisters of Westminster Abbey.

Why was she so honoured? In her own time (or just after it) she was thought by several eminences to be overvalued. Dr Johnson (who was disappointed by her Aspasia in his unsuccessful tragedy, *Irene*) said that she 'got more reputation than she deserved, as she had a great sameness'. She lacked majesty and range; her vocabulary of gesture was restricted to 'lifting up and down of the arms, at almost every period',[36] and putting her hands together too frequently. She had little talent for comedy, although she showed herself determined to prove the opposite. In tragedy, moreover, she failed the heights of Lady Macbeth; and when compared with Mrs Pritchard was found (by Richard Cumberland, for instance) to lack variety in action, expression and vocal tone, and, above all, 'nature'. As Calista, he complained, she did not speak the lines but 'sang or rather recitatived' them, in a sweet, plaintive, high-pitched and rather monotonous incantation. 'It was like a long old legendary ballad of innumerable stanzas, every one of which is sung to the same tune.'[37]

Yet, to many others, her voice had – as Davies put it – an 'irresistible magic'. With Garrick's eye and Mrs Pritchard's soul, said Horace Walpole, it was the essential requirement of the perfect actor. Its soft and silvery sweetness was ranked among the main reasons why Garrick put up with her plaguiness and paid her so highly. (In 1763 he noted in his journal, 'Mrs Cibber has received from us £700 a year beside her benefit, and has everything but the mere garniture of her head found by the managers.') She had enough beauty to assume more of it, on stage. A nineteenth-century historian imagined her as 'an alabaster vase lighted from within';[38] she had eloquently expressive eyes ('in grief and tenderness they looked as if they swam in tears; in rage and despair they seemed to dart flashes of fire'[39]); and looked oddly like Garrick in complexion, face and size, as if they were brother and sister. Although she was somewhat short in stature ('unimportant') for a tragedy queen, she had a good figure ('uncommon symmetry and exact proportion') – and maintained its appearance of youth far into middle age. She was a charmer, both on and off the stage, with no affectations of gentility, and a 'manly constancy' and 'serenity of mind'.[40] According to Tate Wilkinson, she was 'the best Ophelia that ever appeared before or since'; Charles Macklin said that her Juliet was unequalled in expressing love, grief, tenderness or rage. She was an ageless romantic heroine as Ophelia, Desdemona, Juliet or Perdita. But one of her greatest successes was as Constance in *King John*. At the lines:

> Here I and sorrow sit: this is my throne:
> Let kings come bow to it.

'nothing that ever was exhibited could exceed this picture of distress; and nothing that ever came from the mouth of mortal was ever spoken with more dignified propriety.'[41] Mrs Cibber was, indeed, expert in tenderness and distress, a specialist in sweet and suffering sensibilities, as in Belvidera, Calista and Indiana. Churchill addressed her as:

> Mistress of each soft art, with matchless skill
> To turn and wind the passions as she will;
> To melt the heart with sympathetic woe,
> Awake the sigh, and teach the tear to flow . . .

But she could also storm with anger and resentment; go luridly mad, as was expected of a player queen, as in *Jane Shore*, and (to quote *The Rosciad* again), 'freeze the soul with horror and despair.' Charles Dibdin declared that

In all characters of tenderness and pathos, in which the workings of the feeling mind call for the force of excessive sensibility, she was like Garrick; the character she represented . . . she greatly felt, and vigorously expressed . . . Actresses may have had more majesty, more fire, but I believe that all the tragic characters, truly feminine, greatly conceived, and highly written, had a superior representative in Mrs Cibber than in any other actress.[42]

And David Williams, writing in 1772, said: 'The criterion by which I judge of an actor is the degree of power he has of making one forget that he is one. This Mrs Cibber possessed to a greater degree than any one I ever saw.'[43]

Between Nell Gwyn and Sarah Siddons the best-remembered actress on the British stage is Margaret Woffington. Like Nell Gwyn's, her fame depends less on her theatrical achievements than on her sexual prowess, magnified by lubricious gossip during her lifetime, posthumously endorsed by a mildly pornographic hack 'biograpy' (the *Memoires of the Celebrated Mrs Woffington*), and later pasteurized in popular fiction and plays. The legend, like the one surrounding Elizabeth Barry, is itself significant; but Peg Woffington deserves to be remembered not as a scapegoat of Puritan guilt or a heroine of backstage romance, but because she was an artist of fine talent (greater by far than that of Mistress Nelly) and a woman of rare mettle who struggled to win a unique independence.

Margaret Woffington was born in Dublin: that is the one fact about her childhood of which we may be sure. The year was probably 1717, as Janet Dunbar suggests, although the Dictionary of National Biography and Janet Camden Lucey settle for 1714, while her memorial tablet in Teddington parish church records the more flattering but untenable date of 1720. From scraps of legendary and often contradictory gossip a familiar pattern of deprivation and precocious experience emerges. Her father, said to be a bricklayer, died when she was a child, leaving her mother penniless; and although she had some respectable and relatively prosperous Dublin relations (her uncle was probably an organist and Vicar Choral at St Patrick's) Peg was sent out into the street to sell ballads and watercress. But not, it seems, herself. According to the *Memoirs,* which provide lengthy, lip-licking circumstantial 'evidence' of the event, she lost her virginity at eleven, soon after her father's death, to a seventeen-year-old neighbour. But unlike Mrs Gwyn, Mrs Woffington appears to have been a protective, if inefficient, mother (to whom Peg was devoted) with no inclination to prostitute her daughter. She was also a pious Catholic; and this may well have caused her family's alienation from the other Dublin Woffingtons, who were Protestants – as Peg's father almost certainly was.

Peg Woffington was said to have attended a dame school from the age of five until ten. But her main education was acquired in the streets of Dublin's fair city: the kind of instant, crude initiation into economic and sexual realities experienced by all the daughters of the poor. She soon discovered one of the few ladders by which she could climb out of that poverty – the stage. Peg's basic theatrical training began when she was about twelve with a group of juvenile performers ('Lilliputians'), run by a French rope-dancer turned manager, Madame Violante, who had up till then presented 'variety' entertainments with dancers, acrobats, jugglers and other vaudeville artists. Under the tuition of this cosmopolitan old trouper Peg learned to act, dance and improve on her ballad-singing, to such effect that she was cast as Polly Peachum in a miniature version of *The Beggar's Opera*, not long after its record-breaking London run. The piquancy of the contrast between the youthful innocence (or knowingness) of the performers and their underworld characters proved, as Madame Violante had hoped, to be good box-office; and Peg Woffington scored a personal hit. With equal confidence and apparently even more impact she later played Macheath (together with Mrs Peachum and Diana Trapes on the same night). The Lilliputian gimmick was so profitable that Madame Violante revived it for a couple of seasons. In September 1732 she even achieved a fortnight's run in London at the Haymarket, with Peg Woffington signalled in advance as an attraction. These novelties did not please the town; but her early taste of success in show business, combined with her toughening experience on the streets, helped to give Peg an appetite for the independence that its rewards could bring, and the strength to fight for them. In Madame Violante she may well have found, in at least one respect, a stimulating example; for here was the rare spectacle (excluding the brothels) of a woman on her own in business, giving the orders to men and keeping the money they earned for her.

It took Peg years of hard work, soft talk and self-tuition – in the arts of love, no doubt, as well as the stage – before she could recapture her Lilliputian glories. From 1732 to 1736, back in Dublin, she vanished into obscurity, but it seems likely in the light of her success with Madame Violante and her burgeoning beauty, that she found some employment at the theatres in Smock Alley and (from 1734) Aungier Street. Charles Coffey, Dublin author of *The Devil to Pay*, was 'enraptured' by her, and through his influence she was engaged to dance between the acts and allowed to watch rehearsals and performances at the Aungier Street playhouse. One night in 1736 she persuaded the manager to let her stand in as Ophelia, a part she had often watched and had learned by heart. From then onwards she was established as a member of the company, playing in Dublin during the winter, touring the country in the summer. She showed off her figure and her developing skills in breeches parts (*The Female Officer, The Recruiting Officer*); and the turning-point of her career came when in April 1740 she appeared as Sir Harry Wildair, the rakish hero of *The Constant Couple*.

Farquhar wrote the part in 1699 for his friend Robert Wilks, who was unrivalled in it during his lifetime. No woman had yet attempted the role, but Peg talked the manager into letting her try it *and* buying a brand-new satin suit for her to play it in. She was an instant hit, inspiring songs with verses like this:

> Her charm, resistless, conquers all –
> Both sexes vanquished lie,
> And who to Polly scorned to fall
> By Wildair, ravaged, die.

Was Peg's appearance in *The Beggar's Opera* eight years earlier really so well remembered, or was this a helpful puff by Mr Coffey or another interested admirer? There was, in any event, nothing factitious about Margaret Woffington's triumph as:

> A creature uncommon
> Who's both man and woman
> And the chief of the belles and the beaux!

Peg became the talk of the town. But she soon had another city in mind, especially as severe economic depression had begun to afflict not only the poor Dubliners among whom she had been brought up but also the theatre through which she had made her escape. She decided to try her luck in London. There was perhaps another reason for her move: she had been betrayed by a lover from a county family who, after swearing the usual vows of devotion, had suddenly left her for a local heiress. Within a few days of her last performance as Sir Harry, Peg left Dublin for London, taking her new satin suit for Wildair, a velvet gown for tragedies, and twenty-three years of experience, ten of them in the theatre. Drury Lane was then known to be the weaker of the patent houses, so she determined to try Covent Garden first. She called on the manager John Rich at his home in Bloomsbury Square, and went on calling until she was admitted. Once Rich saw her he engaged her on the spot, impressed by her beauty, her shrewdness and her reports (as well as his own) of her Dublin successes. That November Peg made her Covent Garden debut as Silvia in *The Recruiting Officer*; and two weeks later, when London saw her Wildair for the first time, she eclipsed her Dublin hit with an unprecedented run of twenty nights. She followed this with Elvira in *The Spanish Friar,* Phillis in *The Conscious Lovers,* Cherry in *The Beaux' Strategem,* and other comic roles. After only one season she left Rich because he refused to increase her salary, and in 1741 moved to Drury Lane, where she remained for seven years. Mrs Woffington had arrived at the top of the tree. There she stayed, through squalls, heart-breaks and angry attempts by rivals to shake her off, until her premature death twenty years later.

Before we outline the events of those twenty years, let us take a look at Peg Woffington in her prime. To her many admirers she seemed 'the most beautiful woman that ever adorned a theatre', as Tom Davies called her. 'As majestic as Juno, as lovely as Venus, and as fresh and charming as Hebe', so Rich is said to have described her at their first meeting to Sir Joshua Reynolds (Reynolds was among the dozen artists who painted her in her black velvet, her oyster satin and other costumes immortalized in oils). Even George Anne Bellamy, the blonde Irish beauty who was at daggers drawn with Peg Woffington, said in her memoirs that as Cleopatra (Dryden's) 'her beauty (for I must give everyone their due) beggared all description' and that she was 'the enchantress of all hearts' (if not Miss Bellamy's). The face that looks out at us from her portraits, though charged with intelligence, warmth and determination, has a faintly mannish look, somewhat heavy and jowlish. It was in action that her beauty was revealed, buoyant with energy and radiant with authority. With high-spirited vivacity she combined the confidence of queenship: so confident that she could cover her beauty with greasepaint wrinkles as Veturia (i.e. Volumnia) in James Thomson's version of *Coriolanus.* This mark of professionalism seems to have been rare enough for astonished comment. It was a mark, too, of the unaffected humility with which she agreed to have her portrait painted while ill in bed, not long before she died.

Peg Woffington was taller than most of her contemporaries, and had learned to make the most of her height, showing unusual grace and 'majesty' (among the most praised of her attributes). She left her dark-brown curly hair unpowdered. She had long, slender, tapering fingers, using them to considerable effect in mime. Under a high forehead her eyes were dark and sparkling, with heavy, mobile, arched eyebrows admired for their 'peculiar power of inspiring love, or striking terror'.[44] Her nose was rather large and aquiline, which helped to give the impression of regal dignity when required. She had a sensuous, expressive mouth (a nineteenth-century admirer invoked 'the pouting witchery of ever-parted lips'[45]) and the kind of willowy figure that looked just right in breeches parts.

In private Peg Woffington was a witty talker, an enthusiastic reader and a good learner, who rapidly made up for her lack of formal education. 'Her understanding was superior to the generality of her sex,' declared Arthur Murphy, dramatist and compatriot, and she tended to behave as if she believed it. No respecter of persons or privileges (sexual or social) her wit and mimicry were often resented by colleagues of both genders. Tact was not Peg's strongest point, and she never acquired the habit of deference. From childhood she had served as the main breadwinner in her family, a kind of substitute husband and father. Now, in addition to maintaining her mother in some style (Hannah Woffington preferred to stay in Dublin) Peg paid for the education of her sister Mary (always known as Polly); introduced her to London society; tried to launch her in the theatre; and helped her to marry into the nobility. She had made a success on her own at work among men; she had shouldered male responsibilities; and she had seen male irresponsibilities exposed *in extremis* too often to acquiesce in the convention of male supremacy. She could be content, one suspects, with nothing less than a recognition of equality, and she managed to achieve this to an unusual degree (though not without stimulating something of the venom excited in the previous century by Mrs Barry). Yet she was far from being a man-hater. Indeed, she preferred men's company (women, she complained, talked of 'nothing but silks and scandals'); and in many male circles she was welcomed as a boon companion.

It seems fitting that Peg Woffington should score her greatest stage success as a man; and at least one chronicler said that she was 'more like a man than a woman' off the stage. But this describes no more than her unusually resolute independence and self-reliance. She combined 'a female softness and a manly mind'. And in her sexual life there seems to have been no hint of lesbianism; her affairs, real and rumoured, were all with men.

On Peg Woffington's arrival in London she made many new friends. Conspicuous among them were two elderly admirers: Colley Cibber, who replaced Coffey as her mentor, and Cibber's companion, Owen Swiney (or McSwiney), an author and former manager. So continually were they seen in attendance and pursuit that bawdy rumour circulated about 'Susanna and the Elders'. Like much of the scandal about Peg's sex-life this was probably ill-founded; but she herself never seems to have worried what the gossips might say, as long as they did not attack her *work*; and she never attempted to emulate the discretion and decorum of an Anne Bracegirdle or an Anne Oldfield. Not only did she enjoy flirtation but she seems to have relished sex with the right man and made no bones about it – or about turning the tables on male philanderers, 'demanding the right to have affaires as they did themselves, without question or control.'[46] During her first five years in London Peg Woffington took several lovers from outside the theatre: principally, the Earl of Darnley, a young Irish peer with a post in the Prince of Wales's household, and Sir Charles Hanbury-Williams, a wit, politician and dilettante. None lasted the pace. Sir Charles marked his dismissal by Peg with a bitter ode which ended:

> Venus, whose charms rule all above,
> Is fam'd for fickleness in love,
>   And for her beauty's power;
> You are her copy drawn with care,
> Like her are exquisitely fair,
>   Like her a thorough whore.

That Woffington was indeed a whore was the main burden of the *Memoires*. 'A vast number of young and old rakes offered themselves to our heroine, and a vast number were accepted,' its author declared, at twenty guineas a time, with cut rates for deserving cases and those especially well-endowed. Peg catered for deviations, too, we are told. Setting aside the scurrilities of this book, it seems likely that Peg Woffington enjoyed her power over men rather more than her pleasure with them.

> Power, power, my dear, sleeping or waking, is a
> charming thing ... the men'll come when we call 'em
> and do what we bid 'em, and go when we send 'em ...
> they are like other beasts of prey, you must tame
> 'em by hunger, but if once you feed 'em high, they
> are apt to run wild....

So said Peg as Rosetta in *The Foundling*, a comedy written especially for her (the only one known to be staged) by Edward Moore; and the war-game of the coquette was one in which she was frequently employed, both off the stage and on.

One evening after her Wildair had been applauded with especial fervour Peg Woffington swept into the green-room, flushed with triumph, saying: 'By God, half the audience thinks me to be a man.' And Kitty Clive retorted, quick as a flash, 'By God, madam, the other half knows you to be a woman.' This is the most famous of Woffington anecdotes (Quin and other players are often credited with variations on the gibe). It is also perhaps the most misleading. Peg took lovers without humbug, but with fastidious, even imperious discrimination. It was not her sexual appetite that was unappeasable, but her pride in power and independence. She was the kind of woman about whom her fellow actresses say. 'Oh no, he isn't good enough for *her*. She'll *never* be satisfied.'

Some two years after her arrival in London Peg found a man who *was* good enough for her – or so she believed. She first met David Garrick when he was still a stagestruck wine merchant, through his friend and her compatriot Charles Macklin, with whom he shared radical ideas about reforming the London stage. In the summer of 1742, after Garrick's sudden emergence as the leading actor of the new generation, he acted with her in Dublin, and there they started their love affair. On returning to London they set up house together for a time. There was nothing especially novel or daring at that time in such an openly conducted liaison; but one striking difference is that it was conducted on equal terms, for Garrick and Woffington paid the monthly housekeeping bills alternately. They kept distinguished company: Peg was a brilliant hostess to such guests as Dr Johnson, Samuel Foote, Henry Fielding and Fanny Burney, who remarked on her social accomplishments and 'natural magnetism'. Garrick and she were in love. They came close to marriage – so close, indeed, that the ring was bought and the day named (according to Peg's story, at second hand). On the very morning of the day the future bride-groom's hesitations were so manifest that Peg left him, there and then, for ever. Whatever the manner of its ending, the affair was all over by 1745. Garrick marked the break-up with some savage verses, reviewing Peg's past affairs with Darnley and Hanbury-Williams:

> I know your sophistry, I know your art,
>> Which all your dupes and fools control;
> Yourself you give without your heart –
>> All may share THAT but not your soul.

After jeering at her 'thirst for gold', he ended with these lines:

> Some say you're proud, coquettish, cruel, vain.
>> Unjust! She never wounds but cures;
> So pitiful to every lying swain –
>> Flatter or pay, the nymph is yours.

Peg, it seems, kept quiet. She also kept single. After Garrick she seems to have taken few lovers, and she gave up the idea of marriage (although her mysterious relationship with a shadowy Colonel Caesar, which began not long after she arrived in London, continued until her death).

Woffington and Garrick continued to act together, but not for long. Peg was a member of the company with which he opened his historic regime in 1747 as manager of Drury Lane, but apart from personal difficulties in working for a man from whom she had parted on the verge of marriage, she had to endure a guerilla campaign from Kitty Clive, Susannah Cibber and Hannah Pritchard. The Woffington-Clive vendetta had begun soon after Peg's arrival in London. 'No two women in high life ever hated each other more unreservedly than these two great dames of the theatre,' said Tom Davies. In the green-room once they almost came to blows in a verbal battle which provoked two male champions (very unevenly matched in age and strength) to physical combat. Susannah Cibber's enmity was less overt but no less implacable. Although Peg had will-ingly given up Lady Brute and Lady Townly to her in 1745,

Susannah wanted more: she fancied herself as a queen of comedy as well as tragedy. And Hannah Pritchard regarded Peg 'with all the scorn of a plain and respectably married woman for one who was neither',[47] and who was scornful of green-room small talk and womanly confidences. At the end of one season Peg Woffington decided that she had had enough. She never returned to Drury Lane.

It was time, she decided, to develop her talents, to stretch herself on the stage, and so she turned to tragedy. She did so in the knowledge that she had one major, notorious handicap: her voice. In comedy it did not matter so much – on occasion, indeed, it proved to be an asset – that Peg Woffington's voice was harsh, that it cracked creaked and abruptly changed key: 'a most unpleasing squeaking pipe'. This was part of her trademark. When she first played Portia and said of Lorenzo, 'He knows me, as the blind man knows the cuckoo, by the bad voice,' the audience burst into laughter and Peg laughed with them. But it was a different question to turn tragedienne in her early thirties with such vocal eccentricities, when so much importance was placed on the *sound* of the lines, delivered in a declamatory, chanting fashion. But Peg needed the prestige that tragedy brought: she wanted to prove that (unlike Mrs Cibber) she could be at home with both the comic and tragic Muses.

Characteristically, it was not in one of her comic successes but as Jane Shore that she chose to appear for her last benefit at Drury Lane, taking the plunge into new terrain with a certain defiance. A few weeks later, with a no less characteristic mixture of personal daring and professional conscientiousness, she set off with Owen Swiney on a pilgrimage to Paris. She wanted to study tragic acting – and, in particular, the acting of Marie-Françoise Dumesnil, champion of the 'natural' romantic approach (*feel* the character and identify with her) as opposed to the formal classicism and calculated effects of her rival Clairon. Dumesnil was 'the first tragedienne that dared to *speak* on the stage', George Moore asserted over a century later. What Peg Woffington learned from her, if anything, it is impossible to say; but she appears to have known some French (perhaps from her apprenticeship with Mme Violante), and London critics later complained of the bad influence on her work of the great Parisian actress. She may well have been encouraged by Dumesnil's example in her relatively natural style, although she lacked the training and technique to make it work sufficiently well to satisfy English taste.

When Peg Woffington opened at Covent Garden in the autumn of 1748, she started off cautiously with her hits in comedy – Lady Brute, Silvia, Elvira, Mrs Sullen, Mrs Ford, Lady Townly, Rosalind, Phillis and Bellinda; but she also played Isabella in *Measure for Measure*, Portia in *Julius Caesar*, the Lady in *Comus* and Jane Shore; and in the new year she added Veturia, Andromache in *The Distrest Mother* and Calista in *The Fair Penitent*. Not everyone believed that Peg Woffington achieved the leap from comedy to tragedy. Charles Macklin said that tragedy was 'evidently not her forte'. Francis Gentleman called her 'the screech owl of tragedy'. Yet the public was delighted. And, with her new armoury of roles, she seemed to be established at Covent Garden as one of the most powerful threats to Garrick's regime at Drury Lane, and one of the most popular personalities of the London stage.

Before long, however, Peg Woffington found Rich's company no more congenial than Garrick's. Quin, the leading actor, was jealous of her, resenting her invasion of his realm of tragedy. He was jealous, too, of the young Spranger Barry, who arrived at the Garden in the autumn of 1750. With Barry came Mrs Cibber, and old enmities flared. These were fuelled by the high rate of absenteeism among leading players, Susannah Cibber being the worst offender. As the most dependable of Rich's attractions Peg was frequently asked to stand in by playing one of her comic successes; but the manager kept her name on the bills in smaller type than the names of Cibber, Quin and Barry, in spite of her frequent protests. Peg finally refused to do one more good turn by deputizing for the ailing or evasive Mrs Cibber, although Rich had announced her performance. Some members of the audience, apparently misunderstanding the reasons for Peg's non-appearance – or (as she believed) prompted or paid by the manager's family and other enemies – demonstrated noisily against her when she next appeared on the stage. She behaved with characteristic independence, described by Tate Wilkinson:

Whoever is living and saw her that night will own that they never beheld any figure half so beautiful since. Her anger gave a glow to her complexion and even added lustre to her charming eyes. The audience treated her very rudely, bade her ask pardon, and threw orange peels on the stage. She behaved with great resolution and treated their rudeness with glorious contempt. She left the stage, was called for and with infinite persuasion prevailed on to return. She walked forward to the footlights and told them she was ready and willing to perform her character if they chose to permit her – that the decision was *theirs* – on or off just as they pleased – a matter of indifference to her. The ayes had it and all went smoothly afterwards.[48]

But not for long. After three years she turned her back on London and went home to Dublin.

For the next three years, as leading lady of the Smock Alley Theatre under Thomas Sheridan's management, Peg Woffington reigned supreme. There were no rivals anywhere near the throne. Sheridan agreed to pay her £400 for the first season, and it proved so successful that he doubled her salary for the next season. This figure was below the £1000 that Quin demanded at Covent Garden in 1750, but well above the pay of any men on the Dublin stage. There were limits to Peg's triumph. She 'had not that free access to women of rank and virtue which was permitted Oldfield and Cibber',[49] partly because of her sexual reputation (Sheridan, it seems, felt he could not introduce her to his wife) and partly because of her sharp tongue and impatience with cant. But outside those polite circles where the ladies ruled, Peg Woffington was a social success. She was, for instance, the only woman admitted to membership of the Beefsteake Club, at whose weekly dinners she met such men as the Provost of Trinity, the Commander of the Dragoons, the Lord Lieutenant's son and, sometimes, the Lord Lieutenant himself. Later she was elected the Club's President. Moreover, for all her wealth and her success, she scarcely ever missed a performance. She was especially punctilious in playing at the benefit performances of her more obscure colleagues.

Yet, in spite of her social and theatrical victories, Peg Woffington left Dublin after only three years. Why? One cause may have been the political embarrassment of Peg's sudden conversion to the Protestant faith in 1753. In Irish terms, she seemed to have sold out to the English oppressors at a time when popular resentment against the Dublin colonial regime was whipped up by new taxation. What happened was that her old friend Owen Swiney promised to leave her his whole estate if she would renounce her Roman Catholicism (this must have been a verbal promise: it is not recorded in his will). Peg clearly put financial independence above religious loyalty or family allegiance, although the legacy is said to have been no more than £200 per annum. She might well have stayed in Dublin to face the consequences (indeed, such a prospect might have seemed an irresistible challenge) if Sheridan's successors at Smock Alley had been willing to pay her £800 as before. They were not. 'No man has a higher sense of her merit than I have, yet that great salary cannot be given, even to her, the fourth season, because novelty is the very spirit and life of all public entertainment,' said Benjamin Victor.[50] John Rich, however, had no hesitation in re-engaging her for Covent Garden at this 'great' figure, and Peg Woffington now embarked on what was to prove the last chapter of her career. She played all her old parts and several new ones, comic and tragic, including Violante in *The Wonder*, Celia in *The Humorous Lieutenant*, Jocasta in *Oedipus*, Roxana in *The Rival Queens* and Penelope in Rowe's *Ulysses*. In her final Covent Garden season she actually appeared in a *new* play, Hulme's *Douglas*, but Lady Randolph was not one of her successes. By now, however, Peg was seriously ill. Disease struck in May 1757, when she was appearing as Rosalind in a benefit performance, one that she could readily have dodged (as many colleagues did). She struggled through to the epilogue, but at the line 'If I were among you, I would kiss as many of you as had beards that pleased me', she broke down in tears, unable to speak because of pain. She cried out, 'Oh God, oh God,' staggered into the wings, and was never seen on the stage again. She meant to return. There was talk of it from time to time. But three years later, on 26 March 1760, Peg Woffington died.

The *Memoires,* rushed out within a few weeks of her death, attempted to combine character assassination with moral whitewash. Peg Woffington had left the stage, said the author, because she had 'accidentally heard a sermon on the instability of all human enjoyment by his present Grace of Canterbury . . . was quite stricken with remorse and penetrated by sorrow for her ill-spent life.' Thereupon she gave up sex and acting, and devoted herself to social service. This myth of recantation persisted, together with the legend of the insatiable whore, though later authors cast John Wesley and Polly Woffington's husband as the instruments of redemption. It is as if they were determined to humble in death the pride with which Peg Woffington had fought in life, applying the mask of virtue and social camouflage that she had always rejected, turning her into another pious Magdalen who had seen the light. Even now, two hundred years after her burial, she seems to inspire people to seek punishment for her sins. One modern biographer says that the cause of her death may 'very probably' have been 'a tertiary manifestation of latent syphilis'; yet the same (otherwise admirable) author admits that Peg *could* have died from less retributory ailments, like extra-pulmonary tuberculosis or high blood pressure.[51]

That Peg Woffington excelled in comedy seems incontrovertible: not only as Wildair (by which she was best remembered), but as Millamant, Maria and Lady Plyant, coquettes, maids, citizens' wives and ladies of fashion. One critic, Francis Gentleman, said that 'she always seemed too conscious of her personal charms'. Another, John Hill, complained that she mixed 'the concerns and the passions of the woman with those of the actress'. Yet he also wrote that she had 'many of the qualifications of a great actress'.

Mrs Woffington has great sensibility and she has, more than most players of either sex, given a loose to nature in the expressing it; to this she owed the greatest part of her fame as an actress; and in this she always excelled, when her private passions did not interfere.[52]

And as a tragedienne? Her voice was clearly against her. Writing after her death, Charles Dibdin said that it seemed to have been 'the only impediment to her becoming superlatively excellent'.[53] *Only*? Yet those critics who had pointedly attacked her vocal inadequacy nevertheless found one or more of her tragic roles – Calista, or Hermione, or Zara – admirable performances; and she was plainly in command of her audiences in tragedy as well as comedy, in spite of her harsh and erratic speech.

Peg Woffington had, in Chetwood's phrase, 'a most admirable improving genius'; or, as Dibdin put it, she seized 'every eligible opportunity to improve . . . with solicitude and avidity'. She was a working actress, learning as she went along, ready to play nearly any part that she was asked to take. Even if she did not win the allegiance of her professional peers or social superiors on the distaff side, Peg Woffington reigned by force of beauty, intelligence, will power and the incontestable authority of a queen.

4 SARAH SIDDONS

NURSE: What will you do, Madam?
ISABELLA: Do! Nothing, no, for I am born to suffer.
Isabella, or *The Fatal Marriage*

And so poor Mrs Siddons' disorder that we have all been at such a stand about, turns upon close examination to be neither more nor less than the pox given by her husband. What a world it is!
Hester Thrale Piozzi (1792)

'WERE A WILD INDIAN TO ASK ME, what was like a queen, I would have bade him look at Mrs Siddons,' said Tate Wilkinson.[1] During her heyday, from 1782 to 1812, she exercised a far more royal presence in Britain than Queen Charlotte or Princess Caroline, who reigned over her as official consorts of George III and the Prince Regent, and she inspired more homage among their subjects than those dumpy German expatriates could ever hope to command. For thirty years in theatres throughout the country she held the allegiance of audiences. She made them weep with her tenderness and pathos. She made them cower under her 'superb disdain'. She frightened them into hysterics and fainting fits. She awed them with her nobility and heroic virtue. She struck them into submission with the savageness of her contempt, the fury of her rage, the profundity of her despair, the magnitude of the wrongs she endured at the hands of men, as she went mad, or was murdered, or committed suicide. The philosopher William Godwin said that it was 'worth the trouble of a day's journey to see her but walk down the stage' in *The Mourning Bride.*[2] To Byron, who saw her at the very end of her career, she seemed 'the beau ideal of acting . . . nothing ever was, or can be, like her.'³ Four years after her retirement William Hazlitt, who some years earlier had sobbed through her performance as Isabella in *The Fatal Marriage,* wrote that she was regarded 'as if a being of a superior order had dropped from another sphere to awe the world with the majesty of her appearance. . . . It was something above nature. We can conceive of nothing grander. She was not less than a goddess, or than a prophetess inspired by the gods. Power was seated on her brow, passion emanated from her breast as from a shrine. She was Tragedy personified.'⁴ The painter Haydon, who met her when she was sixty-five, said that 'it was like speaking to the mother of the gods.' To him she was 'the greatest, grandest genius that ever was born'.⁵ To the end of her life, and after, she inspired superlatives. She was compared with a torrent, a whirlwind, a tornado. She appeared to be a force of nature rather than a wealthy actress, mother of five, victim of rheumatism, erysipelas, sexual frustration, *and,* perhaps, venereal disease, as well as hypochondria.

For the past century the name of Mrs Siddons has survived not only in the annals of the theatre but also in nooks and crannies of the British folk-memory, among millions who know little more of her, if anything, than that she once played Lady Macbeth, and that she carried the manners of a tragedy queen into domestic life, scaring the daylights out of a draper by asking him in bloodcurdling tones, 'Will it wash?'; and requesting the salad ('Give *me* the bowl') as if she were demanding the daggers from Macbeth. Later actresses on the stage have made bigger fortunes, enjoyed greater power and international fame (Mrs Siddons never acted outside Britain) and displayed a wider professional range. But none has matched the peculiar authority that she exercised in the life of the nation. And none has, in her time, done quite so much to improve the reputation of her profession and the status of her sex.

In doing this Mrs Siddons made no use of 'sex appeal', as conventionally understood. She did not appeal, but *commanded,* as a queen. As a lesser being she radiated the filial virtues of a daughter, the protective tenderness of a mother, and the exemplary fidelity of a wife. When she did appear as a transgressor, it was in the deepest penitential gloom (as in *Jane Shore* and *The Stranger*), long absent from any adulterous beds, and totally deodorized from any lingering intimation of pleasure in the act of love. Even as a camp-follower who had quite recently lived in sin (Elvira in *Pizarro*) she somehow conjured up a halo. 'My sister', said John Philip Kemble, 'has made a heroine out of a soldier's trull.' In appearing to soar 'above nature', as Hazlitt put it, she transcended differences of gender. 'Sex was out of the question,' wrote William Robson. 'Although the face and form were majestically beautiful, it was the *mind* that "burned within her" that gave the charm to the Pythoness.'[6] And the desexing effect was perhaps assisted by what her official biographer, Thomas Campbell, described as 'that air of uncompromising principle in her physiognomy'.[7] Moreover, she could simulate an adamantine courage and strength that were thought to be masculine prerogatives, with a 'male dignity . . . that raised her above the helpless timidity of other women.'[8] This supra-sexual aura made it easier for men to accept her as an equal (or something close to it) off the stage. A sidelight upon that acceptance gleams in Byron's reported remark that he 'should as soon think of going to bed with the Archbishop of Canterbury as with Mrs Siddons.'[9] 'The little development in her of the sexual element is a most noteworthy fact', wrote an Edwardian biographer, 'seeing that a *great actress, a great courtesan* is the generalization to which theatrical history largely leads.'[10] Mrs Siddons's 'sexual element' was not quite as vestigial as Mrs Parsons believed, but it seems true, as the same author says, that she was 'a woman of essentially Puritan nature'.

Off stage Mrs Siddons was not a conventionally pretty woman. Her many portraits show – in common with those of most actresses – a face that, for all its manifest attractions, scarcely seems to justify the eulogies of her as one of the most beautiful women of her time. Yet on stage, in action, this was the effect she produced – and maintained well into middle age. Both her dimpled chin and straight, narrow nose were somewhat too prominent – 'Damn it, Madam, there is no end to your nose,' the exasperated Gainsborough is reported to have said as he painted her. But on stage she glowed darkly, with exotic echoes in her pale, strongly-marked features, under a helmet of dark brown hair: features 'so thoroughly harmonized when quiescent and so expressive when impassioned, that most people think her more beautiful than she is.' Even Fanny Burney, who rated her somewhat coolly as 'eminently handsome', admitted that sometimes she *was* something more – 'a sort of radiance comes round her in scenes where strong heroic virtues are displayed.'[11] And she commanded a great flexibility of facial expression: 'an amazing versatility of countenance',[12] in contemporary terms.

Mrs Siddons was somewhat 'above the middle size': 'not too much so', one journalist assured his readers, but she made the most of her height and, like all great players, she could seem at will to be taller. Until her mid-forties her figure was slender and well-proportioned, with a short, full-breasted torso, eloquent rounded arms and long legs. She triumphed in what critics called approvingly her 'deportment' – the poise of her head above a long throat, her *port de bras*, her gait, her carriage, the way that she held attitudes, placed herself in stage compositions with a painter's (or sculptor's) eye, and 'disposed' her limbs – notably in death-scenes.[13] 'She is sparing in her action', said her biographer Boaden, 'because English nature does not act much.'[14] Yet far from being static and statuesque, as the popular stereotype of her suggests, she could and did move swiftly, violently, or with 'whirlwind grace'. When as Isabella in *The Fatal Marriage* she went mad, she screamed, fell suddenly on her knees, and just as suddenly rose to her feet again (an effect she had to discard when she grew plump and scant of breath).

Mrs Siddons also possessed the essential tool of a great voice, or, more precisely, a voice that she had stretched and strengthened over thirty years into a unique instrument. It was off stage 'naturally plaintive', just as her natural cast of features was grave and melancholic. But she could make it shake with rage, or rise to a wild shriek that 'absolutely harrows up the soul',[15] or throb with sustained tenderness and melting sweetness, or ring sonorously round the walls of Drury Lane or Covent Garden (when they were three times as big as an average London playhouse today). She could vary it 'from the height of vehemence to the lowest despondency, with an eagle-like power of stooping and soaring, and with rapidity of thought.'[16] Yet she was generally praised for speaking with 'correctness' and 'exact propriety'. Almost every phrase, every word, was precisely articulated, although of course not all words were given equal value. Every role included lines with which she was long identified: like her 'heart piercing' cry of 'Forgive me – but forgive me!' in *Jane Shore*; her royal and righteous anger in *Henry VIII*, as Queen Katharine rebuking Wolsey in 'a voice of thunder', 'Lord Cardinal, to you I speak' ('her form seemed to expand and her eye to burn with a fire beyond human'[17]); and the fear, pathos, tenderness, self-pity and other emotions expressed by Belvidera to her husband in *Venice Preserv'd* – 'O, thou unkind one!', 'Part, must we part?', and 'Now then kill me!' being among the most admired lines.

The other main instruments of Mrs Siddons's dominion over her audiences were her large, brilliant, liquid brown eyes. They could be seen to shine or sparkle, or glare from the back of the theatre – or, at least, 'at an incredible distance' – helped by the mobility of her dark and expressive eyebrows ('flexible beyond all female parallel'[18]). They were so powerful, one actor said, that if she gazed at you on stage you would almost blink and drop your own eyes. At moments she seemed able 'to turn them in her head'. And they were 'so full of information that the passion is told from her look before she speaks.'[19]

With her eyes and her 'deportment', Mrs Siddons could mesmerize a crowded theatre without saying a word – just by walking on, or standing still and listening, or *looking*. As Constance in *King John,* 'her very body seemed to think.'[20] As Volumnia, marching silently in a triumphal procession, 'her dumb-show drew plaudits that shook the building! She came alone, marching and beating time to the music; rolling . . . from side to side, swelling with the triumph of her son. Such was the intoxication of her joy which flashed from her eye, and lit up her whole face, that the effect was irresistible. She seemed to me to reap all the glory of that procession to herself'[21] – though 240 people marched in its spectacular pageantry. The peak of her performance as Mrs Beverley in *The Gamester* was her staring, speechless grief beside her husband's corpse. Macready, who played one night with her in Newcastle in the year she retired, wrote that 'her glaring eyes were fixed in stony blankness on Beverley's face; the powers of life seemed suspended in her; her sister and Lewson gently raised her, and slowly led her unresisting from the body, her gaze never for an instant averted from it; when they reached the prison door she stopped, as if awakened from a trance, with a shriek of agony that would have pierced the hardest heart, and rushing from them, flung herself as if for union in death on the prostrate form before her.'[22] This, with the 'bewildered melancholy' of her sleep-walking Lady Macbeth, seemed to Leigh Hunt to be 'two of the sublimest pieces of acting on the English stage'.[23]

Among the more remarkable illustrations of Mrs Siddons's pantomimic power was when as Arpasia, towards the end of *Tamerlane*, she was made to watch her lover being strangled. According to Macready she 'worked herself up to such a pitch of agony, and gave such terrible reality to the few convulsive words she tried to utter' that when Arpasia died the audience thought Mrs Siddons had gone, too. They 'remained in a hush of astonishment, as if awe-struck' for a few moments, then demanded that the curtain should be dropped, insisted on the manager appearing before it, and exacted from him an assurance that Mrs Siddons was still alive and well. It was not only the audience who were scared. As she collapsed, an actor turned to Macready's father, 'looking aghast', and said, 'Macready, do I look as pale as you?'[24]

As Lady Macbeth – and from her first appearance in the role at the age of thirty on 2 February 1785 until long after her death in 1831 Mrs Siddons *was* Lady Macbeth – she used her beauty, eyes, voice, deportment, powers of mime and 'royal loftiness' to their fullest effect. The 'sort of radiance' that Fanny Burney admired shone out on the side of outsize crime. 'The demon of the character took possession of her,'[25] it seemed, when Lady Macbeth came to the line 'they made themselves [*and she paused*] air', at which point there seemed to be in both her look and her voice 'ten times the wonder with which Macbeth and Banquo actually beheld the vanishing of the witches.' At 'Come to my woman's breasts' she spoke in a 'slow, hollow whisper' which sounded 'quite supernatural, as in a horrible dream'. That 'whisper' was like nobody else's: 'distinctly audible in every part of the house, it served the purpose of the loudest tones' when she said to herself, listening eagerly to her husband at his bloody work, 'He is about it.' She smiled – a 'ghastly horrid smile' – at 'That which hath made them drunk hath made me bold' and at the knocking on the door she moved with sudden violence, striking Macbeth on the shoulder, shaking him out of his paralysis of fear and forcing him away. But it was the sleep-walking scene, above all, that people went to see. Shrouded in white, she entered with a 'death-like stare'; put down her candlestick (against all precedent); and riveted the audience by the energy with which she went through the motions of rubbing out the 'damned spot', then passing her hands before her nose and grimacing with disgust as if they still smelled of blood. After 'All the perfumes of Arabia . . .', delivered in a 'hollow, broken-hearted voice', she sighed and gave a 'convulsive shudder – very horrible'. With uncanny immobility she listened intently to the sounds of Duncan's murder being re-enacted in her dream. Then she used to feel for the light, while 'stalking backwards, and keeping her eyes glaring on the house,' making her exit with 'groaning whispers . . . as if beckoning her husband to bed, [she] took the audience with her into the silent and dreaming horror' of her darkened world. The dramatist Sheridan Knowles wrote: 'The chill of the grave seemed about you while you looked on her . . . your flesh crept and your breathing became uneasy.' Years later, asked to sum up her effect for an American actor in one plain phrase, he said, 'with a sort of shudder', 'Well, sir, I smelt blood! I swear that I smelt blood!'

And yet, for all that, Mrs Siddons believed that Lady Macbeth should be played in quite a different way, as she made clear in notes published after her retirement. Macbeth's wife should be, she said, 'captivating in feminine loveliness, no gorgon but frail, with every fascination of mind and person', a woman of strong sexual appetite, deeply in love with her husband, kindled by ambition, suppressing her womanly instincts. This interpretation was not for her to play; indeed, it has been suggested that it represented her notion of Lady Macbeth before the play began, 'a private image helpful in creating her role'. But it was Mrs Siddons's 'fiendish' queen who dominated her successors in the part, until nearly a century later Ellen Terry followed that 'private image' in performance.

Who was the woman behind this supernatural apparition, and where did she come from? Among the most significant differences between Sarah Siddons and her more illustrious predecessors was that she represented the third generation of actors in her family. They were, moreover, provincial actors, part of the emerging national theatre outside London in the early part of the eighteenth century. Sarah was born at an inn in Brecon on 5 July 1755, while her parents were on tour. Her father, Roger Kemble, was the son of a barber, followed his father's trade, and is said to have become an actor relatively late in life, at thirty; but her actress-mother, Sarah Ward, was herself the daughter of an actor-manager who had appeared as a boy with Betterton and who ran an itinerant troupe moving around the West Midlands. John Ward had one distinction: he was, like many of the most zealous enemies of his profession, a devout Methodist, and he ran his company under strict moral surveillance. Roger Kemble joined this company as a novice; eloped with the manager's daughter (John Ward's opposition to the match later foundered on Sarah's iron will); and took over the family business. His eldest daughter went on the stage, in her own words, 'from the cradle'.

In spite of the Vagrancy Act of 1713, by which players could be jailed as 'rogues and vagabonds', and the Licensing Act of 1737, which in effect prohibited them from working outside London, some forty companies of strollers were touring the provinces by the time Sarah was born. Many were little better than theatrical tramps, begging for permission to act and touting for customers, enduring hunger and humiliation in what one actress (Charlotte Charke) described as 'a little dirty kind of war'. The Kemble troupe had become 'considerably more affluent than most of its contemporaries', with a fixed circuit of dates which included not only barns but one or two real playhouses; but poverty was always close at hand, at least in Sarah's infancy.

Sarah's childhood was unsettled by continual travelling from place to place; and her education was inevitably patchy. She attended day-schools in several towns and at least one academy for young ladies (in Worcester) for a time; but she frequently had to rely on her parents for instruction in matters not only of the stage but the schoolroom, too. Her mother gave her scraps of tuition in elocution, singing and the harpsichord; both parents provided lessons in the basic business of acting; and she became an avid reader – indeed, she claimed that by the age of ten she 'used to pore over *Paradise Lost* for hours together.'[26] Although this vaunt of early literary sensibility may seem to rank (in credibility) with the claims to genteel pedigrees by Elizabeth Barry or Kitty Clive, she was clearly a retiring and serious-minded child, and it is probable that, like many others without a settled home, she took refuge in books and their compensating fantasy-world from both the loneliness *and* the gregariousness of family life 'on the hoof' and in the wagon.

Sarah's need for escape was all the sharper because Mrs Kemble was a stately matriarch who enforced strict discipline in her family. She also, like her father before her, tried to apply it in the family troupe: not so much, perhaps, because she 'put respectability above art',[27] but because she was (like John Ward) religious in faith and feeling and because she reacted strongly out of bitter experience against the reputation and treatment of her profession. This 'Volumnia in everyday life',[28] whose portrait dominated Mrs Siddons's drawing-room for many years after she had become famous (Thomas Lawrence, who painted it, called her 'the old lioness') believed that an ordered, virtuous, Christian life was a condition of professional survival and success, especially for her daughters. On at least one of these daughters this belief had a decisive influence. Both Sarah Siddons's parents were handsome and imposing figures; and from her father she inherited consciousness of pedigree and breeding, for Roger claimed to belong to a Herefordshire family – 'a good house, though decayed'[29] – whose forbears included a seventeenth-century Catholic martyr, the Blessed John Kemble.

The Kemble children were exposed to the stresses of a 'mixed' marriage – Roger Kemble was a Catholic, Sarah a Protestant – in which the balance of financial and, perhaps, psychological power was tipped in favour of the wife. (According to contemporary convention the boys were brought up in the father's religion, the girls as Protestants). Yet the marriage seems to have been an enduring partnership. Sarah was accustomed from childhood to the spectacle of successful female authority (no small help in her theatrical image-making). But Roger Kemble must have been of unusual determination and ability, to surmount the handicaps of living in provincial society as a double outsider – an actor and a Catholic – and to cope with his formidable spouse. In later years he tried to discourage his children, especially his sons, from going on the stage; but in their infancy they saved actors' salaries by performing with the family troupe, as most theatre children did before the rise of the modern entertainment industry. All the eight Kembles who survived the early years (nine of the twelve were born in different towns) became – for a time, at least – professional players.

Sarah's first recorded appearance was in 1767, at the age of eleven, in Worcester. We know next to nothing about her life until, at sixteen, a Brecon squire paid court to her. He was favoured by her parents, but not by Sarah. She was in love with William Siddons, a handsome actor of twenty-eight who had joined the Kemble company five years earlier as an amateur. (He was the son of a Walsall publican.) Siddons was dismissed as soon as his suit (which had begun a year or more earlier) was revealed to the Kembles; and Sarah was exiled from the corrupting freedoms of the theatre, so that she could come to her senses in a more wholesome environment. She was employed by an upper-class family as a kind of superior maid in a country house, Guy's Cliffe, near Warwick. Although it has never been quite clear what Sarah *did*, apart from frequently reading Shakespeare and Milton aloud, this was apparently no commonplace slavery of domestic service, but an initiation into a cultured, aristocratic style of life among people who later became her friends and admirers. Lady Mary Greatheed, the duke's daughter and MP's widow for whom Sarah worked, may have been embroidering the past with the emotions of the present when she testified in later years that she 'felt an irresistible inclination to rise from her chair when Sarah came in to attend her'. Yet there seems little doubt that the relationship was intimate and, for Sarah, liberating. The long interval at Guy's Cliffe strengthened her self-assurance and widened her social experience; gave her leisure to read, think and digest her earlier theatrical lessons at a distance from the forcing-house of circuit training, with all its short cuts and traditional tricks; and permitted her to mature for nearly two years in a riper, more serene fashion than would have been possible in the family troupe. William Siddons was allowed to see her, from time to time; and, in due course, she was allowed to marry him. In 1773, at the age of eighteen, she embarked on a matrimonial career of over thirty years, Victorian in its conspicuous virtue (most of the way, at least) and its secret sexual repression. 'Sid' (as she called him) was a gentle, well-mannered man, but an indifferent actor, an inefficient manager of his wife's fortunes and, as it turned out, a somewhat unsatisfactory husband. He was Sarah's first love, and he was her last – almost; certainly the last that she recognized publicly, or even perhaps admitted to herself.

Soon after the wedding the Siddonses left the Kemble troupe, and found employment, off and on, with other companies of rather less solidity. Hard times were relieved by two strokes of luck. In Cheltenham, as Belvidera, Sarah was seen and admired (though far advanced in pregnancy) by the Hon. Henrietta Boyle, who went to the play for a joke, was overcome by tears, and became on the spot a friend and patron. 'Beautiful, rich, fashionable and by way of being a poetess',[30] the Hon. Henrietta gave Sarah good advice and expensive clothes, encouraging her self-confidence, and taking a stage further the education in gentility initiated by Lady Mary Greatheed. What is more, Henrietta's stepfather, Lord Bruce, recommended Sarah to David Garrick. The great actor-manager, then approaching retirement, took no action then. But in the following summer of 1775, when Sarah's repertoire included such prime roles as Jane Shore, Euphrasia, Calista, Monimia, Portia, Imogen, Rosalind – and Hamlet – word of her growing reputation reached Garrick from other sources. He sent out envoys, who reported back with an enthusiasm undimmed by the fact she was once again heavily pregnant. Among her merits, said one influential talent-scout (on the evidence of one performance), was that she had 'contracted no strolling habits'. He reported that 'the woman Siddons', as Garrick had described her, possessed 'one of the most strikingly beautiful [faces] for stage effect' he had ever seen, and that this was 'nothing to her action and general stage deportment'. No other Rosalind in his experience had shown such variety and 'propriety' of expression (meaning that Mrs Siddons knew how to speak in Shakespeare). What was more the Siddonses were a very respectable couple. Covent Garden was also aware of these merits, and had made approaches. But Garrick got in first, or at least more conclusively. And so Sarah Siddons heard the call that every young actress longed for – the summons to act at Drury Lane with the greatest actor of the century. Weirdly enough, it was as a comic rather than a tragic actress that she was engaged. Of the seven characters (out of twenty-three) that she identified to Garrick as her best, four were in comedy; in that direction, she apparently believed, her special talents lay. It was a sign that she was not yet ready for London.

Not until 29 December, shortly (*too* shortly) after the birth of her second child, did Mrs Siddons make her London debut as Portia. It was something less than a triumph. Critics complained that she was tremulous, hoarse and often inaudible, her movements clumsy, her costume ugly, her presence negligible, 'uncertain whereabouts to fix either her eyes or her feet'. Clearly, she panicked. She suffered from under-rehearsal, physical and nervous exhaustion, excess of timidity, and a misjudgment of the Drury Lane acoustics. It was far bigger than any theatre in which she had yet played, and she lacked the experience to adjust the scale of her performance to its 2,200 seats. Thereafter she played seven minor roles, but in none did she capture the town. One play was booed off the stage, in a flurry of riotous brawling. Her only appearance in Shakespeare with Garrick, as Lady Anne in *Richard III*, was dismissed by one critic as 'lamentable', and ignored by the others. Nonetheless, when the season (Garrick's last) came to a close, she believed that she and her husband would be re-engaged. Garrick (so she said) had assured her of this, and had treated her with especial favour, to the anger of his three leading ladies. But during the summer, while acting in Birmingham, she was curtly notified by the Drury Lane prompter that her services were no longer required by the new management. At her first attempt she had failed to meet the expectations of the London audience, the arbiters of theatrical success. She had, in fact, arrived at Drury Lane too early.

This rejection was a crippling blow not only to a young artist's self-esteem, but also to her esteem of colleagues, audiences, managers – and, indeed, men. Mrs Siddons wrote that 'it was very near destroying me.' For the next eighteen months it so 'preyed upon my health' that 'I was supposed to be hastening to a decline.'[31] Perhaps she was exaggerating: she often did, off stage as well as on. But the wounds took far longer than eighteen months to heal. Perhaps, indeed, they always remained open, because she kept them open, as a conscious or unconscious aid to that luminous projection of suffering womanhood that constituted one of her main assets as an actress. And it was Garrick whom she blamed for it all. He had flattered her, lied to her, miscast her, undervalued her, deployed her against his triumvirate of leading ladies for his own managerial ends. There was more than a touch of paranoia in these charges. The fact was that she was not yet good enough; yet she was so fiercely proud that she found this fact hard to endure – so hard that she buried it at the back of her mind. Injustice, treachery, talent unrecognized, love unrequited – these emotions, embellished and intensified in her self-dramatizing inner autobiography, fuelled the fictional griefs and angers of her later victories.

Although Garrick had, so she believed, tricked her and although London had spurned her, it did not take Mrs Siddons long to justify to the leading managers outside the capital those early rumours of exceptional promise, helped by the prestige of having worked with Garrick. She earned high praise (in spite of that 'decline' towards which she said she was 'hastening') in Birmingham, Liverpool, Manchester and York; and within two years she was engaged by the top regional theatre in Bath. She was recommended by the tragedian John Henderson (the outstanding English actor between Garrick and Kean) who said 'she never had an equal nor would ever have a superior.'[32] Soon after her arrival the Bath proprietor John Palmer acquired the Theatre Royal in Bristol, serving both playhouses with one company, who had to travel backwards and forwards between the two cities three times a week. For Sarah it was an exacting and exhausting pattern of work, especially when she was pregnant; and during her four years with the company she bore three children (one of whom died in infancy). She was the main breadwinner, at £3 a week (while the theatre was open, for eight months in the year), an income supplemented by Mr Siddons's much smaller salary from supporting roles and by the proceeds of benefits. It was enough to pay for a nanny-nursemaid, but not for a personal maid. And there was a lot to do. She combined her domestic and maternal responsibilities, her rehearsing and performing thirty roles or more in a season, and her commuting between Bath and Bristol, with an arduous programme of private work. For Mrs Siddons was soon not content to follow traditional interpretations and projections of character within the somewhat perfunctory framework outlined in the brief rehearsals of a stock company. She came to think out for herself the technical and psychological problems of her roles, season by season, however often she played them. She laboured at self-improvement in voice, movement and presentation. Long after she had returned from the theatre, long after her husband had gone to bed, she sat up studying herself in the mirror of her art. Forty years later she wrote, 'That I had strength and courage to get through all this labour of mind and body, interrupted too by the cares and childish sports of my poor children who were (most unwillingly often) hushed to silence for interrupting my studies, I look back with wonder.' Not the least of her complaints was that she had to play secondary roles in comedy. (She still fancied herself in *primary* roles, but by the time she reached Bath she realized that tragedy was her forte.) She was supported by immense self-confidence: as may be seen in her own story that on the night before she was to play Lady Macbeth for the first time she sat down to *study* it for the first time. 'As the character is very short, I thought I should soon accomplish it.' She learned differently that very night – 'the horror of the scene rose to a degree that made it impossible for me to get farther' and she hurried to bed 'in a paroxysm of terror'.[33] Never again did she put off learning a part till so near the deadline. But it is a fascinating revelation of the strength of her belief in her powers, even as a fledgling of twenty, not least in her ability to memorize a role almost instantly. As she enlarged and developed her talent, revealing a rapidly growing power and authority, she acquired influential friends and patrons, including Thomas Sheridan, Mrs Thrale and the Duchess of Devonshire. She enjoyed her ascendancy in Bath; and it was there that she fashioned her royal armour, the home-made queenship that protected her inner self. Bath *made* Mrs Siddons.

When in 1780 Sheridan first invited her to return to Drury Lane, she refused. She seemed content to remain in Bath, dreading a second humiliation in London. Remembering the first fiasco, she said that her voice was not strong enough for Drury Lane. She refused again in 1781. But when the offer was repeated in 1782, she could resist no longer. It was the money, she explained, that was the bait. Yet it was ultimately, one suspects, the challenge to show London that she was right, to avenge her wrongs, to ascend the throne. In one way, the 1775 fiasco had been lucky for her. It prevented the stultification of a too early success.

Mrs Siddons reappeared at Drury Lane on 10 October 1782, at the age of twenty-seven, as Isabella in *The Fatal Marriage*. This time there was no faltering or faintness. Nobody could complain that she was awkward or inaudible, although the day before she had begun to lose her voice under the pressure of nervous anxiety. She had waited six years for this moment, and she seized it with what must have been one of the peak performances in the history of the British theatre. Overnight Sarah Siddons became the leading lady of the stage. She entered her inheritance with sudden and spectacular success, wiping out at a stroke the disgrace of her earlier debacle. One critic acclaimed her at once as 'beyond all comparison ... the first tragic actress now on the English stage'. Among playgoers her triumph was measured by the tears she inspired, the fainting fits she caused, the sighs, groans and even shrieks in the audience. Sheridan himself sat sobbing in a box, on her second night as Isabella. The Prince of Wales and the Duke of Cumberland were seen to cry, too, in that season. Even the King, who could hardly bring himself to watch tragedy, condescended to view the new phenomenon – and came back again, 'vainly endeavouring to conceal his tears behind his eyeglass'. He saw Mrs Siddons five times in January, and summoned her to Buckingham House, demonstrating thenceforward a rare degree of theatrical enthusiasm. The Queen, according to Mrs Siddons, 'told me in her gracious broken English that her only refuge from me was actually turning her back upon the stage at the same time protesting, "It is indeed so disagreeable" ' – which was intended to be a compliment.[34] When she plunged her dagger in her breast, said Boaden, she gave an electrifying laugh, and 'literally the greater part of the spectators were too ill themselves to use their hands in her applause.'[35]

In the three months after her debut Mrs Siddons developed

her mastery over the town as Euphrasia, Jane Shore, Calista, and Belvidera, stock roles with which she had begun her career and which remained the main pillars of her repertoire for the next twenty-five years. Her salary was doubled. She was allowed two benefits, which brought her nearly £1500 – more from two nights than she had gained in four years at Bath. All records were broken at the box office. Tragedy became fashionable again, after being out of favour for years in London. Not least of all her honours was that she was given Garrick's dressing-room. 'It is impossible to imagine my gratification when I saw my own figure in the self same glass which had so often reflected the face and form of that unequalled genius',[36] the genius who had treated *her* genius so meanly. There in his theatre she was to reign supreme among actresses for the next twenty years.

When the London season ended Mrs Siddons embarked for Ireland, setting a pattern which made her rich and brought her national fame. Every summer from then on she acted in Scotland, Ireland or in leading English cities, adding at least £1000 to her annual income and consolidating her reputation. Another part of the pattern was established in her second season at Drury Lane, when she was joined by her brother. John Philip Kemble made his London debut in September 1783, as Hamlet. It was not marked by the thunderclap of success that had greeted Sarah's night of triumph the previous year – indeed, from the start Kemble's acting was the subject of controversy among playgoers and critics – but it launched him on a career that was crowned, within a few years, by the leadership of the British stage. Supported by the management of her brother, as she was to be for three decades, Mrs Siddons now tried Shakespeare. At first she ventured two roles only, for no more than five performances each: Isabella in *Measure for Measure,* and Constance in *King John,* which became one of her prime roles in later years, though at first it was not liked by the critics. (With more immediate success, she played Mrs Beverley in *The Gamester,* which also became a favourite part, and Lady Randolph in *Douglas.*) But in the following season she appeared as Rosalind (a big mistake), Desdemona and her most cele-brated role, Lady Macbeth. And in the next few years she added to her London repertoire Portia, Imogen, Queen

Katharine and Volumnia, the two last ranking with her greatest successes.

From 1784 onwards Mrs Siddons seldom appeared more than fifty times in a season, often a good deal less, never attempting to match the eighty-two appearances of her first season. She was expected to play at least three times a week, for a salary which rose to £50 a week (in the last phase of her career it was 50 guineas a night). By 1785 she was earning up to £5000 a year. Her ambition was to make as much money as she could while she was still in fashion. Her target was £10,000, to buy a country cottage, security for her children and, if needs be, escape from the 'servitude' of acting. This target was reached in 1786. Indeed, she told one aristocratic patron that 'many . . . can give certain proof that I am worth £14,000.' But she continued to act for another quarter-century, while continuing to declare to friends that she was on the point of giving it all up, when she had saved enough to buy a carriage, or when she had put a little more aside for her children.

During this period Mrs Siddons was sometimes absent from the London stage, for reasons of health or money, and for short spells she was out of fashion; but she was never really out of power, even though the basis of her repertoire scarcely changed. She tried new roles, but most were failures. In twenty-seven years she played fifty-four, yet only eight were incorporated into her repertoire. Two of the most notable of these were in revivals – as Agnes in *The Fatal Curiosity* and Alicia in *Jane Shore*. Her outstanding brand-new roles were Mrs Haller in *The Stranger* and Elvira in *Pizarro*. She appeared in flops by such distinguished contemporaries as Joanna Baillie, William Godwin, Fanny Burney, Hannah More and Arthur Murphy (and by a number of old family friends, including Lady Mary Greatheed's son). She also failed in plays by Dryden, Rowe and even Shakespeare. She never played Cleopatra, Beatrice, Miranda, Perdita, Viola or Helena in London; she failed as Rosalind and Juliet; she played Ophelia and Kate (the Shrew) only once; she made little impression as Portia, Gertrude or Cordelia (in Tate's version). Her effective Shakespearean repertoire was relatively small: Lady Macbeth, Volumnia, Queen Katharine, Constance, Desdemona, Hermione (which she did not play till she was forty-seven), and, some way behind in popularity, Imogen and Isabella. She had scant talent for comedy: her tendency to look ponderously sportive earned her the description of 'a frisking Gog'.[37] John Galt wrote of her, 'Nature was insulted when it was imagined that she could laugh otherwise than in scorn.'[38] And even in tragedy her range was limited. Yet looking at her career in historical perspective, she never really lost the supremacy she had established in 1783, buttressed five years later when John Philip Kemble became acting manager, under Sheridan, at Drury Lane. A whole generation was brought up, as Hazlitt put it, in 'the Kemble religion'.

Although Mrs Siddons made few extensions to her repertoire, she remodelled her style to suit the enlargement of the theatres. The new Drury Lane, opened with *Macbeth* in 1794, was over half as big again as its predecessor, holding more than 3600 people. This inflationary architecture, matched by Covent Garden, was inimical to intimate and subtle playing, promoting as it did a more declamatory, statuesque style of performance. Mrs Siddons became, perforce, 'more grand and imposing' in her actions, to signal across the vast spaces of the auditorium. The tenderness of her earlier pathos evaporated. She chose simpler modes of dress. She discarded the traditional head-plumes and in 1795 ceased to powder her hair. She made longer pauses and more deliberate gestures. She imitated 'antique' models, perhaps, more self-consciously. She lost some of the throbbing sweetness and pathos of her earlier successes. In her last decade on the stage she became too stout for comfort and (one would have supposed) for credibility in several roles. She was slowed down by rheumatism and other ailments, by the laudanum she took addictively for them, and, at times, by a weighty sense of her own importance. Moreover, she played no new parts at all. Yet on her retirement in 1812 she was still the unchallenged queen – in spite of everything.

It had not all been plain sailing. Within two years of her initial triumph Mrs Siddons was hissed and barracked at Drury Lane, on the opening night of her new season in 1784. Rumours had spread that while in Dublin that summer she had refused to act for one player's benefit, and had asked £50 to act for another actor whose career had been cut short by illness. When she appeared on the Drury Lane stage she was greeted with what she described as 'universal opprobrium – accused of hardness of heart, of the most sordid avarice, and total insensibility to everything and everybody, except my own interest.' At first she could not make herself heard. When her brother escorted her off the stage, she fainted in his arms. But she returned to face the howling crowd, defended herself in a short speech against 'these calumnies', and the storm subsided. Nevertheless, satirical paragraphs and prints kept up the attack that autumn, and a reputation for stinginess was thereafter inexpungably linked with her fame. (This scarcely seems surprising, for even if the 1784 charges were exaggerated by her enemies Mrs Siddons was, unarguably, far from generous: a hard bargainer, with more than a touch of avarice; close with her money, except in the immediate family circle.) According to Mrs Siddons, she wanted to give up acting there and then, so bitterly did she resent her treatment: 'It will never have those pleasing charms it had before.'[39] She continued in her profession, so she said, for her children's sake alone, and she repeated this statement forty years later in her autobiographical notes with a still burning sense of grievance that she had been 'cruelly and unjustly degraded'. Whatever her protestations, it is doubtful if she could ever have actually left the stage. She did not act to live: increasingly she lived to act.

No Prime Minister, she assured one sympathetic peer at the time, had more enemies than *she* had. She knew, she said, how Pericles must have felt about the Athenian mob: she and Pericles had 'something in common'. The more prosperous she became, the more she required to feel victimized. Her 1784 experience of being booed and publicly reviled served to reinforce her regal armour, and to charge the batteries of that scorn and contempt in which she excelled on the stage.

Thereafter, Mrs Siddons had – like most women of less supernatural ambience and decidedly smaller income – many substantial reasons for sorrow and anger. In addition to her professional anxieties she carried a heavy load of family responsibilities, as the richest member of the clan. She had a deep affection for her father and helped to support both her parents in comfort. Roger Kemble lived until 1802, when he was eighty-one. Sarah died four years later. Mrs Siddons was also a loyal and generous sister. At the beginning of her reign she introduced Elizabeth and Frances Kemble to Drury Lane, though 'she could not make them actresses.' She supported her actor-brothers Stephen and Charles, and her actor-son Henry, in their stage careers. She was closest of all to John Philip, for whose success she paved the way – first, by gaining him a provincial foothold, then by bringing him to Drury Lane. She was a devoted, indeed possessive, mother. After her daughter Maria died, at nineteen, she virtually adopted Tate Wilkinson's daughter, Patty, so strong were her maternal needs (she still had four of her own). Mrs Siddons seems, moreover, to have done her best as an aunt and a grandmother. But to friends like Mrs Piozzi she gave the impression, apparently unwittingly, that her family exploited her, or at least that they did not fully reciprocate the affection she lavished on them and were insufficiently grateful for her labours on their behalf. This picture, one suspects, was one that she often privately hugged.

Off the stage, Mrs Siddons's emotional energies were most effectively ventilated as a daughter, a sister and a mother – not as a wife. She maintained her 'Sid' for most of their married life (he was too mediocre an actor to be engaged at Drury Lane or Covent Garden) but complained that she got little thanks for it and little domestic support, let alone love. Although she publicly deferred to him on some matters ('Mr Siddons is a much better judge of the conduct of a tragedy than myself', meaning 'in manuscript') and paid tribute to the convention that he was her lord and master – as he was, in law – their marriage seems to have deteriorated rapidly from her mid-thirties. Not surprisingly, William Siddons failed to come to terms with his wife's immense fame and his own subjugation to her towering personality. 'She is', he said to her brother, 'too grand a thing for me.'[40] To find himself tolerated (just) merely because of his marriage seems to have destroyed in him the tenderness of the early years. Indeed, his wife wrote when she was fifty that his unresponsive temperament had 'checked my tongue and chilled my heart in every occurrence of importance *through our lives.*'[41] Perhaps, once again, she was exaggerating; but it does appear that, in Roger Manvell's words, 'she was as starved of private affection as she was overwhelmed by public admiration.'[42] That, at least, is how she saw herself, increasingly, as the years went by; and she increasingly resented the fact that all the money she made went to Mr Siddons as his legal right, and that he should urge her to go on making *more* of it while he showed so little ability to handle it (and, indeed, lost much of it in speculations).

Family troubles apart, Mrs Siddons suffered throughout most of her life from poor health, as well as hypochondria. From the age of thirty she was often the victim of nervous exhaustion, sometimes fainting in the wings at the end of a performance. In her theatrical prime she endured 'terrible headaches', erysipelas of the mouth, piles and other anal irritations, severe rheumatism and no less severe sexual frustration. 'A warm heart and a cold husband are sad things to contend with,' Mrs Piozzi wrote of her in 1790.[43] It seems unlikely that Mr and Mrs Siddons had sexual relations after the birth of their seventh child in 1794, and it is improbable that she ever took a lover. Mr Siddons is said, however, to have taken a mistress. He is also said by Mrs Piozzi to have given the Tragic Muse a venereal disease, of which the symptoms were not correctly diagnosed for several years. If this is true, the discovery of what caused her mysterious and tormenting disorders must have come as a traumatic shock to a woman who set so high a value on moral 'purity', priding herself on fulfilling the family tradition established by her grandfather, setting herself apart from the common run of actresses. Mrs Siddons can scarcely have carried self-dramatization so far as to invent the story; and from what other source could Mrs Piozzi have heard it? 'She is all resentment,' wrote Mrs Piozzi in 1792, when Sarah was still no more than thirty-seven. True or not, other ailments persisted, for which her doctor declared that there was no cure – for it was all *nerves*. 'She has martyred herself with unavailing remedies and will try no more,' wrote Mrs Piozzi in 1801.[44] She began to take laudanum with increasing frequency. It slowed her down, but she kept on acting. And acting continued to be her prime medicine, her *raison d'être,* whatever her reiterated threnodies of complaint that she was longing to give it up. She was soon to need it more than ever before.

At forty-seven Sarah Siddons, while acting in Dublin, embarked on an intimate friendship with an actor and fencing instructor, Mr Galindo (Christian name unknown). He was in his early twenties, and married to an actress. Seven years later

Catherine Galindo published a venomous booklet attacking Mrs Siddons for treachery, cruelty, wanton behaviour, 'Satanic barbarity', alienating her husband's affections, and causing their financial ruin, publishing twenty of Sarah's letters as evidence. There *is* evidence, certainly, of the ageing actress's partiality for the charming young swordsman. He was her frequent companion on trips into the Irish countryside. She decided to appear once more as Hamlet, so that she could take fencing lessons from him. To make sure of seeing him on her return to London, it would appear, she fixed an engagement at Covent Garden for his wife, against the wishes of Mrs Galindo (so she later claimed) and certainly of John Philip Kemble, who behaved 'like a madman' when he discovered what his sister had been doing behind his back and said she had been duped by 'persons whom it was a disgrace to her to *know*.' That scheme was dropped, but the Galindos came to London just the same; and the relationship between Mrs Siddons and Mr Galindo lasted for some four years, on notably intimate and even indiscreet terms. Yet the letters published by Mrs Galindo do not support her caricature of the actress as 'one of the most practised hypocrites that ever imposed on the world' – in, for instance, her hysterical accusation that Mrs Siddons deliberately refused to see her daughter Sally on her deathbed, because she wanted to stay with Mr Galindo instead. And during this period in which his affections were said to be alienated, by a woman old enough to be his mother, he sired two children by his wife. After violent quarrels, his relationship with Mrs Siddons ended in 1807. She had lent him a thousand pounds to go into management in Manchester; the venture flopped; and there was trouble over payment of interest, let alone repayment of the loan. Money always mattered a great deal to Mrs Siddons, and her pride as well as her pocket was hurt. She refused even to open Galindo's letter, and ranked the whole experience as another of those agonizing humiliations for which she had been singled out by Providence. Mrs Galindo's bombshell was carefully primed to show that the money could never be repaid and that it was all Mrs Siddons's fault.

It says a great deal for the unique moral aura of her reputation that it seems to have survived, virtually undamaged, the impact of Mrs Galindo's book in 1809; especially as Mrs

Siddons's name had already been linked in scandalous gossip with another young man. Unlike Galindo, Thomas Lawrence was a celebrity, the most fashionable painter of the day. A handsome, romantic charmer, he plunged into one passionate attachment after another without apparently seeking to consummate any of them. This 'spiritual philanderer', as Roger Manvell calls him, had first met Mrs Siddons in Bath as a boy prodigy of twelve. He drew her as Euphrasia and Zara, portraits that became popular prints. Fifteen years later, in his London heyday, he fell in love with her elder daughter Sally (then twenty), and became virtually engaged. While Sally was ill, he transferred his favours to her sister Maria, who was four years younger. He became formally engaged to her, and Mrs Siddons agreed to pay off his considerable debts as a marriage portion. But then Lawrence's affections, while Maria in her turn was ill, reverted to Sally. She refused to accept him, but he pursued her and her mother, creating many violent scenes. If Sally rejected him, he declared hysterically, he would emigrate to Switzerland. He had said exactly the same about Maria, when she was 'sole arbitress of his fate'. He also threatened suicide. Throughout 1798 recurrent emotional fevers and frenzies shook the Siddons family. On one occasion, Sarah said, Lawrence 'paced about for three hours in agonies that brought me almost to fainting three or four times.'[45] Yet the whole bubbling cauldron was somehow kept secret from Mr Siddons, who would have been 'cold and repelling', Sarah was sure, and from John Philip. Sally was intermittently ill, and frequently doped – like her mother – with laudanum. Maria was rapidly wasting away. She died that year at nineteen. On her deathbed she made her sister promise, with her mother as one witness, never to marry Lawrence. In the words of the other witness, Maria said, 'Sally, Sally, sacred be this promise' – stretching out her hand, and pointing her forefinger – 'remember me, and God bless you!'[46] Although Sally was plainly in love with Lawrence, she did not break this promise; Lawrence himself developed enthusiasms elsewhere; but her mother – who had shown, during this prolonged private drama, an intense personal attachment to the artist – was frequently seen in his company, so much so that after Sally's death in 1803 (at twenty-eight), scandalous gossip about their relationship was in full flow. Everyone *knew* that they had run away together, and that a divorce was on the way. Mr Siddons announced in *The Times* that he would pay £1000 for the discovery and conviction of anyone who had been spreading the stories. The storm in the teacup subsided. And the actress and the painter continued their friendship until the end of his life. Not long before his death he fell in love for the last time with a Kemble: Sarah's niece Fanny. Perhaps Roger Manvell is right in maintaining that it was Mrs Siddons that Lawrence had loved all the time, since his boyhood; and that he was for her 'the one deep, if partially unconscious, love of her life,' a love 'uncomplicated by demands on her bed.'[47] Certainly he provided for her an off-stage drama of even more sensational emotion than the familiar roles in her repertoire.

In 1804, the year after Sally's death, Mr and Mrs Siddons separated – not, it seems, because of Sarah's conduct, but rather because he was now so crippled by lumbago that he decided he could only survive by living in Bath, where he could take the waters. Before they parted, Mrs Siddons persuaded him to settle £20,000 on her and undertake to leave the other £20,000 of the estate to her on his death. After this was accomplished (and it surely could not have been had he believed in her infidelity), she wrote to him affectionately 'however we may differ in trifles, *we can never cease to love each other.*'[48] It is hard to accept the reality of this sudden Darby-and-Joan projection, after all the years of sterility and resentment (even if his sexual habits had been irreproachable). And it is also hard to withhold sympathy from Mr Siddons, struggling for self-respect under the shadow of the ever-suffering queen. But now that he was no longer *there,* and she had control of half her fortune, her bitterness seems to have disappeared; and they maintained friendly relations until he died – which happened within four years.

For all the glories of her state, Mrs Siddons had troubles in the theatre as well as at home. Acting in the provinces, she said, was often twice as exhausting as in London. At 'the great points and striking passages' the audiences were slower in applause than at Drury Lane, where it 'invigorated her whole system' and gave intervals for 'assisting the breath and nerve'. What was worse, they sometimes guffawed at moments of high solemnity or shouted out helpful comments. ('Farewell, ye *brutes*', said Mrs Siddons dismissively, on departing from the stage at Leeds.) She often complained at the *labour* of it all, which she magnified in her usual way. 'I have worked harder, I believe, than any body ever did before,' she wrote after a nine hundred-mile tour in 1795.[49] Yet she made a great deal of money; and she would have made far more – the *'immensely immense'* sums she envisaged in 1786[50] – if she had been paid her due salary at Drury Lane. But Sheridan – 'uncertainty personified',[51] as she called him – continually owed money to all his employees, the stars included, skating from one financial crisis to another in an unending flurry of lies, evasions and broken promises. On several occasions his behaviour drove Sarah to go on strike. She refused to act in the 1789–90 season and between December 1790 and January 1792 she made only seven appearances at Drury Lane. She stayed away again several years later, with her brother, who resigned as manager in 1796. Again and again Sheridan charmed them back, as he charmed nearly everybody, though it was four years before John Philip returned to his managerial post with the bait of a share in the theatre. Again and again Sheridan cheated and short-changed them. When the 1797–8 season began, for instance, he owed Mrs Siddons over £2000. When the season ended, the debt was still £1500. Finally, the Kembles could stand Sheridan's conduct no longer. They left Drury Lane in 1802 and after a year's interval moved to the rival house in Covent Garden, where John Philip bought a sixth of the property, reinforcing his status as acting manager and leading actor.

At Covent Garden Sarah Siddons spent the last nine years of her professional life, acting on average about thirty-five times a season in most of her stock favourites. Her reign was marred by a temporary usurpation – the brief cult of the child actor Master Betty, whose hysterical adulation prompted her to a diplomatic withdrawal in 1804–5 – and by two family disasters The first was the fire of 1808, which burned Covent Garden and its contents to the ground. Kemble was ruined, and had to start again from scratch. Mrs Siddons lost all her dresses and jewels, collected and treasured over thirty years, and a veil (valued at £1000) that had belonged to Marie Antoinette. The vast new Covent Garden cost so much to build (about £300,000) that prices were increased for the season of 1809–10. This provoked an explosion of popular anger in violent demonstrations (the O.P. – or Old Price – Riots) that continued for three months, drowning even the Tragedy Queen in organized tumult and derision, until Kemble surrendered and apologized from the stage. It had been a revolt not only against the new prices but against 'the Kemble religion'. The two self-made aristos, emblems of the *ancien régime*, were defeated by the *canaille* (so John and Sarah saw them). Although they continued to act with honour and profit for a few years more (Kemble recovered enough fortune to retire in comfort in 1816) their era was almost over, and they knew it.

Sarah hated the prospect of living without acting, no matter how often she had protested her weariness of the stage. A few days before her last performance in 1812 – on 29 June, as Lady Macbeth, when the audience insisted on ending the play after her sleep-walking scene – she wrote to Mrs Piozzi, 'I feel as if my foot were now on the first round of the ladder which reaches to another world.'[52] In fact, she did not reach that world for another nineteen years. She reappeared on the stage for several scattered performances – mistakenly, perhaps, as Hazlitt indicated, although for many people she still seemed as far beyond criticism as beyond sex. Positively her last stage appearance was on 9 June 1819, for the benefit of her brother Charles. But she was still to be heard for a time giving readings from Shakespeare and Milton at high prices in public, and private readings at home over tea or at evening receptions. She died at her house in Upper Baker Street on 8 June 1831 at the age of seventy-six, having outlived all but two of her children and most of her friends and enemies, but not her legendary reputation as the Tragic Muse.

Why did Mrs Siddons make such an impact on the emotions of her audiences, through thirty years on the stage? Why did she make them cry so much? Why, even as a stout and arthritic grandmother, did she frighten and disturb spectators of all ages, piercing into their own private griefs and nightmares?

One obvious part of the answer is that Mrs Siddons generated *in herself* an unusually high emotional voltage across an unusually wide range, outside the sphere of comedy. She was capable of expressing great joy, tenderness, courage, affection and loving pride, even in her later years, although it was for her displays of anger, indignation, defiance, madness, despair, fear and contempt – all tinged by her regality of presence and personality – that she was perhaps better remembered. 'I never saw so mournful a countenance combined with so much beauty. Her voice, though grand, was melancholy; her air, though superb, was melancholy; her very smile was melancholy.'[53] That helped to make people revel in feeling sad: 'a thrill which more exactly answers the idea of *pleasing pain* than anything I ever felt.'[54]

She herself was seized and shaken by violent emotions, in identifying herself with the women she impersonated. In playing Mrs Haller, her daughter Sally said, she 'cries so much at it that she is always ill when she comes home.' As Belvidera in 1805 she sobbed so uncontrollably in one scene with her brother that her handkerchief was sodden with tears when she got off the stage. 'I never played more to my own satisfaction than last night in Belvidera; if I may so say, it was hardly acting, it seemed to me, and I believe to the audience, almost reality.'[55] At this time there were especial grounds for grief in her private life, for this was the year of the Lawrence imbroglio. Describing one encounter with the hysterical painter, she wrote: 'I was so shaken by his wild transports yesterday that, on rising to ring for some hartshorn and water, I should have fallen upon the floor if he had not fortunately caught me at the instant, and was totally incapacitated to play last night.'[56] But even in less turbulent years she showed a passionate involvement in the sorrows of many of her characters, sending out into the audience driving tides of emotion that made their own inner feelings 'burst from the centre, rage and roar aloud' (to quote a line from Belvidera that Mrs Siddons used to emphasize at full pitch). At Roger Manvell puts it, 'she became possessed, and in consequence came to possess her audience.'[57] Increasingly, she found in the theatre an outlet for the sexual energies and emotional hungers which were smothered and starved at home. It seems likely, too, that in spite of her deference to convention (at least until she was fifty) and her apparent acquiescence in a Divine Will that seemed to endorse the subjugation of women, she was sometimes seized by resentment against sexual discrimination – energized by indignation that she, Sarah Siddons, should ever be treated as no more than a woman. Such sentiments were revealed in, for instance, her bitter comment to Samuel Rogers in 1817 at the public dinner given to her brother on his retirement, an honour never extended to her. 'Well, perhaps in the next world women will be more valued than they are in this.'[58]

Most of the roles Mrs Siddons played had been popular for many years before her time. Her mother had drawn on much the same gallery of wronged, suffering women – victims of male cruelty and inconstancy, trapped by man-made laws and institutions: driven to madness, like Isabella; murder, like Euphrasia; suicide, like Lady Randolph, Isabella, Zara and Belvidera. But it seems unlikely that any of these roles had ever been charged with such emotional intensity. Cumulatively, they suggest a kind of subconscious protest against the condition of women which, fuelled by Mrs Siddons's own personal drives and by her genius as an artist, found an unprecedented response in the hearts of the audience. There was an especial emotional charge, one may suppose, in her delivery of Jane Shore's pathetic condemnation of double standard morality:

> Such is the fate unhappy women find,
> And such the curse entailed upon our kind,
> That man, the lawless libertine, may rove
> Free and unquestioned through the wilds of love;
> While woman, sense and nature's easy fool,
> If poor weak woman swerve from virtue's rule,
> If, strongly charmed, she leave the thorny way,
> And in the softer paths of pleasure stray;
> Ruin ensues, reproach and endless shame,
> And one false step entirely damns her fame.

Roger Manvell is perhaps overstating the case by saying that 'the whole of wronged womanhood spoke through her voice.'[59] Certainly it would be perilous to assume that she saw herself this way, that she cherished any conscious mission to arouse the conscience of society about the treatment of her sex. It is plain, moreover, that she was exceptionally privileged, almost as far above the vast majority of women as the queens she loved to portray. Yet she was, for much of the time, desperately sorry for herself; and it was this grief for herself, rather than her gender, that helped her to exert such power as a Lady of the Sorrows for three generations. In old age she told Thomas Moore that she regretted leaving the stage because 'she had always found in it a vent for her private sorrows, which enabled her to bear them better,' and she had often been given credit for 'the truth and feeling' of her acting, when she was only 'relieving her own heart of its grief'.[60]

Nevertheless, it seems probable that whatever Mrs Siddons thought she was doing, she did to some degree embody for many of the people in many of her audiences their subliminal guilt, resentment and anger about the Women's Question, as it came to be known after her death. There is some evidence for this in the fact that virtually the only *new* plays in which she was a success, through over forty years in the profession, were *The Stranger* (1798) and *Pizarro* (1799), which she first played in her mid-forties and which at once rivalled in popularity her favourites from the stock repertoire.

The Stranger was a free version, rewritten by Sheridan, of a Continental success by the modish German playwright August von Kotzebue. In the world of the Kembles, it had three distinctions (two of them shared with *The Gamester*): it was in prose; it was in modern dress; and it challenged contemporary moral conventions – of the theatre, at least. Mrs Siddons appeared as Mrs Haller, a Countess in disguise who had wronged her husband (John Philip Kemble) by falling in love with another man and running away from the Count (and their children) when the affair ended. Racked though Mrs Haller was by penitence and guilt, buried deep in histrionic gloom, she was a sinful, adulterous wife, and would therefore have been sentenced to death by any right-thinking eighteenth-century dramatist who observed what had happened to other erring wives in the serious drama of the past eighty years. Mrs Haller, however, was reprieved. Not only was she allowed to live, but she was reunited, at the very last moment, with her forgiving husband and loving children. All were reconciled as the curtain fell. Some critics were not reconciled to the message: that the wages of (wifely) sin were not death, after all. *The Stranger* shocked British audiences, morally, as they were not to be shocked until another foreigner upset them a century later, with *Ghosts* and *A Doll's House*. The sense of outrage was not so acute as in Ibsen's case; partly, perhaps, because of the thick layers of pious self-castigating cant in which Mrs Haller is punitively smothered, insisting resolutely that she can only meet her husband after death, when penance has broken her heart. Yet the 'extra-connubial attachment' of the heroine aroused deep disgust.[61] It was prophesied that the time would come 'when not a child in England will have its head patted by its legitimate father.'[62] Even Boaden, one of Mrs Siddons's most ardent devotees, described the play as 'a noble ruin, marking the desolation of our domestic manners.'[63] But Mrs Siddons insisted on playing Mrs Haller and audiences insisted on seeing her in the part, though some also insisted on a different, moral ending. The title-role was one of her brother's favourites.

In *Pizarro*, another free adaptation of von Kotzebue, Mrs Siddons appeared as an adjunct of the conquest of Peru: Elvira, an Amazonian camp-follower, in a large plumed helmet, urging the head of the local resistance movement to kill her former lover Pizarro. Rolla fails in the attempt; when a friend succeeds, Elvira goes to a convent to expiate her guilt. Once again, for the second year running, Mrs Siddons had appeared as an immoral woman who actually *survived*, in defiance of all the canons of stage morality. She not only indulged in 'extra-connubial attachments', but incited men to murder, as well. And still she was let off. Some people thought it was going too far: so did Mrs Siddons. Initially she objected to the part. Then, on the first night, she was in 'an agony of fright' (partly, it was said, because Sheridan had not *quite* finished the play). But there was no cause for alarm. *Pizarro* was performed for thirty-one evenings in succession, an unprecedented run for a play without music. The character of Elvira, and Mrs Siddons's performance of it, were largely responsible for this smash-hit. And Elvira's rhetoric includes some eloquent flourishes on behalf of women at large. Thus:

O men! men! ungrateful and perverse! The beings to whose eyes you turn for animation, hope and rapture, through the days of mirth and revelry; and on whose bosoms in the hour of sore calamity you seek for rest and consolation, then when the pompous follies of your mean ambition are the question, you treat as playthings or as slaves.

Or again:

O man! ye who, wearied by the fond fidelity of virtuous love, seek in the wanton's flattery a new delight. Ye may insult and leave the hearts to which your faith was pledged, and, stifling self-reproach, may fear no other peril; because such hearts, however you injure or desert them, have yet the proud retreat of an unspotted fame – of unreproaching conscience.

Whatever the emotional voltage generated by Sarah Siddons from the contemplation of her private sufferings (real and imagined) and the wrongs of her entire sex, she could not have become one of the wealthiest women at work in Britain without other assets of personality, experience and technique. Some of these have already been described in the opening pages of this chapter. Another key to her success as an artist was her intense, single-minded concentration on the inner life of the woman she was playing and the technical problems of the role, in its conception, preparation and projection. She studied hard, but the study did not often – as in her brother's acting – *show*. She had, it seemed clear, thought long and deeply about her parts as *people,* not merely as solo turns. And she went on thinking about them, no matter how often she played them. 'From the moment she assumed the dress she became the character; she never chatted or coquetted by the green-room fire but placed herself where no word of the play could escape her, or the illusion for a moment be destroyed.'[64] As soon as she appeared on the scene, she impressed the specific reality of her role on the audience. In that first moment, 'her deportment conveyed the mind and circumstances of the being she represented'; and she maintained that illusion until the end of the performance. 'Even when not engaged in dialogue, she never lost sight of her character'[65] – a surprised tribute that throws a revealing sidelight on what other actresses did when not engaged in dialogue. Her voice, her face, her gestures, her walk changed from role to role. It did not matter to her audience that, outside a handful of Shakespearian parts, most of her roles were in fustian drama, or that, for much of her career, she wore 'piles of powdered curls, with a forest of feathers on top of them, high-heeled shoes, and a portentous hoop'.[66] As her official biographer put it somewhat dotingly, 'Where there was little or no poetry, she made it for herself; and might be said to have become at once both the dramatist and the actress.'[67] The plays were platforms for her to work on: to queen it, to weep, to rage, to glare, to declaim, almost to sing – for, in some ways, the theatre of Mrs Siddons was closer to opera than to the naturalistic drama of today.

Mrs Siddons's 'Remarks on the Character of Lady Macbeth' have been described by the Stanislavsky scholar and biographer, David Magarshack, as containing 'all the essentials of Stanislavsky's system'.[68] Like some disciples of that system, she seems to have found evidence in her imagination about characters' appearance and motivation for which there is no warrant in the text: she assumed, for instance, that Lady Macbeth had 'dark blue eyes'.[69] But more helpfully, she had a sharp eye for useful detail in life, art and literature, as her letters indicate. 'To *observe*', said her first biographer, 'is her mental discipline.'[70] He declared that he had seen 'hundreds of touches caught from the real world' in her performances. She studied sleepwalkers, for instance, to perfect Lady Macbeth. William Robson went so far as to say that 'she sought the cell of the maniac and the couch of the dying' for instruction.

How, then, might one try to sum up the secret of Sarah Siddons? There is no simple, single answer; but here are a few clues, in recapitulation. She had exceptional physical assets – in her face, eyes, voice, body and bearing – which she controlled with exceptional skill, sensibility and technical resource. She had, as Leigh Hunt said, 'the air of never being the actress'.[71] She was the part, not the performer. She was not a naturalistic player (as we understand the term), but she made her words seem to be 'the natural expression of the emotion', with a visible 'hesitation and working of the mind'. She had an exceptional stage presence, with an aura of personal dignity, integrity and moral authority: 'the most lofty-minded actress I ever saw', said Charles Mayne Young.[72] All reports of her off-stage life supported this impression, which survived the Lawrence and Galindo scandals in her fifties, and was reinforced by an otherworldly, asexual energy. She contrived an extraordinary 'unity of

1 *Above left* Nell Gwyn: pioneer of the personality cult, she gave up the stage at twenty
2 *Above* Elizabeth Barry: 'mistress of tears' — and of her own destiny
3 *Left* Anne Oldfield rocketed to theatrical fame and social eminence early in the eighteenth century. Although she had publicly brought up illegitimate sons by two successive partners, her artistry was honoured by burial in Westminster Abbey

4 *Above left* Kitty Clive, prima donna of light comedy. 'What Clive did best, she did better than Garrick,' said Dr Johnson

5 *Above* Susannah Cibber, pictured here as Cordelia in the happy-ending version of *King Lear* by Nahum Tate

6 *Left* Peg Woffington whose legendary sexual prowess for long obscured her significance as an artist and as a woman of unique independence. Her most popular roles were in breeches parts, with the traditional titillation of male dress.

7 *Opposite* Sarah Siddons, depicted here by Reynolds as the Tragic Muse, seemed, said Hazlitt, 'Tragedy personified'. She was the most regal, supernatural and misunderstood of player queens.

8 *Opposite* Ellen Terry as
Beatrice, one of her greatest
Shakespearian characters and
most popular Lyceum roles
9 *Right* Janet Achurch,
pictured in 1887, was credited
by Shaw with 'inaugurating'
the Ibsen movement
10 *Below* Stella Patrick
Campbell as Paula Tanqueray,
the Pinero role which brought
her instant fame in 1893

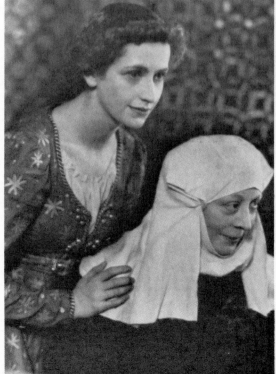

11 *Opposite* Sybil Thorndike as Shaw's St Joan (1924), the supreme experience of her career

12 *Above right* Edith Evans as Millamant in *The Way of the World* (1924), perhaps her major triumph

13 *Right* Peggy Ashcroft and Edith Evans: two player queens together in *Romeo and Juliet* (1935, New Theatre)

14 The role of Queen
Margaret in the RSC *Wars of
the Roses* (1963) is one of
Peggy Ashcroft's finest
creations

design, the just relation of all parts to the whole', as Macready described it; this was, he said, 'one great excellence that distinguished all her personations'.[73] She had a rare command of theatrical technique, but never resorted to obvious stage tricks, as Garrick and her brother John Philip sometimes did. 'You never caught her slumbering through some scenes in order to produce, by contrast, an exaggerated effect in others.'[74] She was a mistress of stillness, silence, *repose*: developed as an aid to the sculptural style of acting, meant to be seen and heard at a distance. Yet this was based on a control of tempestuous energy and vitality, and the ability to make quick transitions in voice and feeling. She had a fundamental simplicity – of mind, spirit and religious faith – that made Kitty Clive acclaim her acting as 'all truth and daylight'. She could work herself up with a 'superb power of self-excitation'[75] that carried the audience with her into a shared catharsis of emotion. She could make them feel more intensely, and feel 'better', not only because they liked the release of tears and the dollops of rhetoric burnished by her oratory, but because she somehow enlarged their capacity for emotion and for envisaging what womankind *could* be. She put a high value upon her work, her family and herself. Because 'she took her great talent for granted, and she took herself seriously'[76] with a public assumption of imperial dignity, audiences acquiesced in her dominion – and in the new social prestige and respectability of her profession.

Let us conclude with Hazlitt, writing three years before her death: 'Mrs Siddons seemed to command every source of terror and pity, and to rule over their wildest elements with inborn ease and dignity. Her person was made to contain her spirit; her soul to fill and animate her person. Her eye answered to her voice. She wore a crown.'[77]

5 VICTORIAN LADIES

Why have women passion, intellect, moral activity – these three – and a place in society where no one of these three can be exercised?
Florence Nightingale (1859)

I have ever found my art a most purifying and ennobling one, and the aim of all my life has been to educate and elevate myself *up to it* ... Whatever gifts I had as an actress were ever regarded by me as a sacred trust to be used for widening and refining the sympathies of my audiences.
Helena Faucit, Lady Martin (1878)

Now that we have a surplus female population it is clear that all women cannot marry, they cannot enlist, nor yet go out to the colonies and become domestic servants. So they sigh after the stage.
George Moore (1886)

IN THE HALF-CENTURY after Sarah Siddons died the theatre was transformed – in its architecture, organization, finance, dramatic repertoire, styles of acting, social status and public support. The grand manner broke down as tragedy went out of favour. Burlesque, extravaganza and melodrama flourished. The advent of gaslight encouraged a growing emphasis on pictorial effect and (in due course) scenic realism, adding a new dimension to the projection of sexual glamour. Both the cost of playgoing and the rewards of acting soared. By the 1880s the theatre had achieved unprecedented levels of prosperity, respectability and social recognition – a process in which women played a leading role not only as performers but as managers.

Some of these trends were already perceptible while Mrs Siddons reigned at Drury Lane and Covent Garden. She had seen these theatres enlarged from homes of the drama into vast arenas of spectacle, melodrama and pantomime, suffering from a kind of architectural elephantiasis which damaged the arts of playwriting and acting, even her own and Kean's. This was caused by the struggle of the 'patent houses' to meet the demands of a rapidly growing urban public while clinging to their monopoly of the 'straight' or 'legitimate' drama against the competition of the 'minor' theatres that mushroomed around London. These minors effectively forced them, in time, out of the realm of straight theatre. In 1843 the anomalous privileges of Covent Garden and Drury Lane were at last abolished. In London, henceforward, the drama – in a widening variety of genres – was staged in a growing number of smaller, more intimate playhouses. The classical and sub-classical repertoire was no longer the pillar of programmes in London or the provinces. Although the more popular plays of the past were revived by actor-managers and their consorts in the West End and on tour, the repertoire system disappeared from the London stage with the development of the long run, which made possible a new level of prosperity for authors, actors and (above all) managers.

Never before had so many actresses, dancers and singers been at work in Britain. Never before had so many women enjoyed such financial independence and personal freedom at work. And this was at a time when, in Florence Nightingale's words, 'Widowhood, ill-health or want of bread, these three explanations or excuses are supposed to justify a woman taking up an occupation.'

Women, when they are young, sometimes think that an actress's life is a happy one – not for the sake of the admiration, not for the sake of the fame; but because in the morning she studies, in the evening she embodies those studies; she has the means of testing and correcting them by practice, and of resuming her studies in the morning. . . .[1]

As an actress, even of middle standing, a girl might earn far more than she could ever hope to be paid as a governess, a nurse or a companion. By the 1880s, Mrs Kendal testified, 'there are a great many who can earn their £300 or £400 a year, and that is a very nice competence for a woman in the middle

class of life. . . . Besides, she has the blessedness of independence, and that is a great thing to a woman, and especially to a
single woman.'[2] Moreover, the social odium of the theatre
having largely evaporated by then, there was (she said) 'no other
calling in which she can keep her own standard so high; no
other calling in which she can set a better example and do more
good' – an irresistible recruiting call to middle-class womanhood in the late Victorian era. Even as late as the 1930s, when
many more jobs were open to women, '£250 a year is quite
an achievement, even for a highly qualified woman with years
of experience,'[3] outside the entertainment industry. A 'highly
qualified' actress might then, while at work, be earning at least
thirty times as much.

Puritan opposition persisted. As late as 1884 the popular
preacher Spurgeon declared that no playgoer (let alone an actor
or an actress) could be a member of a Christian community.
The range of characterization and expression was restricted by
both official and unofficial censorship, compared with, say, the
opportunities of French authors and players. And the drama
continued, for many years, to maintain a double-standard
morality. For most of the Victorian era death (often self-
inflicted) was the usual mandatory punishment for feminine
'impurity' (unless, of course, the actress was speaking or singing
in a foreign language). Ideals of 'purity' were, indeed, maintained with almost evangelical enthusiasm by several leading
players – notably by Helena Faucit (1817–98), the outstanding
Shakespearian actress between Mrs Siddons and Ellen Terry,
and creator of many contemporary roles including Clara
Douglas in *Money* and Pauline in *The Lady of Lyons*. Her
personal *pudeur* may be illustrated by her determination when
playing Imogen with Macready not to show her legs when
dressed as a page. She had the costume made ankle-length.
When Macready ordered it to be altered, because (as he
explained) half the audience would think that Imogen was still
undisguised in woman's garb, she 'managed to devise a kind of
compromise' by swathing herself in a riding cloak. In a fore-
word to the fifth edition of her very successful book on
Shakespeare's Heroines, she explained that in her career she
had tried 'to present a living picture of womanhood as divined
by Shakespeare, and held up by him as an ideal for woman

to aspire to, and for men to revere. Whatever gifts I had as an actress were ever regarded by me as a sacred trust to be used for widening and refining the sympathies of my audiences.'4 Miss Faucit was not only widely respected in the profession but outside it – notably by Queen Victoria, whose invitations to Osborne and Windsor at a time when professional actresses were generally excluded from polite society marked a big step forward towards the revaluation of the theatre's role in the life of the nation.

Less talented actresses found other ways of demonstrating moral standards, like those recalled by Fanny Kemble: 'Many actresses that I have known, in the performance of unvirtuous or unlovely characters ... have thought fit to impress the audience with the wide difference between their assumed and real disposition, by acting as ill, and looking as cross, as they possibly could.'5 Some even refused to play characters in equivocal situations or with unseemly lines. As late as 1900 Evelyn Millard threw up her part in a play (H. A. Jones's *The Lackey's Carnival*) because she would not say, 'I swear to you by my unborn child.'6 But for most actresses that way inclined, such self-defensive Puritanism had come to seem less imperative as the social status of their profession improved, and as attitudes towards women outside the theatre changed.

Among the outstanding actresses of the era (Helen Faucit apart) were Eliza O'Neill (1791–1872), who retired before she was thirty and became Lady Beecher; Maria Foote (1797–1867), who retired in 1831 to marry the Earl of Harrington; Fanny Kemble (1809–93), Sarah Siddons's niece, who at twenty-five gave up a profession she detested; and Ellen Tree (1805–80), who showed greater stamina and had greater influence than any of these. After winning a reputation in England and America she married Charles Kean (son of Edmund) in 1842, and from then on devoted herself to his service in acting, management and matrimony as a selfless paragon of Victorian wifely virtue. A mediocre actor, Charles Kean was a conscientious director who earned a place in theatrical history by his management of the Princess's between 1850 and 1859. With Ellen's help, he re-established the Shakespearian repertoire in London; took the first steps in recruiting a better-educated and more respectable public; and paved the way for the productions of Irving and Tree by his painstakingly antiquarian spectaculars. The Keans are also remembered because it was at the Princess's that Ellen Terry, as we shall see, served her apprenticeship. Forty years later Miss Terry told G.B.S. that nobody in the theatre had taught her anything about acting except Mrs Kean (until Shaw advised her how to play Imogen). Ellen Kean gave up the stage when her husband died in 1868. She followed the Victorian model by demonstrating that she felt she had nothing left to live for, although she lingered on for twelve years.

Two women had a still greater influence on the stage by their enterprise in management. Lucy Vestris (1797–1856) took over the Olympic (between Drury Lane and the Strand) in 1830, after starring in burlesque and light comedy in Paris and London. She was the first actress to manage a London theatre. Among her reforms Madame Vestris (as she was always known) paid salaries in advance, and paid them before other creditors; she put a premium on the welfare and morale of her company and staff; she timed and supervised dress rehearsals, and ensured adequate breaks; she pioneered ensemble playing, or inter-acting; she introduced real properties, real carpets, real curtains, real walls, achieving the first box-set with an unprecedented degree of scenic realism. In the words of Charles James Mathews, whom she later married:

> Drawing rooms were fitted up like drawing rooms, and furnished with care and taste. Two chairs no longer indicated that two persons were to be seated, the two chairs being removed indicating that the two persons were not to be seated. A claret-coloured coat, salmon-coloured trousers with a broad, black stripe, a sky-blue neckcloth with large paste brooch, and a cut-steel eyeglass with a pink ribbon no longer marked the 'light comedy gentleman', and the public at once recognized and appreciated the change.[7]

These reforms were extended and consolidated in the 'regular' drama over thirty years later by another enterprising star of burlesque, Marie Wilton (1839–1921). Like many leading actresses she was an actor's daughter and had been on the stage since childhood, with little chance of acquiring any formal education. Her wit and intelligence, however, were quickly recognized by discriminating theatregoers. Dickens called her 'the cleverest girl I have ever seen on the stage in my time, and the most singularly original.'[8] She was also singularly ambitious to do more than kick her legs and display her gamin charm in burlesque till she was past it. With a £1000 loan from her brother-in-law and the promised support of that writing workhorse H. J. Byron, Marie Wilton took over a near-derelict theatre off the Tottenham Court Road (nicknamed the Dusthole) and under the name of the Prince of Wales turned it, almost overnight, into the smartest showpiece in town. Elegant, intimate, comfortable and efficiently run, Marie Wilton's theatre inaugurated a new era in English comedy by presenting, soon after its opening, the first of Tom Robertson's 'teacup-and-saucer' plays, *Society*. The genteel realism of these miniatures of contemporary life then seemed startlingly fresh and novel by comparison with the dominant staginess of 'domestic dramas', and proved immediately appealing to a new middle-class audience. They saw the mirror held up to them by actors of the same class, like the leading man Squire Bancroft, or something looking very close to it. Marie Wilton created an acting ensemble with the help of Bancroft (whom she married in 1867) and Robertson, described by W. S. Gilbert as the inventor of modern stage management. She increased actors' salaries tenfold; paid for actresses' dresses; ensured that each production was mounted with care and good taste. These 'extravagances' paid off abundantly. When the Bancrofts took over the Haymarket in 1880 they abolished the pit and raised stall prices, first to 7/6, then to ten shillings. Whatever criticisms were made in later generations of this effective rationing by price, establishing the drama as a middle-class preserve, they not only made a fortune for themselves, and introduced a new era of prosperity for actors, authors and other managers, but they secured the social acceptance of the theatre and its arts. They retired jointly in 1885. Bancroft was knighted in 1897. At his death nearly thirty years later he left over £174,000. But it was Marie Wilton who set the ball rolling.

Another major figure of the Victorian stage, who did much in her own way to raise the prestige of her profession, was Madge Kendal (1848–1935). With four theatre generations behind her, the twenty-second child of Tom Robertson's father, she started to act at five. She had already made a name when in 1869 she married W. H. Kendal (five years her junior). Madge Kendal was clearly a brilliant artist of great verve, comic energy and technical precision. She helped her husband to manage their various companies with a disciplinarian but illuminating control, training new players to the high standards the Kendals set for themselves. These standards were moral, too. Not only were lapses in behaviour visited with summary punishment; but if artists who had worked with her appeared in what she considered 'a play of dubious morals', Madge Kendal 'expunged the offender's name from her visiting list.'[9] They seldom played apart from each other, usually as husband and wife, for nearly forty years: 'a Perpetual Joint', as G.B.S. said. 'My husband was never my leading man. I was always his leading lady . . . He stands alone, in my eyes, as Husband, Father and Friend.'[10] She was sixty-eight before he would let her have a latchkey (the year before he died). They seemed paragons of domestic felicity. What else? 'They represented a generation of actors', said Shaw in 1895, 'who had toned their acting down and their dress and manners up to stockbroker-civil servant pitch. This was all very well while it lasted . . . but now the Kendals are replaced by couples equal to them in dress, manners, good looks and domestic morality, but subject to the disadvantage of not possessing in their two united persons as much power of acting as there was in the tip of Mrs Kendal's little finger-nail.'[11] James Agate ranked her among the six best actresses of his experience.

Madge Kendal was created DBE in 1926, the year after Ellen Terry received this honour. She was, almost exactly, a contemporary of Ellen Terry; and, almost precisely, her opposite. To Miss Terry we must now turn our attention. . . .

6 ELLEN TERRY

Women as a rule think a mighty deal too much of themselves.
I'm always trying not to be a nuisance to Henry in the theatre.
Every little Miss there gives him more trouble than I do.

Ellen Terry (1897)

> Man with the head and woman with the heart;
> Man to command and woman to obey;
> All else confusion.
>
> Tennyson, The Princess (1847)

> Great Shakespeare's self with eye and brow serene,
> Might look on thee and say, 'Well done, sweet Queen.'
>
> Marie Corelli (to Ellen Terry)

I have never been admired or loved (properly) but one and a
half times in my life, and I am perfectly sick of loving.

Ellen Terry (1896)

DURING THE LAST QUARTER of the nineteenth century one tall,
grey-eyed, golden-haired, husky-voiced, exuberant, impulsive
woman – with a 'great red' mouth, quicksilver movements, and
large, 'speaking' hands – kept, above all other actresses, the
enthralled loyalty of British playgoers. At the age of thirty-one
Ellen Terry embarked on her reign as consort of Henry Irving
at the Lyceum, and helped him to make it, in effect, the
National Theatre of late-Victorian Britain. It was 'an artistic
alliance of such brilliance and endurance as the European
theatre had never known.'[1] Although for years she was in
private 'the queen of every woman' for Irving, she was not his
partner in real power (he was a lone autocrat) or in official

honour: it was not until thirty years after Irving was knighted that Ellen Terry was made a Dame. Yet she was generally revered till the turn of the century as co-sovereign of the stage. 'Our Lady of the Lyceum', as Oscar Wilde called her, became an institution in spite of herself, idolized and idealized both by members of the cultural elite and the general public. G.B.S. said that 'every famous man of the last quarter of the nineteenth century, provided he were a theatre-goer, had been in love with Ellen Terry';[2] but she was worshipped by women, too, of all classes, in both Britain and America. 'I never knew any woman who possessed to such a degree the art of inspiring affection in her own sex ... she was the friend and confidante of dozens of girls, who adored her and loved to serve her in all sorts of little ways.'[3] For much of her life she reigned reluctantly over a feminine court in which her daughter Edith Craig was regent. Outside it she was, perhaps, the most widely, most persistently loved of any actress who had yet appeared on the London stage – loved long after her youthful beauty had faded; and that her popularity was no merely metropolitan cult was demonstrated year after year in the tours she made with Henry Irving around the provinces and on their frequent visits to the US. She was the highest-paid actress on the British stage, probably the highest-paid professional woman of her time. 'Our Ellen', as she was popularly dubbed, was acclaimed as a great actress, a great artist and a great woman.

Her long dominion was partly due to her beauty, to the fact that this was singularly hard-wearing, and – even more important – to the fact that she did not believe in it. As her son Gordon Craig wrote, with pardonable exaggeration, 'she never looked on herself as clever or a beauty, and so she was never vain and ever lovely.'[4] G.B.S., who did not see her until she was nearly thirty, praised her in her early fifties for having invented a 'new' kind of beauty. Yet to many people she seemed in her youth and early middle age a perfect embodiment of the visions of romantic girlhood or idealized sexuality already projected by Victorian poets and painters: Tennyson's queens made flesh, the Blessed Damozel by gaslight, a 'curious compound of childlike innocence and womanly tenderness', as she was described at forty; mystical, medieval, yet up to date. In her teens she was apostrophized as the living model for the

Pre-Raphaelites, whose Brotherhood was formed the year after she was born. Henry James, whose opinion of her acting was grudgingly dismissive, said that she was (at thirty-two) 'the most pleasing and picturesque figure upon the English stage'; as Ophelia, he observed, she had 'a face altogether in the taste of the period, a face that Burne-Jones might have drawn.'[5] She reminded Beerbohm Tree of 'one of Leighton's women, queen-like'.[6] Other testimonials, as the years went by, invoked Marcus Stone, William Orchardson, Albert Moore, Alma-Tadema. More exotic comparisons were made with Veronese, Bellini, and the Elgin Marbles. When she was nearly fifty she actually appeared as Tennyson's Guinevere (in a play by J. Comyns Carr); and while she had little to do but appear, it was generally agreed that she looked, astonishingly, right, although she had left it rather late. The following year, playing Imogen for the first time, she looked so dazzlingly young at her first entrance that 'the audience gasped – there was a silence, then thunders of applause!'[7] Even in her seventies, says her great-nephew Sir John Gielgud, 'she could still give radiant glimpses of her former glory.'[8] In transcending age, she emanated that intensity of being which made Dame Sybil Thorndike describe her as 'the perfect symbol in her work of what the true theatre is – an instrument which transformed body, voice, clothes, words, all materials, into spirit – spiritual essence.'[9]

Yet this high priestess of the 'semi-sacred' Lyceum, championing with Irving the moral as well as the artistic acceptance of their profession in Victorian respectable society, married disastrously three times, the third time at sixty to a man some twenty-five years her junior. The image of idealized womankind had secretly 'lived in sin' with an artist to whom she had borne two illegitimate children. The symbol of essential theatre had given it up at twenty, 'without one single regret'; had been virtually 'driven back' to it, as she said, two years later; and had renounced it again, apparently without a qualm, for six years.

Ellen Terry's reputation as a great actress, moreover, is based on a relatively small number of significant roles. She came late to Juliet (thirty-six), Cordelia (forty-five), Imogen (forty-nine), Mrs Page (fifty-five), Hermione (fifty-nine), and she never came at all to Rosalind, Miranda, Perdita and Kate, let alone to

Cressida, Constance, Isabella and Cleopatra, which were (or were thought to be) outside her range. Her Lady Macbeth and Volumnia were something less than triumphs. It was on Beatrice and Portia that her Shakespearian fame depended; and, to a lesser degree, on Ophelia, Desdemona (six weeks only) Queen Katharine (a part which left her cold), Viola (one London season) Imogen and Mrs Page. She played in scarcely any post-Shakespearian classics, the nearest approach to one at the Lyceum being Hannah Cowley's *The Belle's Stratagem*, when she appeared as Letitia. She rejected the new drama of the Ibsenite *avant-garde*. As she said in 1902, she did not 'care' to act in any of Ibsen's roles: they seemed 'preposterously *unreal – untrue* to nature.' 'I consider myself very happy and fortunate in having nearly always been called upon to act very noble, clear characters, since I prefer that kind of part, and love Portia and Beatrice better than Hedda, Nora or any of those silly ladies.'[10] And that was after she had been exposed to several years of loving, hectoring, cosseting postal propaganda by George Bernard Shaw. He arrived too late, or Ellen too early, for them to be effective collaborators in the drama, although her role in their 'paper courtship' has given her a more assured immortality than any appearance on the stage.

Ellen's greatest successes outside Shakespeare were as the sorrowful Queen Henrietta Maria pleading with Cromwell and parting from her husband for ever in W. G. Wills's pseudo-historical romance, *Charles I*; Camma, the doomed widow turned priestess of Artemis who poisons her persecutor and herself in Tennyson's *The Cup*; the temporarily wronged Olivia in Wills's adaptation of Goldsmith's *The Vicar of Wakefield* (which G.B.S. believed to be the best nineteenth century play in the Lyceum repertory); the more permanently wronged Margaret in Wills's free version of *Faust*, closer to Gounod than to Goethe but without the music (this was Ellen Terry's favourite non-Shakespearian role). In all of these she exploited to the full her gift for pathos, as a victim of man's inhumanity to woman, readily – sometimes all too readily – reducing her audience and herself to tears. (As Guinevere she cried so much that 'all her make-up was washed into streaks, and she had to leave the stage, her hands spread over her ravaged face'.)[11] At the Lyceum her brilliance in comedy was confined, outside

Shakespeare, to *The Belle's Stratagem* and Charles Reade's
Nance Oldfield, which she bought as a vehicle for herself and
her son, who played her suitor. If the 'greatness' of an actress
is to be judged by the range and variety of her work, and by
her achievement, above all, in tragedy, then Ellen Terry has no
claim to be ranked among the great.

She made no such claim herself. In spite of the mesmeric
effect of her 'invented' beauty – she had, in fact, a rather long
nose, a square jaw, large hands and other deviations from model
prettiness – and the emotional overdrive of her personality, her
apparent incapacity in tragedy was widely observed in her
heyday, not least by Ellen. 'I can pass swiftly from one effect to
another, but I cannot fix one, and dwell on it, with that superb
concentration which seems to me the special attribute of the
tragic actress.'[12] This incapacity was conspicuous in her interpretation of Lady Macbeth. Having been persuaded by Irving
to play the role against her own judgement, she was influenced
by reading Mrs Siddons's views on how it *ought* to be played,
and decided to adapt the part to her own personality. As Ellen
saw Lady Macbeth, she was 'quite unlike her portrait by Mrs
Siddons! She is *most feminine.*'[13] Turning her back on the
'fiend' tradition, she played her as a devoted wife who would
do anything for her man – 'not good, but not so much worse
than many women you know'; a woman seized by ambition for
her husband and for her own queenship, but so overcome by
the reality of Duncan's murder that, thereafter, she crumples
and fades away. Gordon Craig was among the people who complained that there was no terror in the sleep-walking scene.
When Ellen Terry said, 'The Thane of Fife had a wife, where
is she now?', the audience felt, according to her son: 'Poor
Ellen Terry, she is so sorry for the Thane of Fife's wife, and
wondering where she can possibly be now, poor, poor dear.
What a *nice* woman!'[14] She did look magnificent, with red
tresses falling on to a robe of blue and green silk tissue, sewn
with green beetle-wings (in which Sargent painted her). There
were many admirers: one critic declared that 'a creature so
spiritual, so ineffable, has never perhaps been put on the stage.'[15]
Yet to many others Ellen Terry's Lady Macbeth seemed a distant relation of Shakespeare's, and these objectors included such

devotees as Walter Calvert who praised the will power but not the performance.[16]

Gordon Craig believed that his mother could have presented a 'real and painful' interpretation of the role if she had not been so concerned with what the audience expected of her, so reluctant for the sake of the theatre and Henry to move out of her Lyceum niche. Perhaps she *could* have achieved a very different Lady Macbeth. But she seems to have been trapped not only by the demands of the institution and the faithful followers she served, but also by her own championship of feminine character – one reason for her love of Shakespeare was his understanding that women had, she said, more moral courage than men – and her confusion about what 'real femininity' was. William Archer criticized her, in another role, for acting generalizations of the 'womanliness' for which she was so often praised, instead of presenting the womanly particularities of the character she was playing.[17] This 'womanliness' – in which the New Woman in life and art appeared to be so alarmingly deficient – was the submissive, graceful posture of the eternal helpmeet, content to be defended, patronized and exploited by the 'stronger' sex. Yet such an attitude was far removed from Ellen's own style of life. This 'womanly woman' of the stage was (by Victorian standards) unwomanly, even 'manly', at home, in her independence and self-sufficiency; a keen supporter of women's suffrage; a woman who treated her many male friends as equals, not masters.

There seems little doubt that Ellen Terry did display greatness as an artist and as a woman. Yet to describe and judge what she was and what she did in summary fashion – indeed, in any clearcut fashion at all – is more than usually difficult. This is in part because she generally disarmed criticism and defied definition. Overwhelmed by the irresistible force of her personality, most reviewers used over and over again the same eroded terms – grace, beauty, vitality, and, above all, charm, while the adulation accorded Irving was sharply punctuated by a barrage of detailed dissent. Possessing 'in the very highest degree the art which conceals art', she seemed so supremely spontaneous at her best that it was not Acting but Nature on view; and how could one review *that*? Except, of course, to say that Miss

Terry's Nature was graceful, beautiful, vital, sunny and *charming*, knowing that it was never at its best on first nights, 'the incarnation of our capricious English sunlight'?[18] For her 'charm' came to be a dirty word. Perhaps Ellen Terry also resists instant explanation because of what Laurence Irving has called the 'agglomeration of baffling complexities and contradictions in her personality' ...

Her nature demanded the love of men, yet she was happiest as a mother and as the centre of a domestic circle which included no paterfamilias ... She was scornful of pettiness and generous in thought and deed, yet in her train she left a turbulence of small gossip and intrigue ... She was a God-fearing traditionalist, yet she rebelled against the Church and the social conventions. Unostentatious and careless of her dignity or appearance, she had an air which commanded respect; at an early age she had been nicknamed 'Duchess' by her family ... Though she was a mistress of technique and laboured to perfect herself in every part she played, she could, while playing, be overwhelmed by her own emotion. She seldom reached the high standard at which she aimed.[19]

The theatre world into which Alice Ellen Terry was born – on 27 February 1847,[20] in Smithford Street, Coventry, a few yards from the playhouse where her father was working on tour – was not very different from the one in which Sarah Kemble grew up, although it was to change radically during her lifetime. Her parents, like Sarah's, were minor provincial actors, always on the move. Both came from Portsmouth. Ben Terry was the son of an Irish-born publican, and Sarah Ballard was the daughter of a local builder, with a strong Scottish strain in her family. Ellen Terry was probably not *half*-Scots, and may have been no more than a quarter Irish, although she often seemed wholly so in temperament. Christopher St John, the actress-author with whom she collaborated in her autobiography (whose real name was Christabel Marshall) asserted that the Irish-Scots mixture was 'the most illuminating thing' she knew about Ellen. Yet she was acclaimed, repeatedly, as 'essentially English' on the stage, or rather, as Max Beerbohm said in 1906, 'what we imagine to be essentially English.'[21]

Unlike the Kembles the Terrys had no company or circuit of their own, but they, too, had a reservoir of family talent. Six of their eleven children (two died in infancy) went on the stage, and four of them achieved fame. They were brought up in green-rooms, dressing-rooms and theatre digs. Neither Ellen nor her elder sister Kate ever went to school. 'What I have learned outside my own profession I have learned from my environment'.[22] The Terrys seem to have been a happy enough family, and in some respects Ellen – compared with many other theatre children – was unusually lucky, not least in her parents. By the standards of today they were restrictive, authoritarian and over-pious – Sarah Terry was, like Mrs Kemble, a devout Wesleyan – but it is to their protective love that one may attribute their daughters' basic confidence and emotional stability at the beginning of their careers.

Kate began early: she was on the stage at three, singing and dancing. At seven her performance as Prince Arthur (in Edinburgh) was so highly praised that she was offered an audition in London by Charles Kean, then at the start of his historic regime as actor-manager at the Princess's. Kate was engaged, repeated her success as Prince Arthur, and was established as a member of the company. This spectacular ascent up the theatrical ladder temporarily split the family. Mr Terry had to go to Liverpool, where he was engaged to play in the stock company, and Ellen – then five – was sent with him to cook his breakfast and perform other domestic chores, while Mrs Terry went to London to look after Kate and her two sons, Benjamin and George. For Ellen this period of separation from her mother (probably less than a year, though to her it seemed twice as long) provided an early education in independence. Perhaps, as Roger Manvell suggests, it helped to insulate her in later life from the inhibiting pressures of Victorian moral and social conformism. Perhaps, in deepening her intimacy with her father, to whom she was already close and whom she 'took after', the Liverpool little-mothering was a source of her later emotional pull towards older, masterful men. She recalled in her autobiography that in Liverpool he 'never ceased teaching me to be useful, alert and quick', often with the aid of a spanking;[23] and to be 'useful' was her most frequently repeated aspiration in her days of fame. Certainly, Mr Terry gave Ellen, as he had given Kate, a thorough coaching in deportment and speech, and a belief that to play a real Shakespeare part was 'the pride of life'. That he was 'a beautiful elocutionist' (so she remembered him) may ultimately have been of more significance to his daughters than his Irish charm, volatility, gaiety, paternal possessiveness, and marital infidelities.

It was not until the relatively advanced age of nine, however, that Ellen made her theatrical debut – at the Princess's, where her father now played small parts and her mother worked in the wardrobe. On 20 April 1856 she appeared as Mamilius in *The Winter's Tale*; was singled out at once (*The Times* commended her for her 'vivacious precocity'); continued in the role for over a hundred performances; and joined Kate as a member of the company. Her real theatrical education now began, under the stern eye of Mrs Kean. The cocky, tomboyish, self-willed little girl learned to dance, to sing, to walk, and to improve her speech, building on her father's lessons. Rehearsals started privately with Mr Terry at breakfast, continuing in a bus, a shop or in the street on the way to the Princess's. Her working day there began at 10 am, Sundays included, and stretched until midnight (it might even go on till 4 am). She played Puck for 250 performances, a groom in a farce, Fleance, Prince Arthur, pantomime fairies, and many walk-on roles. Ellen was paid (after the first year) thirty shillings a week, of which her parents allowed her sixpence. There were domestic chores, too, for Ellen had to help her mother cope with her father's irresponsibility and to look after the babies who continued to arrive. Marion was born in 1853, Florence in 1855, Charles in 1857, and Tom at some later date. The last, Fred, arrived in 1864, when Mrs Terry was forty-seven. And when the theatre was closed in the summer her work continued, though under less awe-inspiring discipline and with somewhat greater opportunities for fun; for Mr Terry took the family troupe to Ryde each year to perform in seaside light entertainment. By 1859, when the Keans left for America, Ellen had served an invaluable apprenticeship. She had learned, as G.B.S. said, to project her voice into the corners of the house 'without the loss of a syllable or the waste of a stroke'.[24] She had absorbed, without realizing it, an awareness of the Keans' ideals of stage 'beauty' and authenticity of decor (however shaky their practice may have been). She had seen a woman in power as 'joint ruler' of a theatre, though still practising wifely obedience.

In that last Oxford Street season she was as well known as the precocious Kate. They were both born actresses. As one critic wrote:

> They possessed in full that power of abandonment to scenic excitement which is rare even among the most consummate of mature performances. They were carried away by the force of their own acting; there were tears not only in their voices but in their eyes; their mobile faces were quick to reflect the significance of the drama's events . . . singular animation and alertness distinguished all their movements, attitudes and gestures . . . A peculiar dramatic sensitiveness and susceptibility from the first characterised the Terry sisters.[25]

Although only twelve and fifteen respectively, they were frequently 'asked out' in society; and among their most ardent admirers were two men of letters, men of affairs, and men of the world, old enough to be their father (though both were childless): Tom Taylor (then forty-three) and Charles Reade (forty-five). Both were to exert a considerable influence on Ellen's life, especially Reade; not least, perhaps, through his defiance of Victorian convention by apparently 'living in sin' with an actress to whom he was not married. Reade's relationship with Laura Seymour may well have been platonic. Ellen's mother must have believed it to be so, as Roger Manvell suggests, or she would have forbidden her daughters to visit Reade at home. Until she was 'a grown woman', Ellen said, she was always chaperoned on her way back from the theatre – and, no doubt, from any social occasion – by her mother or father. Others found it hard to credit the possibility of comradeship without sex. But in that household Ellen came to see, perhaps, a kind of non-erotic equity in man/woman relations that served her as a criterion in later life. In the meantime she found in Reade (and Taylor) a kind of supplementary father, while Mrs Kean served as an auxiliary mother.

Until she was sixteen Ellen was emotionally dependent on her real parents, although they depended economically on her sister and herself – which may account for some of the confusions in her later attitudes to men as husbands and as colleagues. For two years she toured, under her father's management, with Kate, Mr and Mrs Terry and a pianist in 'A Drawing

Room Entertainment'. This consisted of two short plays in which the Terry sisters acted all the roles, male and female, with many quick changes (Ellen made an impression as a boy with a large cigar). They appeared in Ireland and in the West Country, earning from £10 to £15 a performance, cashing in on their London success and the Kean name. 'I tasted the joys of the strolling player's existence, without its miseries,' Ellen wrote.[26] The girls paid for the boys' education, though the Entertainment did little for their own, except in the handling of audiences.

Ellen's experience was widened and deepened, however, when she went to Bristol in 1862. She was following, once again, the pattern set by Kate, who was engaged as 'principal lady' in the stock company, one of the best in Britain. (Kate had been born in Bristol while her parents were in the company.) Ellen stayed at the Theatre Royal for only eleven weeks, returning in the following autumn for three weeks, but it proved to be a fruitful period: 'the experience of my life', as she called it forty years later.[27] She was remembered at that time as a 'gay, mercurial child', exuberant, saucy and 'absolutely at home' on the stage.[28] But it was there that she learned, as she put it, 'what work meant', playing in a quick turnover of burlesque, comedy, melodrama and farce. Ellen tended afterwards to exaggerate the length and breadth of her Bristol stage education – and Roger Manvell, for instance, mistakenly asserts that she was there for a year – because she was simultaneously 'having (her) eyes opened to beautiful things in art and literature'.[29] The opener was Edward Godwin, a married architect, freelance theatre critic, and secretary of the Bristol Shakespeare Society, to whose house Kate and Ellen went for Shakespeare readings. The conversation, the furniture, the decor, the whole atmosphere made Ellen feel she had 'never really lived. . . . For the first time I began to appreciate beauty, to observe, to feel the splendour of things, to aspire!'[30] In the ferment of adolescence the tomboy was growing into an artist – but away from her own art. She 'went off' acting. She wanted to get away from the theatre, and from all the babies at home. She longed for 'a world full of pictures and music and gentle, artistic people with quiet voices and elegant manners',[31] like those who surrounded Tom Taylor, Charles Reade and Edward Godwin. Meanwhile, she was engaged at one of London's leading theatres, the Haymarket, where she remained for the better part of a year with a company of veteran stylists schooled in the old traditions. 'Their bows, their curtseys, their grand manner, the indefinable *style* which they brought to their task, were something to see,' she wrote.[32] Although in 1906 she classified this experience as a 'lost opportunity' because she had failed at the time to realize just how much she *could* have learned from these elderly players, something surely must have been gained by playing such roles as Hero, Nerissa, Lady Touchwood and Julia Melville. Yet before the winter season was over, Ellen suddenly left the Haymarket in the middle of a run and turned her back on the stage 'without one single pang of regret'. With Tom Taylor's help, she believed she had found her artistic dream-world. She married, a week before her seventeenth birthday, George Frederick Watts, a fashionable, high-minded and neurotic painter, who had painted Kate and herself. He was nearly forty-seven. She wanted to pose for ever, as his model, 'and clean his brushes and play my idiotic piano to him, and sit with him there in wonderland (the Studio'.[33] He wanted to educate her and remove her from 'the dangers and temptations of the stage'.

Questions of age apart, the omens were not favourable. Mr Watts had lived for years, chastely and gloomily, under the patronage of a succession of wealthy women. The most possessive and persistent of these was Mrs Thoby Prinsep, in whose Kensington home he had become established as a resident lion. 'He came to stay three days; he stayed thirty years,' said Mrs Prinsep. Watts had already lived thirteen years in Little Holland House when he brought Ellen back to it as her first married home. Mrs Prinsep soon *knew* that this high-spirited, impetuous, *stagey* girl was not good enough for 'the Signor', as she dubbed him reverentially. The Signor seems to have needed little convincing that this was his predicament: Ellen, he later complained, had 'formed her ideas of life from the exaggerated romance of sensational plays.'[34] He wrote, 'To make the poor child what I wish her to be will take a long time, and most likely cost a great deal of trouble.'[35] For Ellen the 'trouble' proved to involve a good deal of bossy and humiliating nagging from Mrs Prinsep. She was at sea among the denizens of Mrs Prinsep's world, who included such eminent Victorians as Browning,

Tennyson, Disraeli and Gladstone; and she was frequently reminded of her childishness, and her social and intellectual inferiority.

Ellen was, moreover, sexually inexperienced and innocent, to a degree unimaginable by earlier generations, so closely had she been protected by Mrs Terry. During her pre-marital visits to Watts's studio, where he had painted Kate and herself, he had given Ellen her very first kiss. That was performed 'sweetly and gently, all tenderness and kindness', but the *second* kiss was a little different. After brooding on it for a fortnight, Ellen plucked up courage and confided in her mother. 'I told her I *must* be married to him *now* because I was going to have a baby ... and she believed me!!'[36] Watts, on the other hand, clearly suffered from severe sexual inhibitions, even if he was not completely impotent; and it would scarcely be surprising if, as is commonly supposed, the marriage was never consummated (although Watts's most recent biographer believes that it *was*). The virgins were singularly ill-matched.

Ten months after the wedding Watts sent his 'thunderstruck' wife back to her parents. At first she refused to go, but Tom Taylor and others persuaded her. The deed of separation specified 'incompatibility of temper' as the cause. For Ellen it was a traumatic shock, which must have influenced her views of marriage and of men in general. In later life she could say, with characteristic generosity, that the marriage was 'in many ways very happy indeed',[37] explaining charitably that 'I was so ignorant and so young, and he was so impatient.' But then, at seventeen, 'I hated my life, hated everyone and everything in the world more than at any time before or since,'[38] and most of all she hated Mrs Prinsep. She had no desire to go back to the stage, and there was no financial pressure to do so from the family. Watts was giving her £6 a week, 'so long as she leads a chaste life,' and Kate had become one of London's leading actresses. It was not until over two years later in 1867 – when Kate retired from the stage, for ever, into marriage – that Ellen was practically *driven back*'[39] to the theatre by her parents, Tom Taylor, and Charles Reade, for whom she appeared in a new play. But within a year she gave up her profession, her family and her friends. Without telling anyone, Ellen suddenly disappeared from London to live in a country cottage with

Edward Godwin. She was twenty-one, and he was thirty-three.

Godwin was a handsome, masterful, ambitious and imaginative architect and artist with a passion for the theatre, a contempt for commercial criteria of success, and a talent with a touch of genius – 'the greatest aesthete of them all', Max Beerbohm called him – although it was only after his death that his full stature began to be recognized. During Ellen's brief marriage they had met again in Watts's studio. Now a widower, he seemed a 'citizen of the artistic paradise from which she had been ignominiously expelled.'[40] Until she died, forty years after him, Godwin remained the love of her life. He fathered the only children she ever bore, the two brilliant mavericks who were to achieve fame, in varying degrees, as Gordon and Edith Craig. For a time she lived in near-perfect happiness, almost completely cut off from the theatre and her past. It was the major emotional experience of Ellen's existence, indissolubly linked with the new pleasures of country life, the discovery of sex (after the crippling Watts fiasco), and early motherhood, a period that she increasingly romanticized as time went by. The children were illegitimate because she was not free to marry; but she defied the powerful Victorian taboos against such a union with cheerful resolution, passing herself off as Mrs Godwin, taking up gardening and cooking, looking after poultry, and enjoying and spoiling her babies. To Ellen, living in sin seemed at first (especially in retrospect) like living in Eden. It was a time of growth and self-discovery. And it probably laid the foundation for her later supremacy as an artist and her freedom from staginess and artificiality. This was not only because of the profound experiences of joy with her lover and children and the breathing-space it offered from the theatrical treadmill – 'for the first time I was able to put all my energies into living'[41] – but also because Godwin's artistic conscience kindled hers and kept it burning.

This country idyll lasted for six years. But it became overshadowed by fear, loneliness and poverty, as Godwin's financial difficulties increased and his affections cooled. She had to support herself and the children on half the sum that Watts had allowed for herself alone. To earn a few shillings more she copied architectural drawings by candlelight, which probably contributed to the weakness of her eyes (though this seems to have been a family flaw). Bills were left unpaid. Debts mounted. Ellen herself contributed to them: in spite of her later self-portrait as a heroic housewife, her domestic efficiency was probably less apparent to her lover. Oppressed by anxieties about work and money Godwin became impatient, left her alone for days on end, and fell out of love. Matters finally came to a head when the bailiffs were at the door. Ellen had to do something. Under duress (or so she claimed) she came back to the theatre. It happened in what seems to be a totally implausible *coup de théâtre*.

Charles Reade was out hunting in Hertfordshire when his horse jumped over a hedge into a country lane – and there was Ellen Terry, in distress. A wheel had come off her pony-trap. They had not met since she had disappeared from London five years earlier. 'Come back to the stage!' said Reade. 'Never', said Ellen, meaning it. Then remembering the bailiffs and quoting a figure extravagantly at random, she said, 'Not for under £40 a week.' 'Done!' said 'Daddy' Reade. He had a play in the offing again, directed by himself, to be staged at a theatre under his management. And so, on 28 February 1874, Ellen Terry reappeared on the London stage – in Reade's *The Wandering Heir*, followed by a revival of *It's Never Too Late to Mend*, an adaptation of his best-selling novel.

In spite of her two illegitimate children, and her six years of self-exile, Ellen was back in favour at the top. She had been pretty: she was now beautiful, and already 'heartwise', as G.B.S. put it. She was still ostracized by her family, who were deeply shocked by her 'immorality' (though Marguerite Steen insisted that, once she had left Godwin, the breach was healed) and by such family friends as the Revd. Charles Dodgson (Lewis Carroll). With his notorious penchant for little girls, he had been attracted to Ellen since he saw her debut as Mamilius, and had obtained an introduction to the family. He had photographed the sisters in adolescence. And he was still an ardent admirer of Ellen's acting: in *The Wandering Heir* she was, he noted in his diary, *'simply wonderful'*. But he 'held no conversation' with her or her family, who were tarnished by guilt through association: 'she had so entirely sacrificed her social position that I had no desire but to drop the acquaintance.' Yet there was no public scandal or press gossip about Miss Terry's private life. Although unrepentantly and irreversibly in love, she did not flaunt her unconventional behaviour. Relatively few people knew how her 'lost' years had been spent. Ellen herself seldom talked about them, even to her intimate friends; even thirty years later, in her autobiography, she still kept secret her relationship with Godwin.

After the split from her family, Ellen's proxy fathers – Tom Taylor and Charles Reade – became of even more importance to her. Taylor, who felt a strong sense of responsibility for the Watts fiasco, was in many ways (so she said in her autobiography) more of a father to her than her 'father in blood'.[42] He lavished advice and hospitality on her (as he had on Kate, his favourite); he used his considerable influence, indefatigably, on her behalf; he found parts in his own plays for her; he stood by her in times of trouble. Yet Reade, though a less kindly and less altruistic man, was perhaps a greater influence on Ellen Terry. In old age, making a list of 'My Friends', she put his name first (followed by Bernard Shaw's). And 'Daddy' Reade was surely more than a little in love with her, in a rather more than fatherly fashion. However innocent it may have appeared for a man of sixty to enjoy, for instance, playing blind-man's-buff at home with a beautiful actress of twenty-six, there was a strong if unconscious erotic element in their relationship, on Reade's side at least. He described himself in his notebooks as 'looking coldly on from the senile heights', but admitted that Ellen was 'downright fascinating'. To her in later life he seemed 'a stupid old dear, and as wise as Solomon', both 'unjust' and 'generous', 'impulsive' and 'passionate'. At the time of her return to the stage, in particular, Reade was an explosively candid critic of her work, bombarding her with notes about the details of her performance not only in rehearsal but after the first night, sending her messages from the pit between the acts. The flow of directions seemed unstoppable: he advocated 'ardent' exits, with a 'personal' rush; he stressed the need for variety of pace; he made her come to realize the importance of every line, every detail. Though sometimes a maddening mentor, he was a valuable one. She listened and she learned. But she would not listen when he, like other friends, urged her 'unjustly' to leave Godwin, with whom Ellen had now moved to London (to a house that was soon invaded by bailiffs).

It was probably through Ellen that Godwin was now given his first job in the professional theatre – as archaeological adviser to a production of *The Merchant of Venice*, in which Ellen was invited to play Portia (Mrs Kendal not being available). This was another milestone in her career. After ten years of modern drama (mostly by Tom Robertson) the Bancrofts had decided after Robertson's death to venture on Shakespeare at the Prince of Wales, their fashionable little playhouse off the Tottenham Court Road. The experiment was, as Beerbohm Tree said, 'the first production in which the modern spirit of stage-management asserted itself', but commercially it was a fiasco. Although the scenery and costumes were admired by a discriminating few, drawn to the theatre partly by Godwin's name, the production was visually too far ahead of its time. The Shylock was disastrous. And Ellen Terry, though unanimously praised, was not enough to save the play from closure after a run of only three weeks (compared with the three months, at least, expected by the Bancrofts). But this *Merchant of Venice* was, as Sir Squire later claimed, the 'foundation-stone' of Ellen's mature career. To the London critics she seemed to have acquired a new authority in technique, personality and beauty, combining poetry, charm and naturalness. Whistler and Wilde were among the friends she made through this performance, though she received some criticism from Henry James and John Ruskin. More important than the notices or the tributes, however, was what happened to her *inside:* 'the feeling of the conqueror', as she later described it, 'elation, triumph, being lifted on high by a single stroke of the mighty wing of glory'.[43] 'This is different. . . . It has never been quite the same before'. It was never quite the same again.

Ellen Terry stayed for one season only with the Bancrofts. After *The Merchant* she made a fresh impact as Clara Douglas in Lytton's *Money* ('It is not acting, it is nature itself,' said the *Daily Telegraph*.) When she appeared for one night only in another Lytton favourite, *The Lady of Lyons*, a leading critic talked soberly of 'the advent of genius'. Some months later she and her children finally split from Godwin 'by mutual misunderstanding'. They moved out to rooms in Camden Town, and after a few weeks Beatrice Phillips, who had been 'studying' with Godwin, moved into his house as his legal wife.

There were to be other men in Ellen Terry's life, but none ever replaced Edward Godwin. 'She loved (in the true sense of the word) one man only – and for ever.'[44] After the shattering heartbreak of her banishment (for that was what it amounted to, whatever her own share of responsibility for the collapse of their relationship), she armoured herself against being hurt again. She invested her love, even more passionately than before, in her children. She searched for somebody, something, to *serve*, to harness and exhaust her energies. Two children were enough: she had before her the object lesson of her mother's self-sacrificing quarter-century of births and mis-carriages. The English stage thus gained by her griefs. She also looked for a husband, not for herself so much as for the sake of her children, to give them a legitimate name. Not until nearly two years after the split from Godwin was she free to remarry; but in September 1877 George Frederick Watts, prompted, perhaps, by her friends and by a belated sense of guilt, obtained a decree absolute on the grounds of her adultery with Godwin. Shortly afterwards she married Charles Wardell, who was acting with her at the Court Theatre under the name of Charles Kelly.

Ellen's new husband, an ex-soldier, was a manly 'bulldog sort of man', one of those 'men of brawn' who (according to the editor of her autobiography) competed with 'men of brains' for Ellen's affections throughout most of her life.[45] He seemed to be the 'hefty protector', the 'practical daily assistant', and the emblem of respectability that she and her children required. Certainly, the marriage brought social recognition. Edith and Teddy (as Gordon Craig was called by his mother) had a new name, the sins of their mother's past were forgiven by those who knew and disapproved, and they met their grandparents, aunts and uncles for the first time. Wardell was also a clever actor. Clement Scott said that he 'promised to be one of the best artists of his kind in London'. Ellen – with whom he toured the pro-vinces for three summers – believed that his Benedick was, perhaps, better 'for the play' than Irving's. Yet she soon realized, as she told G.B.S. years later, that it was a 'mistake' to marry merely to give the children a name; and within three years the marriage ended in a judicial separation.

Wardell's heavy drinking has been cited as a cause of this marital failure, although it may rather have been a result. He suffered acutely from jealousy, but Ellen may well have given him reason to be jealous, with her irrepressible enjoyment of male camaraderie and homage. Moreover, he put a high value on his acting and his husbandly role, and tried to insist on being Ellen's leading man both on the stage and in life. That proved to be an impossibility, even if it is not true that she refused to consummate the marriage. In the words of Gordon Craig (whose life as Edward Wardell was brief) his mother was clearly 'not a marriageable person',[46] and this renewed fiasco improved neither her chances of success in further experiments, nor the children's prospect of acquiring a father. When they separated she sent Wardell three-quarters of her weekly salary, and after his death in 1885 she paid off his debts and supported his first wife's sisters for some years – which indicates not only Ellen's unquestioned generosity but also some sense of guilt about her sham marriage. By the time it had collapsed she had embarked on a new partnership in the theatre, and also a new partnership in life, of an odd but enduring kind.

During Ellen Terry's engagement at the Court under John Hare's management she achieved one of her greatest successes in *Olivia,* with a title role hand-made for her especial talent, and became recognized as a leading 'emotional' actress in a characteristically ambivalent 'strong' situation, characteristically deodorized in the *dénouement.* The summit of her performance was the moment when she changed abruptly from love to loathing, as her seducer Thornhill reveals that their wedding ceremony was a trick. 'I *am* your wife! What a horrible silence. I am *your* wife! Speak! The light of day comes in on me. Where shall I hide my shame?' And, a few moments later, Ellen – who had lived blissfully in sin for six years – had to say: 'We cannot go home – I dare not meet mother – I must not kiss the innocent children. Sophy (her sister) would take a taint from my very touch.' And, with a cry of 'Devil!' she struck out at him. Everything, of course, turned out to be quite all right, really: it had to be, on the Victorian stage. The marriage *was*, after all, legal, and Olivia could kiss her sister without infecting her.

The Court regime also brought three men into her life, though not all at once. The first was the unfortunate Wardell. The second was Bernard Shaw. Ellen's performance as Lilian Vavasour in *New Men and Old Acres* (written for her by Tom

Taylor some years earlier, though 'created' by Mrs Kendal) so impressed G.B.S. that she seemed 'the woman for the new drama which was still in the womb of Time, waiting for Ibsen to impregnate it,'[47] or so he claimed years afterwards. It was a 'piffling' play, he admitted, but he could still see and hear Ellen 'crying like mad' in it in memory.[48] They did not meet until twenty-four years later, and then only fleetingly, but Shaw was to become an influential friend through a unique 'paper court-ship'. The third man was Henry Irving.

Irving had acted briefly with Ellen Terry eleven years earlier, but had never since seen her on the stage. He still had apparently not seen her work when in July 1878 he engaged her as his leading lady at the Lyceum, where he was about to embark as manager after seven successful years as its leading actor. As Clement Scott noted, he was looking for 'a beautiful, talented, popular, amenable Queen to set by the side of the Lyceum King'.[49] By then, in spite of the gaps in her experience, she had played over eighty roles (only two in major Shakespearian parts). Perfectionist though he was in so many matters, he seems to have relied on her reputation – currently crowned by *Olivia* – and on the recommendation of a close friend, Lady Juliet Pollock. The gamble (not least, on her amenability) was justi-fied. With her help he dominated the British theatre for the next twenty years. In doing so, he dominated Ellen Terry's life and moulded her career. She had found both the independence and the subjection that she needed. She had found a way to be, supremely and permanently, *useful*. She was not in reality a queen but a perfect consort.

Henry Irving was not only a great actor but a great director and showman. He set new standards of theatrical illusion, of unity in make-believe, pioneering the darkening of the audi-torium, and brought stage design into line with dominant trends in Victorian art (in the first half of his reign, at least) with the help of inventive lighting, using gas and limelight long after electric light had been installed in other London playhouses. His productions excelled in romantic effects, as the background not only for his own performances but for the appearances of Ellen Terry, on whose taste and flair he came to rely in making stage pictures. He stamped his bizarre, single-minded auto-cratic personality, and his sense of mission, on the Lyceum and his company. They were dedicated to the service not only of Irving's ego but his art, and to the greater honour of that art by the nation and the recognition of the theatre's proper place in society. He made the old playhouse off the Strand into a temple of dramatic art, the dramatic art of Henry Irving and (at a somewhat lower level of priestly ritual) Ellen Terry. Irving did great things not only for the Lyceum but for the British theatre at large. What did he do for Ellen? And what did she do for herself at the Lyceum?

To begin with, Irving made Ellen Terry more of a national figure than any previous actress in English history, not excepting Mrs Siddons. At his side she received the homage paid by audiences, season by season, at the Lyceum and also on the semi-royal progresses through the provinces, conducted on an unprecedentedly lavish scale for some four months nearly every year with a large company in a special train. She was acclaimed in the United States on seven long tours with him. She acted as his hostess at Lyceum banquets to royalty and high society, entertaining artists, politicians, poets, friends and admirers from many walks of life (even the Church). She shared in Irving's reflected glory; and although, unlike him, she was awarded no official honours during their collaboration, she won a glory of her own. In doing so, she won new honour for her profession and her sex. In historical retrospect the honour seems all the harder won when viewed against the knowledge that the marriages of both Henry Irving and Ellen Terry had broken down (Irving's wife, whom he had left in 1871, would never divorce him) and against the inevitable gossip that they were lovers in private. 'In our profession', as Ellen wrote sedately, much later, 'behaviour is everything.'[50] Whatever the facts of their off-stage private relationship, discussed below, the maintenance of their public roles as pillars of the Victorian social and moral establishment may well be reckoned among the most notable histrionic achievements of these two rebellious Bohemian eccentrics. It was probably because, in her son's words, she was 'not only a queen of the stage but a good rebel, too', that she was so successful in the end.

Irving also gave Ellen Terry freedom from financial insecurity as the breadwinner for herself and her children, for twenty years. She knew what she would earn (£200 per working week, unchanged through the period). She also knew that (unlike Mrs Siddons) she would get it punctually, and that she had no need to bargain or to price her talent. Irving also guaranteed a rare degree of artistic responsibility. Ellen knew that the setting of her work – costumes, scenery, music, lighting – would be organized to as high a standard as Irving could conceive, and that though she might often improve his conceptions she did not have to carry the burdens of management. While she recognized the ruthless force of his egoism, she had a profound admiration for his work as an artist, and for his commitment to the theatre.

Irving loved her, and in her own way she loved him. It cannot be *proved* that they were ever more than loving friends: they destroyed nearly all their letters to each other. Biographers have argued persuasively that there was no sexual consummation, or at least no affair, not only because of the chronic lack of time and opportunity in their very busy, very public lives but also because of the immense risk to their whole enterprise, which would have been destroyed by any revelation of sexual scandal or by the birth of a child. But, according to Marguerite Steen, Ellen said that she had been Irving's mistress since the very first night of the first Lyceum season.[51] And his endearments in the few surviving letters suggest something more than backstage comradeship. As late as 1891 he was writing to her as 'My own dear wife, as long as I live.' New evidence may still be unearthed, but does it matter? It seems likely that, in any event, regular sexual pleasure was low in the priorities of both Ellen Terry and Henry Irving, and that the extraordinary intensity of their theatrical impact, at their peak, derived much of its high voltage from sexual sublimation. What mattered to each, in different ways, was the unusual persistence through many years of mutual trust and intimate understanding, in work and in life. Irving served as a kind of father to her children, whose careers he helped and whose work he encouraged. To Gordon Craig, especially, he was a guiding influence: his 'master'. (And she did her best to help Irving's sons.)

Most important, Irving gave Ellen Terry unequalled opportunities for personal service. She served as a buffer between him and the company; as a magnet to artists, writers and composers; as a hostess to eminent Victorians and personal friends; as an adviser on design, costume, lighting and casting;

as a counsellor on domestic problems; and, of course, a box-office drɛ w – in whatever parts he asked her to play. She wrote protestingly to Clement Scott in 1885, after his enthusiastic notice of *Faust*, 'You are wrong, dear friend – quite, quite wrong. I am not a great actress, I am not indeed. I am only a very useful one to Henry.'[52] To Shaw she was 'a born actress of real women's parts condemned to figure as a mere artist's model in costume plays which, from the women's point of view, are foolish flatteries written by gentlemen for gentlemen'.[53] It was 'a heartless waste of an exquisite talent. What a theatre for a woman of genius to be attached to!'[54] As always Shaw was overstating the case. He wanted Ellen to act in his own plays, as he made abundantly clear in their brilliant exchange of letters, published after her death.

But Ellen Terry knew perfectly well, and was willing to accept, the weaknesses of her place in the Lyceum world. She liked to be used, as long as she was loved for it. The repertoire was planned, primarily, to provide roles for Henry Irving. He was the main box-office draw. Few plays were staged in order that Ellen could extend *her* range and develop *her* technique, although Irving made sure that she was kept in view of her public. In all too many of the twenty-seven plays in which she appeared during her Lyceum quarter-century, there was little for an artist to do except to exercise hypnotic charm and provide loyal, decorative support for Henry. She was never allowed to play Rosalind (which she longed to do) because there was nothing for him in *As You Like It*. She could no longer play Desdemona after 1881 because Irving said he would never risk Othello again. Her Viola, which she first played at thirty-seven, was, though one of her greatest roles, soon dropped from the repertoire because Irving's Malvolio was not well received. She had to wait until she was nearly sixty to play Mistress Page – because Irving could not trust himself as Falstaff – and Hermione (because he had never seen himself as Leontes). Although he loved her off the stage, and treated her with courtesy – almost equality – on the stage, he put his work first, always. His sense of priorities was illustrated when, after admiring at rehearsals a blood-red cloak in which she proposed to appear as Lady Macbeth after the murder, he silently appropriated it for himself; or when, after Ellen had decided for her first appearance with him as Ophelia to wear black in the mad scene, she was instructed that 'there must be only one black figure in the play, and that's Hamlet.' The moral of this incident for Ellen was that Henry had 'a finer sense of what was right for the *scene*'.[55] And she defended him in her autobiography against the charge that she was given too many 'second fiddle parts' by arguing that she had her share of 'first fiddle ones'. In Juliet, Beatrice, Camma and Olivia she had 'finer opportunities' than Henry in the same plays ;and although she might have had bigger parts elsewhere, they might not necessarily have been *better* ones, while if they were in plays by contemporary authors 'my success would have been less durable.'[56] The public, she knew, must take part of the responsibility. They wanted to go on seeing her as Portia, Camma, Beatrice and Olivia, not as Lady Macbeth – let alone any of the New Women that G.B.S. said she ought to play. She did all she could with the plays available ('dropping back into the pictorial', as Shaw put it, when in difficulties). Not until she was in her fifties was an alternative drama visible (on moral grounds, some of the best roles of Bernhardt and Duse were disqualified for English actresses). Then it was too late; and, in any event, she believed she could not desert Irving. She was a product of the empirical teach-yourself, learn-as-you-go-along tradition, which depended for its vitalizing continuity on a wide variety of parts to learn in. Until she joined Irving, Ellen Terry had a relatively wide experience, in spite of her long absence from the stage; from 1878 onwards her scope was narrow and self-repeating.

After twenty years, however, Irving's love for Ellen Terry cooled; he formed a new intimate friendship (with Mrs Eliza Aria); and Ellen became decreasingly useful in the mounting disasters that finally overwhelmed their Lyceum Camelot. First, in the early 1890s, the Lyceum began gradually to go out of fashion. Although receipts were falling, even in the provinces, and costs were rising, Irving insisted on maintaining the same standards. His health began to fail. New plays of the right Lyceum kind were increasingly hard to find. He was criticized by the champions of the new drama, most ferociously by Shaw, who publicly as well as privately deplored his 'waste' of Ellen Terry. Within a year a fire had destroyed the sets for forty-four of his productions – a crippling loss; he was seriously ill for the first time in his life; and in handing the Lyceum over to a syndicate, to relieve himself of financial responsibility, he sealed its doom. About this time he asked Ellen Terry to visit him at Bournemouth, where he was convalescing. He wanted to tell her that his health was broken and that he was 'ruined'. The remedy was easy, said Ellen, rallying her powers of buoyancy. They could make a mint of money by acting together all over the world, without a company, doing Shakespeare. Irving coughed and hesitated in embarrassment. No, he said, he had already made his plans, and there was no room for Ellen in them. He was going to tour the provinces with a few successes which had no roles for her. So, for the present, there was no work for her at the Lyceum. 'You can, of course, er, *do what you like.*'[57] It was a bitter shock, although Ellen characteristically saw the humour of it – or, no less characteristically, claimed that she did. At fifty-two she was out on her own, 'rudderless', after more than twenty years of loving friendship and artistic collaboration. Yet she realized that Irving was under exceptional stress; she knew that Irving believed he could do nothing else, for himself and his work, and she still tried to serve him. A year later she was writing in her diary that 'for the first time' Irving had begun to appreciate her 'very long service, to know I am valuable'. They worked again at the Lyceum, on provincial tours and in America. But the inevitable end was imminent. They acted together for the last time in 1903, as Shylock and Portia once again, at Drury Lane. The Lyceum closed that year. Two years later Irving was dead.

By then Ellen Terry had already appeared with other actor-managers. In 1903 she went into management herself, for the first time, in order to advance her son's career. She invested her talent and most of her savings in his production of Ibsen's *The Vikings,* which was disastrously mismanaged and in which she was disastrously miscast as Hiordis, a kind of Scandinavian Lady Macbeth. ('Her womanly wiles, her rippling laughter, her sense of fun have no proper chance of employment,' complained *The Times.*) The second production, *Much Ado About Nothing* – in which she played Beatrice at fifty-six – did not recoup her financial losses; and these were increased when she toured the provinces with another play, *The Good Hope,* in which she was also miscast and which was selected largely, it seems, for family reasons – it was translated from the Dutch by Christopher St John, the intimate woman friend of her formidable daughter Edith. These experiments ended Ellen Terry's brief career as a manager in London.

Her post-Lyceum experiences in the Edwardian era were by no means all so infelicitous. Two contemporary dramatists, Barrie and Shaw, wrote plays for her. And she achieved some success in *Alice Sit by the Fire* and rather more in *Captain Brassbound's Conversion*, although both were dramatic trivia with few opportunities for the actress to show why she had led her profession for so long or why, in the year of *Captain Brassbound*, the fiftieth anniversary of her stage debut should be so triumphantly honoured not only by theatre people at home and abroad, but by leading politicians and other public figures. Duse, Réjane and Bernhardt were among the artists who paid tribute to Ellen at her jubilee; Winston Churchill presided at the jubilee banquet; and some £9,000 was raised to replenish her fortunes. Her greatest achievements in the years without Irving were as Mistress Page and as Hermione, for Beerbohm Tree at His Majesty's; her Shakespearian lecture-recitals ('with illustrative acting') which began in 1910 in America and continued until 1921 ('the living, laughing, triumphant, scornful words of a great actress who is proud to be a woman', said *The Times*); and her autobiography (published in 1908), which she wrote with the help of Christopher St John. (Its greatness was not recognized until after the publication of the Shaw-Terry correspondence in 1931 and the book's re-issue, re-edited, in 1933.)

Ellen Terry's creative life in the theatre, however, had ended before the First World War. After the close of her reign at the Lyceum she lacked direction, a sense of purpose, a way of being *useful;* and, more than ever before, the capacity to remember her lines. There was no replacement for Irving; but during the London run of *Captain Brassbound's Conversion* she met James Carew (née Usselman), an American actor whom she married in Pittsburgh the following year while on tour. He was in his mid-thirties: she was sixty. Was she looking for a new loving friendship; a substitute for her beloved son (who, after *The Vikings*, spent most of his life self-exiled across the Channel); a cause to serve; or, simply, an injection of vitality, through the

regeneration of sex? Whatever she was looking for, she did not
find it. Within two years there was a judicial separation, once
again. The marriage may never have been consummated, a
persistent rumour about all Ellen's alliances which may be
founded on fact but may also be prompted by a dogged reluctance to believe, even among those who never saw her in her
Pre-Raphaelite days, that Guinevere liked it. James Carew
remained a devoted friend until her death. In Shaw's words,
'one may say that her marriages were adventures and her
friendships enduring.'[58]

During the First World War Ellen Terry appeared in music
halls in scenes from *The Merchant of Venice* and *The Merry
Wives of Windsor* (with Edith Evans). She made the first of
five forgettable films. She gave her lecture-recitals. Her last
appearance in a full-length play was as the Nurse in *Romeo
and Juliet*, suffering severely from amnesia. Thereafter her
theatrical life dwindled away in recitals, gala appearances, and
one-night stands; but the Terry legend persisted, partly kept
alive by the continuing proliferation of talent in this astonishing
stage dynasty. Ellen needed to go on making money because she
still needed to be *useful* to her family and others to whom she
had given so generously for so many years; but she had, eventu-
ally, to surrender, and to end her days in the care of her
devoted, possessive, tormented and long-undervalued daughter
Edith, among emotional crises and family feuds which rumbled
on long after her death – at her cottage in Smallhythe, near
Tenterden – on 21 July 1928. She left behind her Edith and
Gordon Craig; £10,000 (an astonishing sum, considering her
age and her commitments); and a reputation that has grown in
the succeeding years – as an artist, as a writer, and as a woman.

Fifty years later, the enigma of Ellen Terry's 'secret self' persists.
Roger Manvell describes her as 'one of the great liberating
personalities of her time',[59] yet she might also be viewed as a
symbol of feminine servitude: the freedom that she enjoyed at
home she did not seek at work. She never realized the full
potential of her talent, caught as she was in a changing theatrical
system and an unchanging emotional alliance; yet she displayed
a degree of independence in her job, and made out of it a
fortune, beyond the dreams of most women in and out of the

theatre. Shaw called her 'the most modern of modern women', yet she clung to the Victorian theatre of mystery, pathos and heroic fustian. She was often overwhelmed by tears when playing in it; and yet these were sometimes tears of laughter, when she was convulsed by the absurdity of it all. (As she said in *Nance Oldfield*: 'Tears, you'll make me die of laughter with your tears!' and she underlined this three times in her copy of the play preserved at Smallhythe). She seemed devoid of personal ambition; but (as she wrote about Lady Macbeth) she believed that the desire to be a queen was 'true to women's nature, even more than a man's, to crave power – and power-display,' and she enjoyed her own queenship, I believe, almost as intensely as she tasted so much else in life.

She asserted frequently that 'I have always been more woman than artist,'[60] as if being an artist was somehow unwomanly, but part of her unique power *on* the stage derived from the quality of her life and personality *outside* the theatre. Ellen had 'an enormous sense of fun', not least about her acting and the misfortunes in her life. Although she privately suffered, like so many artists, from extremes of despondency as well as exhilaration, she could make her audiences feel that they were her friends, even her lovers. She seemed to lack any jealousy or ambition, professional or private (or her career might well have been very different). She was unusually tolerant and generous: to those who had wronged her (like Watts); to those hated by society (she was among the few who dared to praise Oscar Wilde publicly after the trials, and she championed Shaw when he was detested by most of her profession); to social casualties and hard-luck cases (she poured out money through the years in quick response to any emotional appeal); to talented young actresses in straits (she helped Lena Ashwell, Violet Vanbrugh and Lynn Fontanne among others with money, advice, introductions and accommodation in her own home). She was a passionately devoted mother, a loyal friend, a very *good* woman, with an appetite for life that bursts out of her autobiography and many of her letters ('some of the best in the language', as Virginia Woolf said).

'If it is the mark of an artist to love art before everything, to renounce everything for its sake, to think all the sweet, human things of life well lost if only he may attain something, do some good, great work – then I was never an artist,' Ellen Terry wrote in her autobiography.[61] This is to oversimplify her. Shaw put it more accurately when he said that in the 'ready sacrifice' of her talent to her domestic responsibilities and to Irving's Lyceum she 'never really sacrificed her inner self. In sacrificing her art she sacrificed only a part of herself. Irving's art was the whole of himself.'[62]

She looked marvellous. She was, Shaw said, 'an artist in dressing originally'. She learned from Watts, Godwin and others 'the painter's beauty of line, harmony and rhythm',[63] in addition to the actress's traditional reliance on facial beauty and the make-up box. She moved gracefully and swiftly, with an 'easy rhythmic swing'. She was all movement, her son said of her. 'Even with her head in a bag she would have captured the house.'[64] She seemed, at her best, utterly natural. It was this quality that repelled Henry James in the 1870s, and attracted G.B.S. in the 1890s. She spoke with impeccable enunciation and resonant intensity, yet in acting Shakespeare she sounded, it was said, as if she had just been talking to him in the next room. She showed a poetic imagination, a refinement of taste and sensibility, yet she could emit vitality and energy with rare intensity. She had an acute theatrical intelligence, coupled with emotional wisdom. She was, essentially, a *giver*: 'never at any moment did we expect her to overwhelm us with the thunder and lightnings of rhetoric, but always with *largesse*.'[65] 'She gave partly because she could not help loving to be loved,' as Sir John Gielgud says[66]: a key to much of her life on and off the stage. But she also gave because she could not help giving: because that was a form of self-expression and fulfilment.

When she was asked, late in life, what was needed for success on the stage, she replied: 'First, a good heart, and then ... Imagination, Individuality and Industry ... You can get on without beauty, but it is impossible for an actress to achieve any distinction without Imagination, Individuality and Industry.' Ellen Terry had all these in abundance, with beauty, too. And the beauty sprang, unquenchably, from her secret selves.

There is, after all, a greater dramatist than Shakespeare, Ibsen or Shaw. There is nature ... Now and again nature creates a new part, an original part ... That was Ellen Terry's fate – to act a new part. And thus while other actors and actresses are remembered because they were Hamlet, Phèdre or Cleopatra, Ellen Terry is remembered because she was Ellen Terry.[67]

It was, as Graham Robertson said, the best part of this great artist. Or, as Gordon Craig put it, 'Ellen Terry played but one part – herself, and when not herself she couldn't play it.'[68] But *which* self? 'Even I myself', she wrote, 'know little or nothing of my real life.'[69] In one of her letters to Shaw, she said: 'I suppose I *must* look well on the stage, for they all say so. I'm glad. I think it is because though I may *seem* like myself to others, I never *feel* like myself when I am acting, but some one else, so nice, and so young and so happy, and always-in-the-air, light, and bodyless.'[70]

PART TWO

7 EDWARDIANS AND AFTER

On the stage all the advantages fall to what our forefathers called the spindle side. A moralist of the last century struck the balance between the sexes in this matter when he said that an actor was less than a man, an actress more than a woman.

A. B. Walkley (1899)

It is no longer thought a venturesome thing for a girl to go on the stage, nor does she lose caste by so doing; the fear and the contempt have both vanished ... An actress is in no fear of open molestation, however she may be beset by insidious means. In every respect her position is improved. If her calling brings her into disrepute, it is generally her own fault.

Georgiana Hill, *Women in English Life* (1896)

The player-woman, once despised, shall stand
A power for good, a glory to the land.

Clo Groves (1890s)

Give me actresses from the gutter!

Sir Herbert Beerbohm Tree (1895)

THE LINEAGE OF PLAYER QUEENS was, until the turn of this century, usually theatrical or otherwise *déclassé*. Most British actresses were 'born in a basket'. The daughters of actors or managers, they began to act in childhood and learned their craft in stock companies or the repertoire of Covent Garden, Drury Lane and the 'minors'. These avenues of training were closed by the collapse of the old provincial circuits, restrictions on child labour and the introduction of long-run economics in London. Meanwhile, the new middle-class mania for theatricals,

both amateur and professional, widened the areas of recruit-
ment. Increasingly after the 1890s actresses were the daughters
of vicars, stockbrokers and civil servants. They began to act
with amateur groups, went to drama classes and elocution
lessons, made their stage debut in their late teens or early
twenties, and gained their early professional training ad hoc
through small parts and understudies in London runs and the
touring versions of West End hits. For a novice of, say, 1900
the experience on offer was far scantier and shallower than
for her counterpart at any previous time since 1660. Whatever
the flaws of the patent-house and stock company system, it
offered to many beginners a wider variety and bigger turnover
of roles, and a quicker, less haphazard way of acquiring the
groundwork of their trade, than could be provided by a theatre
based on long runs and provincial tours. Whatever the social
advantages of the new respectability, moreover, it brought to
the stage the deeply ingrained middle-class inhibitions about
making a scene, letting oneself go, getting emotional, and, in
general, *showing off*. And although the non-theatrical education
of the new intake of actresses was generally far better than
ever before, they were not necessarily any less 'intellectually
naïve' (Shaw's indictment) than their predecessors. The demand
for a theatre that was in touch with the political and social
movements of the time was put forward by no more than a
handful of New Women on the British stage.

Outside Britain there was, indeed, a wider spectrum of
contemporary drama with a wider range of dominant roles for
women. This was demonstrated in the London appearances of
such great exotics as Ristori, Réjane, Bernhardt and Duse,
whose glittering gallery of queens, empresses, courtesans and
more or less New Women contrasted strikingly with Madge
Kendal's well-bred ladies and Ellen Terry's romantic heroines.
The example of their work was, however, no more widely
followed than the example of their lives, largely on the same
grounds of morality. Much of what these grand soloists said
and did on stage would have been unacceptable to the public
and most critics if performed *in English*, even if actor-managers
could have acquiesced in the consequent reversal of the balance
of power between the sexes. Some women went into management themselves to attempt such a reversal, with varying

success. Others made reputations in a few of the Bernhardt and Duse roles. More won fame and fortune in the fat parts that were available in late Victorian melodrama and near-melodrama. 'Woman – the wronged wife, the woman with a past, the New Woman – dominated the drama in the early nineties. What a boon she was to rising actresses!' But, as Lynton Hudson adds, 'Mrs Grundy was ever on the alert. Her vigilance was responsible for many stage suicides or alternatively illogical happy endings.'[1] With the censor's help, double-standard morality was energetically maintained in the modern drama as staged by the expanding British theatre industry.

Some of the most talented of the new British and American actresses, however, were standard-bearers of Ibsen and other European dramatists shunned by the trade and, often enough, threatened by the Lord Chamberlain. Ibsen was ludicrously miscast as a feminist, not only by the baying critics who savaged the belated London productions of his work in the 1880s, but also by some of his most ardent early champions. But he did give to intelligent artists, many of whom *were* feminists, the chance to play women a cut above the usual Angels in the House (immolating themselves and their moral perfection in marriage); or Women with a Past (due for punishment, humiliation and possible execution); or pseudo-Shakespearian Historical Personages; or the good sports, good sorts and good chaps who, together with virginal flirts, dairymaids, old maids and other stereotypes, constituted a large proportion of the Weaker Sex (on stage) some seventy years ago. In Shaw's words, Ibsen seemed to 'lift' women in the drama into 'serious and sometimes heroic figures, who exercised moral influences and religious influences; responding to these influences from others; and struggling with all the currents of the thought of the day.'[2] A generation of women from the professional classes who had begun to think for themselves outside the old domestic limits found a leader, a teacher and an entertainer in Ibsen's main apostle, George Bernard Shaw.

One major actress of the pre-1914 era was Janet Achurch (1864–1916), to whom Shaw gave the credit for 'inaugurating' the Ibsen movement, but who stemmed from older traditions. With at least two generations of theatre behind her, she had acquired a wide experience – in pantomime, melodrama and

Shakespeare, on tour with Frank Benson, Genevieve Ward and Beerbohm Tree – before at twenty-five she took the historic step of playing the first Nora on the British stage. To do so she had to put on *A Doll's House* herself, with her second husband Charles Charrington. They had no money of their own for such managerial exploits: to raise the tiny capital required they signed a two-year Australian contract and mortgaged their joint salary of £25 a week. Extended from seven matinees to twenty-one, the play was a *succès d'estime* for Janet Achurch if not for Henrik Ibsen; in Shaw's eyes she remained the 'only' Nora, while for William Archer she surpassed Duse in several aspects of the role. (Significantly, perhaps, she was the only member of the 1889 cast who bowed to the audience at her first entrance, as G.B.S. noted in horror.) Janet Achurch went into management again to introduce *Little Eyolf* to Britain (1896, Avenue). Shaw wrote *Candida* with her in mind (although by the time she was free to play it, he said, she had 'grown out of the part'[3]); he cast her as the first Vivie Warren (though that production failed to mature); and she was the first Lady Cicely in *Captain Brassbound's Conversion* (1901, Strand). She had beauty (of what G.B.S. called 'the Wagner heroine type'); emotional power on the Bernhardt scale (while giving the impression that there was far more in reserve); vehement intelligence, inventive energy, 'untameable impetuosity and originality' (Shaw again).[4] Archer wrote in the early 1890s: 'Beauty and mobility of face, dignity of carriage, strength and suppleness of plastik [*sic*], sincerity and intensity of emotion – all these qualities she possesses in an extraordinary degree.'[5] Janet Achurch was, said G.B.S. in 1895, 'the only tragic actress of genius we now possess'.[6] She was appearing at the time in *The New Magdalen*, a revived piece of fustian by Wilkie Collins about a fallen woman.

The flaws in this 'genius', however, became apparent at a distressingly early age. Archer said that 'What she chiefly lacks is *ear*: she does not hear her own voice.' More perilously, she did not always listen to her artist's conscience, but more often to the promptings of her greed for personal success. Illness reinforced the effects of ill-directed ambition. Janet Achurch was seriously ill in 1892 and again in 1895, when typhoid brought her near to death. She never fully recovered her strength, or fully sustained her early promise. In her early thirties she took to morphine and to brandy, with damaging effects upon her work. Financially she was extravagant, feckless, and often in debt. Shaw's wisely pleading letters to her at this period light up the reasons for her decline (and illuminate a warm side of his nature usually concealed from the public). She needed, desperately, a kind of management and direction that her husband could not supply (though G.B.S. described him in the 1890s as the best stage manager of 'true modern drama' in London).[7] 'When she is not brutally tamed she smashes everything to pieces. Even then there is something momentous in the fact that the audience *dares* not laugh. . . .'[8] She seemed lost in the common run of West End trivia : 'London wants a fleet of penny steamers and not a Great Eastern,' Shaw wrote to her.[9] Yet she was not a Shakespearian queen, either. When she played Cleopatra, G.B.S. complained, she despised all royal ceremony and artificiality and relied in 'modern republican fashion' upon the force of her personality, which was not enough – most conspicuously in her delivery of the verse. Cruelly he wrote in 1898, 'Janet was an illusion: the reality is Mrs Crummles.'[10] She was then only thirty-four. She retired before she was fifty. Three years later she died. If she was, as G.B.S. insisted, a woman of genius, it seems not only 'ridiculous' but tragically wasteful that her talent should have been so dissipated 'for want of a manager.'[11] But it was also, surely, for want of a company, for want of a theatre, for want of a repertory in which an actress of genius could find a place.

The second major British actress of the pre-1914 theatre was Mrs Patrick Campbell (1865–1940), another case of burnt-out promise. Although she lived until the Second World War, she reached her peak before the First. Shaw acclaimed *her* genius, too; wrote *her* many letters (a paper courtship that seems, by comparison with Ellen Terry's, often stagey and revealingly sentimental); and offered *her* roles in his plays (she refused Candida and Cleopatra but accepted Eliza Doolittle, a part that G.B.S. had written for her). Like Janet Achurch she desperately needed a manager. Her life is, in Graham Robertson's words, 'a record of talent thrown away, wasted time, lost opportunities.'[12]

Beatrice Stella Tanner had an unsettled middle-class childhood in suburban London. Her mother was the daughter of an exiled Italian count, her father an English contractor who had (so she said) made and spent two fortunes. In marrying at seventeen Stella did not escape from genteel poverty. Mr Campbell, to whose name she gave theatrical immortality, was a man of no fixed occupation who, having failed to fix on one after five years of marriage, disappeared with mysterious suddenness to the Colonies, leaving his wife with two infants. He went, officially, either to 'seek his fortune' or under doctor's orders. Although his health may have improved, his fortunes did not. Mrs Campbell needed money urgently, so she went on the stage. At twenty-three she became a professional actress. Almost from the start she behaved like a player queen, though she did not always act like one.

Mrs Patrick Campbell (as she was called to the end) had no theatrical training, beyond some performances with an amateur club in the Dulwich area. Her assets were an Italianate beauty; dark, luscious eyes; a deep, throaty and seductive voice; a quality of 'voluptuous felinity'; intense personal magnetism; and a determination to have her own way. Like many intelligent amateurs with natural presence and personal charm she picked up technique swiftly as she went along, but often dropped it when out of sorts and never learned to use it consistently, as second nature. She never acquired stamina, or the ability to take her work really seriously for long.

Stella Campbell served her apprenticeship at the top by playing leading roles in Shakespeare: not with seasoned actors on professional stages, but in the open air with the Woodland Players, a company recently established by Ben Greet (see p. 177), who drew upon the new reserves of stage-struck bourgeoisie. They toured the country in summer giving performances in such appropriate pastoral locales as the Botanical Gardens in Birmingham, the grounds of King's College, Cambridge and the lawns of some of the statelier homes of England, where Mrs Pat began to make influential friends in high society (pursued throughout much of her career with a concentration she could not always devote to her roles). She then played for two years in Adelphi melodramas, which led to her first big opportunity and her greatest success: as the central figure of *The Second*

Mrs Tanqueray (1893, St James's). At twenty-eight, Mrs Patrick Campbell became a celebrity virtually overnight. In Paula Tanqueray, most famous of all those late-Victorian ladies with sexual skeletons in their cupboards, Arthur Pinero showed a fashionable London audience for the first time a *contemporary* courtesan (albeit retired). Although his play was both vilified and extolled for its supposedly revolutionary audacity in unveiling a *demi-mondaine* trying to go straight, the breakthrough that he made (with Mrs Pat's help) was not so much to Ibsen but rather to Dumas *fils* and the freedoms of Parisian boulevard drama (usually bowdlerized for British consumption). It was, moreover, incontestably moral (or Mrs Kendal would never have touched the role): Paula had to pay the usual wages of sin by the final curtain. But its leading lady was hailed as a new outsize theatrical phenomenon.

During the next twenty years this phenomenon was seen in London, New York and the provinces in some forty-three roles, some for a matinee or two, few for more than a couple of months. Among the most notable were those of a radical, New-Womanish agitator turned nurse and living in sin with a patient, *The Notorious Mrs Ebbsmith* (1895, Garrick), a piece of Pinero fustian that then seemed even more audacious than *Mrs Tanqueray*; the bed-ridden wife of a Norwegian faith-healer in Björnson's *Beyond Human Power* (1901, Royalty), a role in which she triumphantly held the audience's attention without moving her body or raising her voice for an entire act; and Melisande, in Maeterlinck's misty poetic drama. Mrs Pat first appeared in *Pelleas and Melisande* with Forbes-Robertson for a series of matinees (1898, Prince of Wales): Burne-Jones designed her golden gown, and Fauré wrote the music. Six years later Sarah Bernhardt, at sixty, took the male role, and they acted together in London and on tour Mrs Pat attempted several of Bernhardt's own parts: Fedora, which put so great a strain on her voice that she left the cast within a few weeks; Zoraya in *La Sorcière* (performed only in the States); and Magda, a fiasco in 1895 but a success in later revivals. For all her spectacular and sirenish allure (her 'languor' was frequently commended as Bernhardtesque), she was not firmly in the *monstre sacrée* class. Nor was she in the Shakespearian class. After failing with Juliet, Ophelia and Lady Macbeth, under

Forbes-Robertson's management (1895–1899), she tried the Works only once again – *Macbeth* in 1920 – proving her incapacity to speak verse.

Mrs Pat was more successful in Ibsen. In the first British production of *Little Eyolf* she won plaudits first in the tiny, crone-like role of the Rat-Wife and then (taking over from Janet Achurch) as Rita Allmers, although G.B.S. registered dissent from the general approval in one of his more lethally ironic passages of dramatic criticism. There was little dissonance among the hosannas when she appeared in the second *Hedda Gabler* to be seen in Britain (1907, Royal Court). Although it was staged for only a few matinees, this role became one of the pillars of Mrs Pat's later repertoire, and her performance is remembered by admirers as one of her principal claims to be ranked among the great.

During this period Mrs Campbell also went into management. At the Royalty in 1900–1 she staged many new plays by European dramatists: Björnson, Rostand, Echegaray, Sudermann and Maeterlinck. It was, said *The Times* in 1901, 'the nearest thing we have in London to that "repertory theatre" which is being so much talked about'. (The Royalty closed for a week in 1900 when that shadowy figure, Mr Campbell, finally disappeared: he was killed on active service in Africa.)

Mrs Patrick Campbell was not only a celebrity and a star but already by 1900 something of a legend: a legend decorated by her inventive and malicious wit, and swelled by rumours of her amours, battles and assorted outrages. She would wreck a performance for the sake of a practical joke, and destroy a play's run out of pique or boredom. Her capacity for self-mockery and self-destruction persisted to the end. Yet it seems that, whatever the resilience of her fame as a *personality*, her career as an *artist* was 'in a sense, very nearly over'.[13] As Alan Dent pointed out in his biography (to which these pages are deeply indebted), she played no parts of real significance between 1901 and 1911. Then, in 1911–12, she had the unusual experience of two long West End runs. In *Lady Patricia* (Haymarket) she was, in A. B. Walkley's words, 'the most delicious, absurd, fascinating and fantastical of mock-heroines', burlesquing her own extravagances; and in *Bella Donna* (St James's), that hard-wearing corn-in-Egypt melodrama about a wicked adventuress poisoning her husband, she mobilized her resources as a *femme fatale* while muzzling her sense of humour. With *Pygmalion* (1914, His Majesty's) she reached what Mr Dent describes as 'the end of her heyday',[14] playing Eliza with an age-defying 'chutzpah'. Thereafter the career of Mrs Patrick Campbell slid slowly downhill through a string of earlier successes revived with flashes of genius but frequent power-failures.

This is the disturbing spectacle of a talent in limbo, a temperament out of control, an art betrayed by the enemy within. Could Stella Campbell have reached the summits of the theatre, ever, under discipline and direction? It seems possible. She was, Alan Dent maintains, a great actress 'by instinct rather than by profession'.[15] Sir Ralph Richardson, George Rylands, Cecil Beaton and others quoted in Dent's biography testify to the extraordinary impact of her work, even in her old age. As late as 1928, when she appeared briefly on the outskirts of London as Ella Rentheim in *John Gabriel Borkman*, she seemed to James Agate 'the best tragic or emotional actress in the country. In the sheer acting sense, by which one means the marriage of spirit and the technical means to convey that spirit, Mrs Campbell has no rival on our stage.' He ranked her among his six great actresses, with Réjane, Bernhardt, Duse, Ellen Terry and Madge Kendal. At her death in 1940 *The Times* observed: 'In the acting of women with brains and with natures complex, strange or highly strung she had not her equal on the English stage.' And, in a letter to *The Times*, John Gielgud wrote: 'As with all really great artists it was a joy to see her move and hear her speak. On the stage she expressed poetry with every gesture of her hands, and the objects which she touched in playing a scene suddenly seemed to gain immediate significance and life.' If only she could have *cared* more: if only, like Ellen Terry, she had ever thought of being *useful*: if only she had believed, just a bit more, in the theatre: if only there had been a theatre in existence that might, just might, have kept her at work, in harness, in transmission. . . .

Since the Edwardian heyday of Mrs Patrick Campbell the veneration of actresses has reached unprecedented levels of credulity, absurdity and capital investment. In the cinema dozens of miniature talents have been inflated into monstrous, global, ephemeral reputations. 'Greatness' has been detected in a long parade of perishable love-goddesses, one-string virtuosos and outsize personalities who are not so much great actresses as great anarchs, professionally temperamental and amateur in nearly everything else. It is among these idols, perhap, that the successors of Mrs Patrick Campbell are to be found. As the theatre has contracted – and in the past sixty years it has shrunk radically in its reach and volume – so it has been less able to tolerate spoiled-child show-offs, peacock paranoiacs and professional idlers (although elements of these three roles are perhaps essential to theatrical success).

If the regality of a player queen is to be measured by the number of her subjects and the size of her fortune, then it is among the 'popcorn Venuses' of the cinema industry that one must seek the heiresses of Sarah Siddons and Ellen Terry. It is to films and television that hundreds of actresses look first for bread and butter, let alone for fame and fortune. To many artists, stage acting is a part-time indulgence. To millions of TV viewers it is an anachronism, appealing only to the elite and the elderly middle-class. Yet it is still only in the theatre that for better or worse, glory or disaster, an actor or actress can make direct contact with an audience, a connection without which they are incomplete as artists. It is in the theatre, above all, that the audience may share the rare magnificence of great acting, an experience of instant excellence, truth and joy to which there can be no parallel in the cinema or in the television rooms.

In historical perspective the survival of the British theatre after the First World War seems miraculous, faced as it was by competition from films, radio, records, tape, television and many other modes of passing the time, for the custom of millions outside the traditional limits of the play-going world. In spite of massive hazards and paralyzing handicaps the theatre has not only been preserved but transformed, against all reason and economic realism. There are three main explanations for this miracle: the occasional availability of those unique emotional pleasures and spiritual insights indicated in the preceding paragraph; the exceptional incidence of exceptional talent; and the slow and staccato flowering of an alternative theatre, in opposition to or parallel with the commercial system. That system was until some sixty years ago the only system; and by 'commercial' we mean nothing more pejorative than speculative management, gambling on the public's readiness to pay, measuring success by the box-office gross, running plays only as long as takings remained above an agreed economic figure. When the century began, all British theatres had been built and were run in the expectation of private profit. Subvention by local or central government was unknown.

Although the commercial system was prosperous and its geographical range far wider than that of the mixed economy of the 1970s, its aesthetic and social range was narrow. What it distributed and encouraged was boulevard drama, star-vehicles and light entertainment. There was little scope for new ideas in production or design, for Ibsen, Shaw and other major dramatists, for most of the classic repertoire. Even Shakespeare was rationed. So, in the decade before World War I, a reforming movement – miscalled 'repertory' – gathered momentum (see p. 180) Joint priorities were the encouragement of new English plays, especially plays of 'ideas', and the liberation of Shakespeare from current stage tradition, according to the reforming gospel of William Poel and Harley Granville Barker. Most activists believed that the theatre should be recognized as part of every civilized community, and many held that it was, and should seem to be, a mirror of the times, rather than the mirror of a star's ego. Although the initial impetus of the repertory movement petered out during the war, and the conservative forces of show business (including the business of star acting) reasserted their dominion, the Edwardian ideals persisted fermentingly for the next half-century. Their influence is apparent in the lives of the three major actresses of our time, on whom we concentrate in the following chapters. Even more conspicuous, however, is the influence of Shakespeare. In spite of the widened horizons of the drama, compared with the repertoire on which Peg Woffington, Sarah Siddons and Ellen Terry thrived; in spite of Ibsen, Chekhov, Shaw and all the later dramaturgical talent of the century, marvellously diverse as it is – the school and the final test of greatness for actresses, no less than actors, has been found in the works of an Elizabethan actor-manager who never wrote a part for a woman.

8 SYBIL THORNDIKE

Acting is something apart from just plays. It's another art.

Sybil Thorndike (1961)

When you're an actor you cease to be male or female . . .

Sybil Thorndike (1957)

You know, you get frightfully cocky, but if you haven't got that in the theatre, if you don't feel, 'I've got something to say that nobody else on this earth knows how to say,' I don't think you're any good.

Sybil Thorndike (1965)

FOR OVER HALF A CENTURY Dame Sybil Thorndike (1882–1976) was a British institution; and yet she was never less than a gloriously and intransigently individual human being. Among the better loved of national figures she has remained marvellously uncontaminated by prolonged exposure to Public Relations. With her clear blue eyes, broad forehead, determined chin, her voice throbbing and swooping through clusters of clauses, her conspicuously golden heart and her utter lack of affectation she appeared as a reassuringly indestructible incarnation of the theatre's essential humanity and social conscience. An ardent left-winger and convinced trade unionist, she helped to establish Actors' Equity in 1930 and was for years a loyal though never doctrinaire supporter of the Labour Party. She appeared, no less notoriously, as an exemplar of happy marriage and motherhood: the limelight shone often on her unique sixty-year partnership with Lewis Casson, the careers of their four children, and the family reunions of this theatrical dynasty.

Dame Sybil was not only a great lady but a great turn. As her son John Casson wrote in his admirable portrait of *Lewis and Sybil*, 'Sybil has never really stopped performing and it is always a superb performance on the largest scale. But this doesn't mean for a moment that she is insincere. In fact, it means just the opposite. . . . To be with Sybil is to see everything through an enormous emotional magnifying glass.'[1] Among the more sceptical and conservative members of her profession this noble totem was gently mocked for her instant readiness to sign appeals, her inability to see any incompatibility between her Socialist feelings and her Christian beliefs, and her legendary reluctance to speak a harsh word about anyone she ever met. The marshmallow layer of Dame Sybil's reputation did, indeed, hide such endearing imperfections as an explosive temper, an occasionally astringent tongue, a masterly (if rarely exercised) capacity for scene-stealing and an understandable pride not only in her stamina but in her ability to keep up with 'the moderns'. She is too fine an artist to be devoid of egotism, though she may at times have seemed too good to be true.

It was on Dame Sybil's character rather than her work that attention focussed in her later years, with the help of television; and among her most popular achievements was the role of Saint Sybil, earth-mother extraordinary and almost-perfect wife, 'a star not only of the stage but life' (as Sir Alan Herbert put it). In this role she won recognition and affection outside the theatre as a national character.

Here, however, we look at her work *in* the theatre. And it seems necessary to preface this survey by reasserting that while Sybil Thorndike was a paragon of sincerity, she was also a brilliant technician. Technique was never an end in itself for her. Yet although she liked to talk of herself in her eighties as an 'amateur', and one of her selves was always (in John Casson's words) 'an outsize, skylarking, amateur romp',[2] she was a professional to her fingertips and a dedicated artist with a passion for work. In that work, outlined below, she learned greatness.

Sybil Thorndike was one of those high-minded, high-spirited daughters of the manse who brought to the stage at the turn of the century an invigorating sense of moral purpose and family camaraderie. She was born on 24 October 1882 in Gains-borough, Lincs, where her father was curate. Egged on by his wife, and helped by his fine singing voice, Arthur Thorndike became within two years a minor canon of Rochester Cathedral, and it was in that world that Sybil grew up. Two brothers and a sister joined her in the next twelve years. Russell (born in 1884), Eileen (1890) and Frank (1894) were all to follow her into the theatre.

To the stability of her vicarage childhood Dame Sybil owed, perhaps, something of that unquenchable optimism of her later years. The Thorndike family atmosphere was imbued with music. Not only was the Canon a good singer but his energetic wife sang, played the piano and was 'an excellent organist'. In addition, Father read Shakespeare and poetry to the children; Mother read them stories ('like a play', said Sybil); and both parents were admirers of Henry Irving and Ellen Terry. As infants Sybil and Russell (her closest intimate for years) began to create their own theatre in the attic, with no parental opposition. Sybil made her amateur debut at the age of four. From then onwards, she declared in her eighties with characteristic self-mockery, 'I always felt that I could do everything much better than anybody else, as an actress.'[3] With Russell she played at religion, too: holding services, preaching, conducting High Mass (with a bicycle pump), celebrating Communion (with cough mixture). The rituals of the church, and the social surround of Anglicanism in a cathedral town, were a part of their everyday life. The accessibility of God, too, was taken for granted. And there were other propitious influences, some equally without precedent in the lives of most of her theatrical predecessors. These included a Sunday school, where she taught from the age of ten; a 'Shakespeare class' at her grammar school, run by an enthusiastic teacher; a dancing class, at which her mother played the piano; and her own piano lessons, to which she became thralled. At thirteen Sybil was admitted to the Guildhall School of Music, travelling to London once a week for a lesson. An aunt gave her a grand piano, and an upright piano was installed as well so that her mother could play duets with her. Mrs Thorndike was passionately, almost obsessively ambitious for her eldest daughter. Neither Caesar nor Bona-parte, said Russell, could surpass his mother in ambition. To promote her daughter's piano studies she removed Sybil from school, employing a governess (shared with a neighbouring family) to continue her general education. Sybil applied herself to an austere discipline starting every morning at 5 am with a cold bath, and including five hours' practice. The work-ethic, implanted early, never wilted. It took in poetry, too. Mr Thorndike memorized a few lines every morning while shaving. Sybil decided, 'What father does, I do', and kept up the habit for most of her life.

'I dedicated myself to the Lord and to the piano.'[4] Over the grand hung a huge crucifix, presented by her mother. But in her late teens Sybil Thorndike discovered that when she played in public she suffered agonies of anxiety. Her body, nerves and emotions seemed to be reacting against years of competitive tuition. She developed crippling pains in her left wrist at the onset of any concert. And when she was twenty she reluctantly gave up her vocation, feeling like a failed nun. At Russell's suggestion she decided to be an actress instead, and joined him in training for the stage.

The Thorndikes began their professional training at the most stable (if not the first) of the small, empirically organized schools that emerged in late-Victorian times in response to the demand from the new middle-class invaders for the kind of basic stage education that had once been supplied inside the stock companies. They went to the Academy of Acting just off the Strand founded by an experienced actor-manager, Philip Ben Greet. B.G. was not only a pioneer of open-air and neo-Elizabethan Shakespeare but was also a pillar of the Actors' Church Union, with a fervent belief in the Bard as a moral oracle affiliated to the C. of E. For the Thorndike family this religious zeal was one scoring point in Ben Greet's favour. Another was the bait that suitably qualified students would start their careers in one of his touring companies (in his heyday he had twenty-five on the road at once). After three unexacting terms Sybil Thorndike made her professional debut with Greet's Company of Pastoral Players, a successor to the Woodland Players in which Mrs Patrick Campbell had gained her first Shakespearian experience nearly twenty years earlier. Sybil's first role was Palmis in Gilbert's *The Palace of Truth* on 14 June 1904, and she played it not in a theatre but, unthinkably for predecessors in past generations anathematized by the universities, at Downing College, Cambridge. A few weeks later she embarked for America, unchaperoned, for more alfresco theatricals under B.G.'s wing. At twenty-one her sexual naïveté was even greater than her inexperience of the stage. 'Nobody could be innocenter than I was.'5 Before she left home her parents debated whether they should acquaint her with the facts of life, but resolved that she would be all right without knowing them. All right she apparently was. In spite of her disposition to fall in love with (as she put it) 'anyone who looked actory and exciting',6 Sybil Thorndike was too hard at work on the treadmill of her apprenticeship, playing one-night stands all over the U.S. for nearly a year, largely in Shakespeare. Obediently she followed such Greet precepts as the need to 'learn everybody's part, because you never know when you may have to go on.' During this and a subsequent tour she claims to have played 112 parts, sometimes half a dozen in an evening, both male and female. In *Hamlet*, for instance, she appeared in different parts of the States as the Queen, Osric, Ophelia, Rosencrantz, Lucianus and other nameless Danes. 'Dispersedly, she was all the Gentlewomen, half of the walkers-on, and most of the Cries of Women (off).'7 She learned by doing – and overdoing.

In 1907 Sybil Thorndike had to cut short her second American tour because she lost her voice, and she was warned that she might never be able to act again. The initial crisis was caused by swallowing a piece of fluff, and she recovered after being prescribed six weeks of absolute silence, but she suffered for many years thereafter from vocal weakness. This was partly caused by overstrain and overwork, playing so many roles in the intractable acoustic conditions of open-air staging with so little preparatory training. 'I've always tried to do more than my voice would carry.' Perhaps there might also have been in this disability an echo of the tension behind her wrist-trouble as a pianist: the shadowy symptom of an inner refusal to obey her will. In time these difficulties were solved; but during her first two decades on the stage Sybil Thorndike had to work hard for vocal control, care and maintenance. She had to fight, too, to discipline her emotionalism, a violence that sometimes erupted in shouting and near-caricature. She also felt the need to improve her figure and her clothes, 'to make myself look respectable, which was always so hard for me.'[8] She was careless about appearances; lacked chocolate-box prettiness or sirenish sexuality; was more of a hearty than a theatre intellectual; and retained an aura of English gentility long after she left the cathedral close. As she put it in her eighties, with Sybilline exaggeration, 'I was too much a vicar's daughter, and still am.' But whatever unflattering images of herself Sybil Thorndike nursed in her mid-twenties, they did not correspond with the impression she made on the man she met and married in 1908. As he had a life-long influence upon her work, he merits a brief introduction here. . . .

Brought up in North Wales, away from the Home Counties suburbia where so many of the new generation of players were recruited, Lewis Casson was the son of a bank manager and organ designer who had a passion for music and Anglo-Catholicism. Casson himself resolved to be a priest, and worked to pay for his theological training first as a teacher in London then in his father's organ business, until he changed course and made the theatre his church. He turned professional actor late, when he was nearly thirty, after performing in a number of amateur productions. Through them he met the visionary loner William Poel and his young disciple Harley Granville Barker, and was fired not only by their approach to acting and producing Shakespeare but also by their concepts of the theatre's social and moral functions. With no training or experience beyond his amateur work, but endowed with a finely modulated voice, keen intelligence and natural authority, Casson was engaged for a number of plays in the Vedrenne-Barker regime at the Royal Court between 1904 and 1907. When that experiment ended he followed Barker to his abortive season at the Savoy; and then in 1908 joined the first British repertory company established the previous year by Annie Horniman in Manchester. It was there that Casson got to know Sybil Thorndike, and that, through him, Sybil Thorndike got to know a set of theatrical and social values that was to mould the rest of her life.

Sharing the left-wing views of Shaw and Barker, and 'for ever driven onward by an inexorable sense of duty',[9] Lewis Casson believed passionately in the importance of establishing an alternative to the commercialism of the West End and the carbon-copy banality of the touring network. He was among the most ardent acolytes of the repertory movement, for which the Royal Court regime and the Horniman company were brave harbingers of a new dawn. Against the domination of the long run, the repertory crusaders set the policy of a 'strictly limited number of consecutive performances' – limited on the grounds of aesthetics and morality, not economics; consecutive because no conceivable theatre could as yet hope to afford 'true' repertory – as practised currently in Europe by state and civic theatres and in the previous century in Britain by the patent houses and stock companies. Against the domination of stars, the movement set the ideal of a 'permanent' company at the service of the author – notably, the classic and contemporary authors that commercial managers could not or would not stage. Against commerce, it set art; against glamour, sincerity; against entertainment, enlightenment. Casson was inspired by Shaw's vision of the theatre as 'a factory of thought, a prompter of conscience, an elucidator of social conduct, an armoury against despair and dullness, and a temple of the Ascent of Man.' He believed, too, in the Ascent of Woman; and Sybil Thorndike soon joined the Women's Social and Political Union. She discarded the conventional conservatism in which she had, unthinkingly, grown up, although she remained deeply Christian in her allegiances. Lewis Casson opened up new perspectives on her profession, her society and her sex. He became not only her husband and the father of her children but her mentor, coach and (for much of her life) manager and leading man. As an actor, Lewis generally played second fiddle to Sybil: as a director he helped to keep her energies under control and to stretch but not split her talents. Both were powers in their separate rights, strong and often stormy personalities, united in an incomparable partnership.

During the six years before the First World War broke out Sybil Thorndike enjoyed a plethora of formative experiences, including the birth of three children (John, Christopher and Mary) and two seasons (1908–9, 1912–13) with Miss Horniman's company. Between these Manchester engagements the Cassons worked in another short-lived repertory experiment in London, launched at the Duke of York's by the American impresario Charles Frohman, with Granville Barker as one of the directors. After its collapse they spent most of the year in the U.S. under Frohman's banner, making some urgently needed money in Maugham's *Smith*. Among Sybil's twenty-seven (mostly minor) roles in repertory was the goddess Artemis in Gilbert Murray's translation of the *Hippolytus* of Euripides, her first appearance in Greek tragedy. Murray became a close friend who, she said, 'profoundly affected' her life. But most of her parts were in naturalist plays by contemporary British authors such as Allan Monkhouse, Stanley Houghton, John Galsworthy, St John Ervine, Elizabeth Baker and Granville Barker: the avant-garde drama of ideas, social criticism and domestic realism. Among the New Women played by Sybil were Maggie Massey in *Chains*, Beatrice Farrer in *Hindle Wakes*, and (on tour) Candida, remembered by Basil Dean as the best in his experience. Her biggest part and greatest success was as Jane Clegg in St John Ervine's play of that name about a long-suffering wife who makes a bid for independence from her lying, philandering husband after inheriting a small legacy. 'Men is men,' says her odious mother-in-law, 'and there's an end to it. You just 'ave to put up with them.' But Jane answers, 'I don't believe in putting up with things unless you can't help yourself. I want to know things. I hate being told to do things without knowing why I should do them. It doesn't seem right somehow to have a mind and not use it.' There, through Sybil Thorndike, spoke the protesting voice of the women's movement and the brave new repertory world. Jane was a role to which she returned many times in later years.

It was not, however, through the drama of the 'Manchester school' that Sybil Thorndike was to find fulfilment as an actress. The turning-point of her career came shortly after the outbreak of war when Ben Greet invited her to work with him in Shakespeare at the Old Vic under the wing of Lilian Baylis. Sybil came to play Adriana in *The Comedy of Errors* and remained for four seasons, briefly interrupted by the birth of her second daughter Ann. During these years the Old Vic established itself by desperate improvisation, incredibly hard labour and fantastic faith as 'the home of Shakespeare and opera in English'. Nearly all the Works were staged, some of them every year, and Sybil Thorndike took leading roles in a dozen of them: Viola, Rosalind, Portia, Beatrice, Imogen, Constance,

Ophelia, Queen Margaret, Mistress Ford, Princess Katherine and Lady Macbeth. With huge delight she also played male roles, because so many actors were in uniform (including her husband and two brothers): Prince Hal, Launcelot Gobbo, Ferdinand, Chorus, Puck and the Fool (in *King Lear*). She also appeared in such classic comedy parts as Lady Teazle, Kate Hardcastle and Lydia Languish; as Everyman (the annual revival of this medieval morality play became an Old Vic institution); as Peg Woffington in *Masks and Faces,* Nancy in *Oliver Twist,* Columbine – and even Miss Baylis herself in a house-revue. All for ten shillings a performance.

For Sybil Thorndike this was an invaluable supplement to her early pastoral training in the classics. Unlike the stock companies' theatres, the Old Vic had no scene-dock, painting-room or flies. There was virtually no wardrobe, and what did exist had to be shared with the opera company. For decor a few stock cloths and props were used over and over again. The two 'star' dressing rooms were little bigger than sedan chairs; many of the cast had to change in the top boxes, the saloon or the wings; and there was no running water. The building had no proper foyer, box-office or stage-door. And the manager had apparently never read a play by Shakespeare or seen one professionally performed until Ben Greet brought the Works precariously to life on her stage three times a week. Yet the opportunities were tremendous, and Sybil Thorndike seized them with both hands. She already knew the debits and credits of B.G.'s rough-and-ready production methods; yet there was a great deal to learn not only from the plays, in all their diversity, but from the audience. A rare *rapport* (never, unhappily, known to the Horniman troupe) developed in wartime between the auditorium and the stage, an atmosphere of community fermented and maintained by Lilian Baylis. With the help of this extraordinary woman (who became a close friend), her extended family, Shakespeare and (Miss Baylis would add) God, Sybil Thorndike – who in Manchester had seemed, to at least one critic, 'frost and ice' – not only thawed out but warmed the whole theatre with her awakened talent and her glowing personality, making up for arrears of experience, discovering new selves inside her. Press notices were at first scarce (the Vic was off the critics' track) and, later, rarely detailed; nor were they always favourable. Dame Sybil's first Lady Macbeth was, for instance, criticized because her voice was too light and her face too small: she was, some said, unsuited to tragedy. Yet the word spread that a clever and powerful talent was on display in the old building near Waterloo Station, the only place in London to see and hear most of Shakespeare's plays (if you didn't mind roughing it).

It was the Old Vic, said James Agate in due course, that made Sybil Thorndike a great actress. Yet it was not until she had been seen in the West End, both in Greek tragedy and commercial kitsch, that the ultimate accolade began, intermittently, to be used. She first appeared as Hecuba in Gilbert Murray's translation of *The Trojan Women* at the Old Vic in a series of matinees in the autumn of 1919, while playing at night as the heroine of a Drury Lane melodrama. *The Trojan Women,* directed by Lewis Casson, was so well received that the Cassons staged it at the Holborn Empire (matinees only); and the success of these few performances encouraged a group of backers to launch Sybil and Lewis into management at this music hall on a matinee basis. Sybil reappeared as Hecuba, followed this as Candida, and then played Medea, in Murray's translation of Euripides. She scored another *succès d'estime,* but the interest in Greek tragedy, however well performed, was that of a minority within a minority. The *Medea* was withdrawn a couple of weeks later. When its successors (both new plays) failed to draw the crowds, the Cassons' first managerial venture collapsed. It had lasted for two months (matinees only). Sybil Thorndike had won a star's notices, but they could not guarantee a star's box-office business. She returned determinedly to Euripides in the next decade (1922, 1923, 1924, 1925, 1927, 1929) in London matinees or on tour. Her Hecuba and Medea are cited by theatre historians among her finest achievements. Yet this fame depends upon no more than a handful of scattered performances in London. There was no organization that could keep them before the public, and the Cassons themselves could afford to mount only sporadic productions. She was leading where the public did not want to follow: this happened to Lewis and Sybil repeatedly in the 1920s, not only with the Greeks. It made no difference that, to some critics, *Medea* should seem 'intensely modern' and Euripides 'positively feminist'; that others should talk of greatness. For Sybil Thorndike the time was out of joint.

To W. A. Darlington, as he explained in *6001 Nights*, her Hecuba and Medea were 'nothing short of a revelation'. Part of that revelation was the neglect of such 'true tragic grandeur' by the public; and the fact that to be accepted by them she had to lower her sights. Mr Darlington suggested that Sybil Thorndike had arrived at this point in her career too late, perhaps ten years too late, to develop her full powers. She could have become 'a great, a really great, tragic actress ... given a quicker rise and a more sympathetic and theatre-wise public.'

I saw her touch greatness, certainly as Hecuba, perhaps as Medea, and I hoped that these achievements were the prelude to others greater still – but they were not, they were her peak. Never again did I experience with her that sense of surrender which is the involuntary tribute that one pays to emotional acting at its highest pitch.[10]

It was not until the Second World War that the only British actress of the century to succeed, to date, in Greek tragedy (leaving aside the still-vexed question of Gilbert Murray's success in translation) was able to work in it for more than a few afternoons in London, or on tours abroad. She was then nearly sixty. This was achieved by state subsidy through the newly established CEMA (of which Lewis Casson was later appointed the first drama director). In the Welsh towns and villages that the Cassons visited in the 1940s the *Medea* was received with delighted enthusiasm (while *Candida* was, contrary to Old Vic predictions, a failure). Perhaps the audience outside London for the Greeks might have been much bigger than even the Cassons had supposed; but the commercial system that dominated the theatre could not afford to invest in such a possibility. A few of the more imaginative and enterprising London managers (principally Bronson Albery) backed the Cassons; and the Cassons themselves frequently backed new plays and neglected classics. Characteristically, they would mount a series of matinees as soon as, or even before, a play was safely running. But they found it impossible to maintain a repertoire of their own, as the Keans and Kendals had done, in the hit-or-miss anarchy of the West End. Shakespeare proved to be almost as risky as Euripides, as they learned from their *Cymbeline* (1923), *Henry VIII* (1925) and *Macbeth* (1926). The pre-1914 dreams that they had shared with Granville Barker (now a lost leader) had not yet been realized in London, and still seemed Utopian to nearly all the handful of repertory companies struggling to survive outside the capital. Nor, perhaps, could the restless, swerving energy of Sybil Thorndike have been tethered to one place, even a place of her own with Lewis. As she said to Russell, 'I simply couldn't have a policy. I only want to be lots of different people. Isn't that what acting's for?'[11]

Perhaps the Cassons' most consistently successful venture in management, achieving the teamwork and continuity (at least) of their early ideals, was their lease of the Little Theatre between 1920 and 1922 in partnership with José Levy. Their repertoire included neither Euripides nor Shakespeare nor the contemporary naturalists: it was devoted to grand guignol shockers, largely translated from the French. The players, who included Athene Seyler, Nicholas Hannen and Russell Thorndike, understudied each other, rehearsed assiduously under Lewis Casson's direction throughout the run of each bill (changed every ten weeks) and enjoyed themselves among the mounting horrors until saturation point was reached – the audience seemingly expected each programme to outdo its predecessor in ghastliness – and there were rumblings from the Lord Chamberlain's office about the moral dangers of frightening the public quite so effectively for quite so long. While it lasted, Sybil Thorndike revelled in the chance to play twenty-five 'different people'. Not all her roles were ghoulish: she played Punch's Judy, and a Parisian *cocotte* working as a lavatory attendant. But among the horrors in which she was involved, on one of London's smallest stages, she had her eyes gouged out with a knitting needle; she was crushed to death under a moving ceiling with her lover; she was stabbed in the back and stuffed into a trunk; and she watched her lover devoured by wolfhounds. Sybil was not only a glutton for punishment: she gassed a former lover who could not make up his mind to commit suicide; she killed her brother because he had invented a new bomb; and, after being brought back to life by her father, she strangled him with one hand in a thunderstorm. Working in grand guignol satisfied her itch to overdo it: to pull out the stops of passion and terror with a gusto for which there was no elbow-room in the contemporary drama, and no audience in the classics. By releasing her pent-up inner violence it had a therapeutic effect: during this Little season she was freed from nightmares that had plagued her for years. And it gave her a commercial success, after so many unprofitable critical triumphs.

One of the most enterprising of the Cassons' ventures after their grand guignol was the first public production of Shelley's tragedy *The Cenci*, which had been banned for a century by the Lord Chamberlain. This was staged, as was *Medea,* in matinees at the New during the Cassons' appearance at night in *Scandal* (a domestic drama adapted from the French). Sybil Thorndike's afternoon performance as Beatrice in the winter of 1922 not only brought a fresh sheaf of critical tributes (Maurice Baring declared that here at last was a tragic actress who achieved magnificence) but also led to her greatest theatrical success. Her acting in the trial scene convinced Bernard Shaw that she was his St Joan. For some time he had been planning to write a play about the Maid of Orleans: now he got down to it, without telling the Cassons. But Sybil had long wanted to act St Joan, and they tried to get a play about her from Laurence Binyon. He withdrew when the news of G.B.S.'s project came out; Shaw, the Cassons and Bronson Albery joined forces; and *St Joan* opened at the New in March 1924, with Lewis playing de Stogumber and co-directing with G.B.S. The Cassons had invested all their money as well as their talents in the play, although they did not believe it would bring box-office results. Up till now Shaw had not proved 'commercial'. But *St Joan* was a smash-hit. 'Here, at last, was serious Shaw that was also Shaw for the million.' And here was a part perfectly adapted to Sybil Thorndike. John Casson says:

Of those who saw her play Joan none will ever forget the final moment when Shaw's poetry and her acting became fused together in, 'O God that madest this beautiful earth, when will it be ready to receive thy saints? How long, O Lord, how long?' Somehow her Saint Joan has to be seen essentially as she sees herself, or rather as she would like to be able to see herself.... When the part is exactly right for an actor as he sees it, and when he has the technical skill to perform it, then he gives a great performance and attains a supreme sense of fulfilment. This is exactly what happened to Sybil as Saint Joan. Everything was exactly right for her in wish, hope and belief and she had the skill and drive to express it.[12]

It was not, however, her most assured critical success at the time, although after the play's first night the size and radiance of Sybil Thorndike's performance grew in the memory of those who saw it and in theatrical legend. (She only played Joan in London once again, briefly, in 1931). The fact seems to be, as W. A. Darlington wrote twenty-five years later, that although many critics then thought that Sybil Thorndike had not done full justice to a great opportunity, it had become clear as time went by that the opportunity was not so great after all, and that Sybil had done far better than the critics realized in avoiding both the sentimentality that Shaw dreaded and the theatrical deflation threatened by his irony and anti-climactic epilogue.

Whatever Sybil Thorndike thought of the notices, acting in *St Joan* was one of the supreme experiences of her career. According to her biographer Elizabeth Sprigge, it had 'a profound and lasting effect upon her life and her attitude to theatre.'[13] It brought her national fame, and a vast new range of public work. It also spurred her on, through the next decade, to find another comparable role; but that discovery was never made. *St Joan* remained unique, the summit of Sybil Thorndike's work. When its broken run was finally ended at its third theatre by the General Strike of 1926, she was forty-three. She had already played about 225 parts (accepting her figure of 112 in the pre-1914 Greet tours). During the next half-century she added more than a hundred new roles to that total, while repeating several of her earlier successes. Apart from playing in Shakespearian comedy and tragedy, she appeared in Greek tragedy; medieval moralities; eighteenth-century comedy; melodrama; revue; drawing-room comedy; domestic drama; and plays usually labelled as poetic, historical, expressionist, naturalist and plays of ideas. In Ibsen, Kaiser, and Clemence Dane; Euripides, Priestley and John van Druten; Coward, Eliot and N. C. Hunter; Sheridan, Shelley and Margery Sharp; Claudel, Chekhov, Shaw and Maugham.

Before attempting to sum up Sybil Thorndike's achievements, we will look briefly at the later shape of her career. The Old Vic looms up in it from time to time as a landmark. With Lewis Casson she played a short season at Hammersmith for Miss Baylis in 1927–8, while structural alterations were made in the Waterloo Road; she returned for one play (*The Knight of the Burning Pestle*) in 1932; for *Coriolanus* (with Laurence Olivier) in 1937; for *King John* (at the New) in 1941. Between 1944 and 1946 Dame Sybil worked with the Old Vic company at the New, under the direction of Olivier, Richardson and John Burrell, as Aase in *Peer Gynt*, Catharine Petkoff in *Arms and the Man*, Queen Margaret in *Richard III*, Marina in *Uncle Vanya*, Mistress Quickly in *Henry IV, Parts 1 and 2*, Jocasta in *Oedipus Rex* (translated by Yeats) and the Justice's Lady in *The Critic*. These performances brought her work in the classic repertoire to a splendid close; but she continued to give excerpts from great roles of the past in her recitals throughout the world.

In the West End, after their own three box-office failures with Shakespeare, Dame Sybil appeared only once more in the Works between the wars – as Emilia, with Paul Robeson and Peggy Ashcroft in *Othello* (1930, Savoy), a critical triumph for the leading actresses. Elsewhere in the 'commercial' theatre, however, Dame Sybil had few financial or artistic successes; and indeed, she worked a good deal outside London in the provinces and on tour in South Africa and Australia. She found two new plays by Clemence Dane, *Granite* and *Mariners*, that she liked immensely. Both were written with the Cassons in mind but both ran for a few weeks only, in 1926 and 1929 respectively, although Judith in *Granite* became one of her favourite roles on tour. (As a farmer's wife on Lundy, Dame Sybil rashly promises herself to the Devil, who materializes one stormy night out of the sea as Lewis Casson, a sinister stranger who pushes two successive husbands off the adjoining cliff and takes possession of her. In *Mariners,* less melodramatic but no less gloomy, the marital balance of power was reversed.) Sybil Thorndike's main new role in the 1930s outside Shakespeare was as Mrs Alving in *Ghosts*, but she played this for a few weeks only (at the Hampstead Everyman) and later on tour. In John Casson's view it was, after Joan, her best performance.

With *St Joan* (and, perhaps, the later *Waters of the Moon*) *Ghosts* was the only play in which he could watch his mother and forget that he was her son.

By 1932, John Casson estimates, his parents had reached a 'plateau' in their career. There were no more 'great leaps forward'.[14] By the end of the decade, Sybil Thorndike had given up the quest for another Joan, and had 'begun to come to terms' with the commercial theatre.[15] She did so, says John Casson, by 'the simple expedient of turning every part she played into a kind of crusade for herself.'[16] The first of these was in Emlyn Williams's near-autobiographical *The Corn is Green* (1938, Duchess), as Miss Moffat – based on the indomitable school-teacher who had realized Williams's talent and coached him out of working-class servitude and on the road to Oxford. She had been a New Woman, fighting single-handedly against social prejudice and ignorance; and in combining social idealism, emotional uplift and maternal devotion the role seemed to have been made for Dame Sybil. This inaugurated what W. A. Darlington described as 'an astonishing gallery of portraits of contemporary ladies, all subtly varied and minutely observed.'[17] Among the most memorable were Mrs Linden, the trapped wife of a provincial professor in Priestley's *The Linden Tree* (1947, Duchess), arguing against the new egalitarian world in which Dame Sybil herself so ardently believed; the lonely, aristocratic, Schumann-playing widow in *Waters of the Moon* (1951, Haymarket), burning primly in ferocious silence; and the gallant, poignant, lovable Mrs Anson in *A Day by the Sea* (1953, Haymarket), 'everybody's mother' (as she was described) as well as Sir John Gielgud's, with Lewis Casson (at eighty-two) yet again beside her.

It is time to return to the Shakespearian pinnacles. Dame Sybil was at her best, in maturity, as Katharine in *Henry VIII* ('Anything more noble, more dignified, more womanly or more truly heroical ... it would be impossible to imagine,' wrote Agate in 1926); and as Constance in *King John* ('queen among tragedy queens', said Ivor Brown). But it was as Lady Macbeth, of course, that she faced her greatest test and achieved her biggest reputation. She has been acclaimed as the Siddons of her generation. In this respect, at least, the comparison seems inapt. As J. C. Trewin observes in his study of Sybil Thorndike's work, Lady Macbeth is a part that she 'fought with through the years and never quite established, stamped into the records.'[18] Certainly she did not stamp it indelibly, as Sarah Siddons did, into the prose of observers. After her first Old Vic attempt she did not play Lady Macbeth until 1926 at the Princes. Lewis Casson's production (closer to Tree than to Poel) was doomed by the sudden illness of Macbeth (Henry Ainley); and although Sybil was widely praised, her performance was not an unqualified success. She was indubitably royal: on that all were agreed. 'Every inch the queen', even in the sleep-walking scene. But *The Times*, while praising her 'technical faultlessness' and 'high accomplishment', noted that she failed 'to stir the blood or to freeze it'; and James Agate, while commending her 'mind and commonsense in the intrigue, majesty at the banquet, and pathos at the end', regretted that neither of the Macbeths 'exhibited any sense of awe, superstition or poetry. They were not in touch with any world larger than themselves.' Sybil Thorndike was not happy with her own performance, but she did not give up trying to play 'the Scotch lady' outside London (although never again in the West End or at the Vic). She tried on tour in South Africa (1928–9), Australia (1932) and Wales (1940–2), when she also appeared as a witch and the cream-faced loon. 'I've never got her quite right yet,' she wrote in 1938. Perhaps one may look for a clue to her difficulties in her early simplification that Lady Macbeth is 'very like all women who are quiet and violent and want the best for the one they love.'[19] Another, more central clue is the fact that Lady Macbeth is among the most overvalued roles in the classic repertoire, and has come to assume a dangerously disproportionate significance in the career of British actresses who have believed that they must conquer her – or fail the ultimate test. Nonetheless, we should record that a discriminating connoisseur of Shakespearian acting over half a century, Gordon Crosse, estimated that, after Ellen Terry, Sybil Thorndike was the greatest actress he had seen; and he based this assessment largely on her Lady Macbeth.[20]

In 1969 the great Casson partnership was finally broken by the death of Sir Lewis (knighted in 1945). That same year marked not only an end but a beginning, when Dame Sybil inaugurated

the theatre named after her in Leatherhead (and did so, characteristically, as a dirty, down-and-out she-ancient, not one of her
*grandes dames o*r player queens). This may be ranked with
other official and academic honours – DBE in 1931, CH in 1970
and five honorary degrees (from Manchester, Edinburgh, South-
ampton, Surrey and Oxford) – as tributes not only to her acting
but to her personality and her profession: tributes that until
well into this century would have been inconceivable as paid
to a woman, let alone to an actress.

Like Mrs Siddons, Sybil Thorndike has triumphed without
sexual magnetism, erotic charm (what Ivor Brown called 'the
Cleopatra flame') or the ability to project the lyrical passions
of romantic love. ('I've never really liked love parts,' she told
her biographer.)[21] Her beauty in earlier days was not easily
marketable; and her 'masculinity of style' might well have
proved a box-office liability. The same could be said of her
readiness to attack any part; her persistent faith in the ideals of
repertory; her determination to explore new roles and new
directions.

In her middle years Sybil Thorndike sometimes appeared to
suffer from heartiness, over-emotionalism and misplaced
earnestness. She was inclined to be heavy-handed in comedy,
forcing the pace. She found it difficult to relax, to come to terms
with her inner violence, to restrain her surging feelings. 'I do
everything too much.' Yet without losing power and authority
she acquired a new control, warmth, grace and serenity, turning
her voice into a splendidly versatile instrument with a 'searching
utterance that pursues every word, lets no vowel escape it, slurs
nothing, flashes up the sense.'[22] She combined regality and
simplicity, attack and an eloquent quietude. She could mantle
herself in moral grandeur, and blaze with fun. She had the rare
gift of projecting *goodness*: 'she can make righteousness not
only tolerable, but adorable.' 'Essential truth is the secret of
her acting,' wrote Michéal MacLiammóir.

Essentially English she is yet nationless, essentially of her period
she is timeless, a classic creature, golden and brave as a lioness,
with a face to reflect every mood of human experience and a voice
poured into her throat by the winds of Heaven.[23]

A great actress? What is certain is that she was (to paraphrase Kenneth Tynan on John Gielgud) far greater than the sum of her parts: a woman who touched greatness in her life and her work, and in so doing helped countless people in three generations to a better understanding of themselves and their society, a magnified enjoyment and compassion, and a sense of what the theatre is all about.

9 EDITH EVANS

We take the truth from the great actors of the last generation
and try to pass it on to the next.

Edith Evans, 1971

UNLIKE SYBIL THORNDIKE (as in most respects) Edith Evans has
always appeared to be a loner: a woman set apart, veiled in
the mysteries of her art, persistently private, devoutly self-
centred. Never a public figure outside the theatre in the Thorndike mould, seldom giving interviews, making few films and
(until her eighties) largely ignoring television, she has maintained an aristocratic detachment from the circuses of show
business. While lending her support to liberal causes, and serving as president of such organizations as the Society for Theatre
Research and the Society for Cultural Relations with the USSR,
she is not a public speaker or a political animal. The gossip
columns and women's magazines have had little joy of Dame
Edith. She refused for many years to write her autobiography or
collaborate with a biographer, until Mr Bryan Forbes assumed
this role in 1975. 'My heart has been broken – shattered bitterly
and abysmally – several times', she has written; but such experience has been kept secret, and at eighty-six she could smile
superbly, 'as if she has never known what unhappiness is like.'[1]
Characteristically, she managed to hide her wedding in 1925
from the press for nearly ten months. During their ten-year
marriage George Booth, her husband, was invisible to the public
and, for long periods, to her as well. He was a petroleum
engineer who worked much of the time in Venezuela. They had
no children. After his death in 1935 she did not remarry. She
is an ardent Christian Scientist. Until Mr Forbes's biography

appears, little more than that will be known about Edith Evans's off-stage life.

'There's nothing of the exhibitionist in me,' she has said.[2] 'There never has been. I would have been an artist whatever I did, but I don't think I *had* to be an actress.' Never stage-struck, seldom going to the theatre in her girlhood, she was not drawn to it as a way of life by the glamour or the adulation. Yet adulation there has been in abundance for half a century, from fellow-players, authors and artists, from critics and connoisseurs of the stage, from a loyal public which has shown more than a touch of homage – and awe, for she has kept her distance from her subjects outside the theatre. There can be little doubt that Edith Evans is a queen of players. Arguments may continue about whether she is the greatest actress of the century, or, perhaps, the only great British actress of her generation. But however that is measured or defined, the quality of greatness in her work, uniquely achieved and incomparably sustained, seems beyond dispute.

In spite of her surname Edith Evans is not (as journalists have often assumed) of Welsh origin: her immediate background was Home Counties middle-class, towards the lower end of the scale. Her father, a minor official in the Post Office, was a Londoner; her mother (and grandparents) came from Surrey. There was no theatre in the family. An only child, Edith was born in Belgravia on 8 February 1888. She was brought up in Ebury Street, where Mrs Evans ran a boarding house (more to keep herself occupied, according to her daughter, than because of financial pressures); educated nearby, at the school attached to St Michael's, Chester Square; and apprenticed as a milliner in a shop round the corner, just before she was fifteen. Hats comprised the daytime world of Edith Evans for ten years, by which time she had risen to a weekly salary of thirty-five shillings. She had, at first, no ambition to be an actress. It was for social, rather than theatrical reasons, that at sixteen she joined an evening elocution class in Victoria Street, not far from home. But Edith was befriended by her teacher, Nell Massey; and after Miss Massey moved to Streatham in 1910 and founded an amateur group, the Streatham Shakespeare Players, Edith Evans acted in its productions. They won something of a name in the growing amateur movement. One evening in the autumn of 1911 William Poel visited the Streatham Town Hall to see their performance of *Much Ado About Nothing*. The Beatrice, Mr Poel told Miss Massey, was the best he had yet seen. She was Edith Evans. That encounter led to the young milliner's appearance the following summer in Poel's revived production of the sixth-century Indian drama of *Sakuntala*. This was presented in the Examination Hall of Cambridge University, and Miss Evans (deep in character) played an Old Female Hermit. Poel decided to try her out for his next Shakespearian revival, *Troilus and Cressida*, which he intended to be the last for the Elizabethan Stage Society in a series launched over thirty years earlier. At first, showing his customary preoccupation with distaff casting, Poel tested Edith Evans for Troilus; but that part went to Esme Percy and it was as Cressida that she appeared at the King's Hall, Covent Garden on 10 December 1912. With Poel as Pandarus, and support from the Streatham Shakespeare Players, she was launched on her great career – for three performances only (repeated at Stratford-on-Avon in the following May). The young director W. Bridges-Adams wrote to Poel, 'I wish I knew how you contrived to teach an amateur to give such a perfect and such a classic performance: it seemed to create Cressida once and for all for this generation.'[3]

Progress was slow at first for the milliner. Her Cressida was admired by another inhabitant of Ebury Street, the author George Moore. He gave her an introduction to Lord Howard de Walden, who had an interest in the Haymarket, and when this came to nothing – she was advised to stick to her hats – Moore got Edith Evans a role in a Sunday night production of his play *Elizabeth Cooper*. This was not, as he had wished, the leading role, because the Stage Society, which was presenting the play, jibbed at casting an amateur with so little experience. Instead, she played a maid, so well that (according to Moore's biographer, Joseph Hone) 'it became the best part in the comedy.'[4] Thereafter Edith Evans gave up millinery for ever. A leading management offered her a contract at £2 10s a week and at the advanced age of twenty-four she became a professional actress. During her first five years Edith Evans had plenty of time to learn, from life and from the theatre. She played three roles for Poel – Knowledge in *Everyman,* a tonsured bishop in *The Trial of Jeanne d'Arc,* and Gertrude in the Second Quarto *Hamlet* – and several character parts elsewhere, 'much older and more peculiar' than her, though all of the same gender. Unlike so many of her predecessors she got no training in the provinces, which, she believes, was just as well: 'I was very imitative, and I should have picked up all the bad points quicker than anyone.' But the opportunities to learn by doing in London were reduced by the trivialization and commercialization of the West End resulting from wartime conditions. Edith Evans's first main chance was her choice in 1918 to work with Ellen Terry, then seventy-one, playing Mistress Ford in the basket scene from *The Merry Wives of Windsor* and Nerissa in the trial scene from *The Merchant of Venice,* at the Coliseum and on a tour of provincial music halls. Edith Craig had recommended her as the only one of the younger generation who could 'stand up to Mother'. Mother – who inscribed in her autobiography, 'To Edith Evans – a girl after my own heart' – not only increased her weekly salary from £5 to £15, but advanced her theatrical education. Edith Evans also learned from Elsie Fogerty, voice teacher and founder of the Central School, to whom she has given credit for her remarkable vocal control. And she gained diverse experience in several West End runs and special one-off performances of works such as Byron's *Manfred,* Yeats's *The Player King* and *Venice Preserv'd.*

By the time Edith Evans was thirty-five, ten years after her professional debut, she had played no more than thirty roles, thirteen of them in Stage Society, Phoenix Society and other club productions. She seemed handicapped by her late start and her lack of conventional beauty (although these may be seen, in retrospect, to have been assets for such an artist). When Sybil Thorndike gave her a letter of introduction to Lilian Baylis in 1919 she was ignored by the formidable manager of the Old Vic, who rang Sybil some days later to protest: 'How dare you send me such an ugly woman.' But the rare talent of Edith Evans now began to be recognized. In 1921 she was cast as Lady Utterword in the first British production of *Heartbreak House,* initiating a long-standing Shavian link. In the following year her performance in a piece of West End trivia, *I Serve* – as a maid who takes the place of her mistress – was fervently acclaimed. Herbert Farjeon hailed her as 'the most brilliant and accomplished of English actresses.' From then onwards Edith Evans was seldom short of critical incense. Clouds of it billowed over her in the next decade.

A turning-point in her career came in 1923, when she rejected a West End part in Maugham's *Our Betters* (at £35 a week) to play (at £8 a week) in the Birmingham Rep. The occasion was a major theatrical event, the first British production of Shaw's five-part cycle *Back to Methusaleh*; and Edith Evans appeared as the Serpent, the Oracle, the She-Ancient and the Serpent's Ghost. These taxing, innovatory roles led her to the top of her profession. After seeing her at Birmingham Nigel Playfair cast her as Millamant in his Hammersmith revival of *The Way of the World*. This production made theatrical history by its revaluation of Congreve, with the decisive help of Edith Evans, who was now discovered by a wider public. Her triumph in the role was complete. Arnold Bennett described it in his journal as 'the finest comedy performance I have ever seen.' Nigel Playfair wrote, some years later:

here is a character rendered sublime by the poignancy and sincerity of its wit . . . there never has been on or off the stage a woman so sublime in the same way . . . it is a most extraordinary tribute to Edith Evans that she was able to take on her shoulders the weight of such an enormous conception, and play it almost as if the conception were purely her own rather than the author's. . . .[5]

The performance was greeted with unanimous hosannas in the press. Agate wrote:

She has only two scenes, but what scenes they are of unending subtlety and finesse! Never can that astonishing 'Ah! idle creature, get up when you will' have taken on greater delicacy, nor 'I may by degrees *dwindle* into a wife' a more delicious mockery . . . And 'I nauseate walking', and 'Natural, easy Suckling!' bespoke the very genius of the humour. There is a pout of the lips, a jutting forward of the chin to greet the conceit, and a smile of happy deliverance when it is uttered, which defy the chronicler. The face, at such moments, is like a city in illumination, and when it is withdrawn leaves a glow behind.

That face was championed against the insensitivity of London managers: 'if she does not possess rare beauty in the highest sense, then I know not that quality.' So much for Miss Baylis.

That shrewd eccentric had by now changed her mind about the 'ugliness' of Edith Evans. A year later, after an inept (as she thought) performance as Helena in *A Midsummer Night's Dream* at Drury Lane, Miss Evans decided that she still had a lot to learn about Shakespeare. The best place to learn was the Old Vic, so she asked Miss Baylis if she could work there *now*. As the theatre's director, Andrew Leigh, was enthusiastic about such a prospect; Lilian agreed – but with misgivings: Edith Evans was setting a precedent by being the first 'West Endy' actress to appear in the Cut. The manager's fears seemed justified at first. Plunged into the most intensive programme of work in her career, Edith had to carry it out in conditions very different from those of the West End playhouses to which she was accustomed. The old building had been improved since Sybil Thorndike's day, especially in backstage amenities and efficiency, but it was still manifestly ill-equipped and under-capitalized for a theatre mounting some thirty plays and operas in nine months. The discomfort, the amateurishness and the dinginess were not, however, Edith Evans's main problems. These were the volume of work, the lack of rehearsal time, the size of the theatre and the resistance of the audience, which watched with critical expertise this elegant invader of their family circle. It was not until the third play of the season, *The Taming of the Shrew,* that she came to terms with the audience; was accepted; and, by many, adored. In an interview she said that she was learning from them how to broaden her effects, 'how to be simple and direct and sincere.' It was as if, she said, forgetting about Drury Lane, she had been acting till then in a tiny room. 'At last I can stretch out my arms without knocking down an ornament; at last I can shout without bringing down the chandelier.'

During her thirteen roles in those hard-working months at the Old Vic Edith Evans's talent soared and stretched. Her Queen Margaret in *Richard III* was extolled by Farjeon as 'like a figure from the grand old past of Shakespearian acting ... a gigantically-hewn fragment of acting on the epic scale.'

Here is a titanic emotional achievement, not pitched in the key of realism, which is comparatively easy, but in the key of heroism, which is so much more difficult and so much more exhilarating . . . Her towering passions have a sublime sculptural quality. As she advances on Richard, you could swear that she holds a thunderbolt in her upraised cursing arm . . . here is an actress who can teach all our other actresses not only how to be witty, but how to curse and weep.

As Cleopatra ('the most terrifying challenge she had met')[6] she seemed miscast: not so much Shakespeare's as Dryden's queen (whom she had already played in a Phoenix Society production). With Rosalind she overcame all resistance, in the witty exhilaration of a springtime beauty; she extended her range into broader comedy, with infectious relish, as Margery Eyre in *The Shoemaker's Holiday*; and she crowned her season as the Nurse in *Romeo and Juliet*, cloaking her quicksilver in rough heartiness, wearing the character with such an intensity of being that the play 'appeared to move round her.'

When Edith Evans left the Old Vic in May 1926, seventeen pounds lighter in weight, she carried with her the secret of her marriage in the previous September and the reputation of being an actress in the great tradition. She could (said the critics) walk and talk like a queen and like a peasant, too; she was 'the quintessence of gaiety', yet could blaze into monumental rages; she not only had magnificent diction but also revealed new meanings in classic texts. Edith Evans had now shown a versatile authority in Shakespeare, Restoration comedy, Shaw and the commodity drama of the West End. This was the mixed terrain on which she concentrated in the period before the Second World War broke out. And, all the while, she kept uncommonly quiet off-stage.

Though her work pursued a less erratic and wasteful course than that followed by many contemporaries, there were – as there are in every actress's career, even in a better-organized theatre – misjudgements, disappointments and missed opportunities. It seems strange, for instance, that she should have appeared only once in Ibsen. Shortly after leaving the Old Vic she played Rebecca West in a *Rosmersholm* transplanted to an English setting, staged by Barry Jackson for three weeks at the

Kingsway. She was praised by some critics for rising to 'the very heights of tragic despair'. Agate described it as her best performance yet, full of 'the most subtle gradations of feeling' and 'the very finest art'. But this was not only Edith Evans's first appearance in Ibsen: it was also her last. Her own three ventures into management with new plays (in one she played Delilah for four performances) were disastrous: she was as fallible as other stars in picking plays for investment of her money and her talent. Yet without a stage of her own or a national theatre to work for, she had to go on taking pot luck in the entertainment industry, hoping for the best from her managers, her colleagues and her audience, giving the best of herself from character to character. She played some thirty-five roles between 1926 and 1939; and, considering their theatrical context, the level of artistic and commercial success was unusually high.

Edith Evans wisely returned to Restoration comedy in several productions during this period, notably as Mrs Sullen in *The Beaux' Stratagem*, first at Hammersmith in 1927, then three years later at the Royalty. As Farquhar's witty Lichfield beauty, weary of marriage and provincial life, she scored a success equal to that of her Millamant, to whom some critics preferred it (as did Nigel Playfair). St John Ervine went so far as to assert authoritatively that she surpassed Anne Oldfield. She went back to *The Way of the World* some months later at Wyndhams; played Laetitia in *The Old Bachelor* (Hammersmith, 1931) – a slender part in a weak play; and in 1936 she returned to the Old Vic for the most surprising event in Miss Baylis's bizarre career – Tyrone Guthrie's production of *The Country Wife*, described by the chairman of the Old Vic Governors as a 'masterpiece of smut'. Donning a blue wig as the randy Lady Fidget, and looking (said Agate) like 'a Rowlandsonesque cartoon of Britannia turned bawdy', she moved through Wycherley's *doubles entendres* with a controlled extravagance and a stately zest, immensely dignified. Vividly summing up this aspect of her career, J. C. Trewin wrote:

Other players have explored the Restoration. One feels that Edith Evans has always been there before them, eager as a resident to show them around. She can let a sentence stream out upon the air, a silken scarf unfurling in a light wind. She can let the voice crackle exquisitely through an intricate pattern, a mazy damascene, or else flash a speech home with a thrust-and-twist that closes the door and turns the key. It becomes the voice of the period ... Edith Evans has set the Restoration to her own music.[7]

In Shakespeare she had two relative failures during this pre-war period – as the Shrew (1937, New), 'a tornado that exhausted itself too soon'; and as Viola (1932, Old Vic), who was generally judged too close to the Restoration, too heartless, outside her temperamental range. But her 'vulgar and lacka-daisical' Emilia, in the same short Vic season, seemed to many observers a definitive performance, which made clear Emilia's hidden life with Iago. 'When she cries "Help, help, ho, help – the Moor has killed my mistress. Murder, murder!" ' I don't believe Mrs Siddons could touch her. It is like a bellow from the mouth of Melpomene herself.' Edith Evans, moreover, extended two earlier successes. In 1932 John Gielgud persuaded her to appear as the Nurse in *Romeo and Juliet* for the Oxford University Dramatic Society. It was his first production, the first venture of the Motleys as designers, and the first of many occasions on which Edith Evans and Peggy Ashcroft were to work under his direction as friends and collaborators. In prais-ing Miss Evans's 'contributory masterpiece', the critic of *The Times* wrote:

She has the walk of an old woman, the hands of a sly one; and all the nurse's experience of ribaldry and affection are in the curious tortoise-like movements of her head. Never a strain, never an affectation; laughter proceeding naturally from character and all controlled; in movement, in speech, in the light of the eye, above all in restraint masterly.

Two years later Edith played the Nurse again on Broadway in Katharine Cornell's production, making the New York con-quest that she had missed on her American debut in 1931 (as Florence Nightingale in *The Lady with a Lamp*). And in the autumn of 1935 she returned yet again to Verona in Gielgud's production at the New, with Peggy Ashcroft, the Motleys and two Romeos (alternating with Mercutio) – Gielgud and Olivier. In the ten years since she had first played the Nurse Edith Evans had lived her way deeper into the character and the words, and emerged 'as earthy as a potato, as slow as a cart-horse and as cunning as a badger' (as W. A. Darlington memorably described it). This Nurse was 'massive with the accretions of an experience that has left her fundamentally shallow-pated ... a mighty achievement in characterization never irritatingly elaborated, and in elocution governed continually by internal word-sense.'

Rosalind was the other Old Vic success of 1925 to which Edith Evans returned – at the same theatre, in the 1936 Guthrie season. One danger seemed obvious. She was forty-eight. But whatever doubts the audience may have brought to the theatre, they were soon dispelled. In theory this Rosalind was 'too old, too worldly, too robust and too plain. In practice it was glowingly feminine, full of moodiness, caprice, gay deception, wit and frank sensuality, much of this with a wink at the audience,'[8] an endearing effect which helped to cancel apparent anomalies of age (Michael Redgrave, her Orlando, was twenty years her junior) and seemed a plausible ploy of the original Ganymedes. Redgrave and Evans took fire from each other, and their mutual admiration helped to evoke the right Arden of the heart. Some people objected to the deliberate artifice of Esme Church's production, in which Rosalind appeared as a transvestite Blue Boy in a Watteau park, and to the ways in which (somewhat as in her Viola) Edith Evans kept sentiment in check. For other witnesses, as for Laurence Kitchin, 'there was genius at work.' Tyrone Guthrie wrote, a quarter-century later:

from beginning to end the performance swept one along on the wings of a radiant and tender imagination. It was a comment upon womanhood and upon love, more interesting and moving, not less, because it had the ripeness and wisdom of experience. It was a feast of spoken music – a revelation to me of how Shakespearian verse, when wonderfully spoken, gilds the meaning of words and opens the windows of the imagination in the way which the theatre uniquely can, but seldom does. This was a great performance.[9]

In Edith Evans's third speciality, Shaw, she again returned to earlier successes, playing three roles (not the Oracle) in *Back to Methusaleh* (1928, Royal Court) and Lady Utterword in 1929 (Malvern) and 1932 (Queen's). She found a new role in the first British production of *The Apple Cart* (1929, Malvern and Queen's) as Orinthia, one of her longer runs (ten months) though not one of her richest parts. During the early 1930s Shaw wrote *The Millionairess* with her in mind, but she declined the chance of playing Epifania Fitzfassenden in 1935. Four years later she changed her mind, but the production never reached London because of the blitz.

Few new plays featured in Edith Evans's career between 1926 and 1939, but some provided her with rich opportunities for characterization as well as achieving commercial success. Outstanding among these were *Evensong* (1932, Queen's), in which she appeared as Irela, a selfish, arrogant, ageing prima donna; *The Late Christopher Bean* (1933, St James's), which gave her the chance to play a simple-hearted Welsh maid; and, less profitably but perhaps most theatrically rewarding, *The Old Ladies* (1935, New), directed by John Gielgud. As a crude and sinister old crone who scares a genteel coeval to death, her performance seemed 'a slow nightmare of macabre genius'.

Edith Evans's finest work in new roles was done under Gielgud's leadership, playing for the first time in Chekhov and Wilde. As Irina Arkadina in *The Seagull* (1936, New) with Peggy Ashcroft as Nina and Gielgud as Trigorin, she revelled in acting a self-entranced actress (akin to Irela, but created by a master). This shimmering, peacocky portrait of a vain, attitudinizing and possessive woman was, as Gielgud wrote later, 'full of the most subtle touches of comedy, alternating with passages of romantic nostalgia' and punctuated by 'sudden outbursts of tenderness';[10] although James Agate described it as 'quite rightly without one atom of heart to it.' Heartless, indeed, was Edith Evans's other major pre-war creation: as Lady Bracknell in Gielgud's production of *The Importance of Being Earnest* (1939, Globe). Her magisterial snobbishness, crushing in its impact on stage yet featherweight in finesse, was all the funnier because it seemed perfectly *natural*, even though Lady Bracknell is a confection of artificial comedy, beyond realism. Behind the extravagantly imperious cross-examinations about pedigree and fortune lay the personal and social truth of the aristocratic world so elegantly mocked by Wilde. Dame Edith gave to him, as to Congreve, Farquhar and Shaw, the service of exact, imaginative attention to the text. Her most celebrated vocal flourishes (like the soaring, astounded *ha–a–andbag*) were not decorative trills but notes inseparable from the entire composition; and this itself became integrated under Gielgud's baton into a superbly balanced display of ensemble playing. (This was an effect that the film version did not, perhaps could not, recapture.) And, for all her later achievements, Dame Edith does not appear to have given such another team performance.

With the outbreak of the Second World War, a turning-point or a stopping-place for everyone, we may pause to look ahead. Over thirty years of work still lay before Edith Evans, in spite of interruptions by the pressures of war and the effects of illness. During this long period she played twenty-five roles, nineteen of them for the first time, in addition to wartime appearances in revue in London and for Forces audiences, for whom she also toured in *Heartbreak House* (as Hesione Hushabye). We can touch here on no more than a few of these performances, but they are somewhat easier to select than in the earlier years. She made few conquests of new territory comparable to those before 1939; and her revisitations of some pre-war successes did not, for all their rewards, extend her range. To some observers, indeed, they seemed to illuminate its contraction. Her second Cleopatra (1946, Piccadilly) was something less than a triumph: still closer to Dryden than Shakespeare, in spite of her mastery of language, defeated for the first time by age (at fifty-eight). Her Queen Katharine (1958, Old Vic), her Queen Margaret and Nurse (1961, Stratford) seemed smaller creations than their predecessors to many of those who could make comparisons and wanted to. Yet to others the latter performance seemed a consummate expression of character through the lines, exuding a radiant intensity of truth, demonstrating a mastery of timing, control and inner realism that set a model to younger players. For a post-war generation it gave, wrote Alan Brien, a 'proof of her genius' not apparent in *Richard III*. Philip Hope-Wallace said, 'This is the Nurse as Shakespeare might have dreamed of seeing it played ... Each syllable has a perfect identification with the character.'

Some of Edith Evans's best post-war work was done, once again, with the Old Vic (at the New in 1948, for the war-damaged Waterloo Road building had not yet been reopened). In returning to Restoration comedy and to Chekhov, she saved

the Vic's plummeting fortunes in that season. As the raddled
Lady Wishfort (Millamant's aunt) in *The Way of the World*
she brought to life a character that Hazlitt had commended in
half a sentence for amusing 'grossness', sacrificing her assump-
tions of beauty and elegance for the hoggishness of a beldam
who declares at her toilet-table, 'I look like an old peeled
wall' – and so, magnificently, she did. Although the dazzle of
this acting, among what T. C. Worsley described as the 'attendant horrors' of the production, inevitably unbalanced the play,
it was a joy to see and hear. As Mr Worsley wrote

> . . . when Dame Edith Evans speaks, the words cascade and check,
> pause and then gush, straight from a living person who has always,
> you are convinced, spoken just so. How she confounds Dr Johnson,
> who pronounced of Congreve's plays: 'His characters are commonly
> fictitious and artificial, with very little of nature, and not much of
> life.' This Lady Wishfort has so much of both that, laughable,
> ridiculous and ridiculed as she may be, she is yet not a mere figure
> of fun. She touches our pity as well as our laughter.

Pity and laughter were stirred again by Dame Edith's second
Old Vic role that season: Madame Ranevsky in *The Cherry
Orchard*, in which she showed once more her profound expertise
in exploring emotional shallows. She brought on to the stage the
whole of the woman's past with a wistfulness that was never
allowed to obscure her selfishness, an effortless charm that left
unsugared her essential pettiness.

During the past thirty years many dramatists have hoped to
see Dame Edith in their work; some have written plays for her;
nine have seen her act in them, not always with delight. She
has persistently shown a sublime charm and mesmeric technique
(most dazzlingly, perhaps, in Christopher Fry's *The Dark is
Light Enough*, 1954), though sometimes in imperfect adjustment to the text (as in Enid Bagnold's *The Chinese Prime
Minister*, 1963); nor has it always been enough to keep the play
running (as in Robert Bolt's *Gentle Jack*, 1963). Commercially
and theatrically, she achieved more success in less ambitious
work like N. C. Hunter's *Waters of the Moon* (1951, Haymarket), in which – as another of her glamorous, shallow
sparklers – she made every entrance seem (said J. C. Trewin)
'a short guide to stagecraft'. As a selfish, stylish and possessive

chatelaine she helped to give Enid Bagnold's *The Chalk Garden* (1956, Haymarket) the air of a classical revival (wrote Kenneth Tynan). But Dame Edith's prime hit in a new play was as Lady Pitts in James Bridie's *Daphne Laureola* (1949, Wyndhams). One of the most treasurable passages in her later work occurred in the first act, when as the drunken, fashionably dressed wife of an octogenarian millionaire, she sat alone at a table in a restaurant, steadily sipping brandy in silence, and suddenly burst out singing (Massenet's Elegie). This turn was followed by a virtuoso monologue about Life and Lady Pitts delivered to the other diners, among whom was a romantic Pole who fell instantly in love with her. (The presence of male adorers in a plot may well have helped Dame Edith in choosing plays. In order to be irresistible, she has only needed the author to say so.) Heart-rending, haunting and funny, this performance showed Edith Evans at the height of her powers, as T. C. Worsley said. He was wrong in predicting that the play would be revived many times in the future. Wrong, at least, so far. Who would have believed half a century ago that a National Theatre company would revive Noel Coward's *Hay Fever* (as it did in 1964)? And that Edith Evans, returning for the last time to the Old Vic, would score a personal triumph in it as one of those incurably egotistical actresses whom she has so frequently incarnated, though seldom with such comic brilliance as she did at seventy-six in the old playhouse in the Cut?

How may one attempt, in conclusion, to sum up the work and define the secret of such an artist? One may not. How can one isolate and describe the union of truth and technique that seems, in performance, indivisible; the embodiment of one artist in a hundred selves, all different yet all made with the same craft, instinct and sensibility; the self-knowledge and self-confidence required for the continual tightrope-walking between illusion and reality, being and seeming? One cannot. What can be done (as in earlier pages) is to recollect in tranquillity some pleasures of the Evans phenomenon, and make a few guesses about their origins.

Consider, finally, the spectacle of Dame Edith at the age of eighty-six on the Haymarket stage in 1974, no longer working in a full-length play but giving a recital, in which poems and passages from a few of her more celebrated roles were inter-spersed with music from the Friends of the entertainment's title (*Edith Evans . . . and Friends*). Smiling in a vacuum, stripped of the protective illusions of an acted text around her, she exhibited for all her frailty a tenacious magic and hypnotic presence. Amused and amusing, she communicated an extra-ordinary sense of *celebration*: out of nowhere, a bubbling joy. And the key to that, it seemed, lay not so much in the sustain-ing self-love of a great performer but in the still-potent voice. That voice has sounded, so often, on the very edge of laughter; a joyous gurgle that takes a sudden sword-edge; curling and floating, gasping and gliding, streaming and soaring, cooing and cursing; pausing in an eloquent silence. As Kenneth Tynan wrote in 1953:

> She can bring tears to your eyes by the sheer splendour of her voice, which she brandishes like a string of emeralds; the beauty of each vowel hangs in the air, lingering a moment longer than any other actress could have made it, assuming a crystalline shape in the mind, and then melting away. . . .

With that voice she has expressed a rare feeling not only for the sound but the sense of language. Christopher Fry says:

> She once told me that she has no sense of humour but a sense of fun – and perhaps it's the having fun with what she is saying that can make the simplest sentence sound witty. There's often a touch of surprise in her voice, as though meeting the words was like going into a strange room and suddenly finding it full of old friends.[11]

There has seemed to be a kind of imminent laughter in many of Dame Edith's characters, not only in her voice but in her eyes, her mouth, her gestures, her attitudes and her personality.

Yet, as we have seen, it is not only in comedy that she has triumphed. From role to role she has retuned her voice, remade herself, with a rare sureness of instinct: a felicity of *composi-tion*; a capacity for instant truth. 'Edith never speaks false,' testified a leading director. She senses exactly what she can say and do in the creation of a character, loyal to the life she feels in it and to her own verities. 'By thinking you can turn into the person if you think strongly enough,' she has said: a method closer to Christian Science than to Stanislavsky. It is not only the spiritual essence but the clothes of that person to which she has brought her divining artistry. As Lena Ashwell said of her, forty years ago, 'By dressing to the part she becomes the part, as surely as it becomes her.'[12] Part or person: how does one draw the line? By behaving, one might simply say, as an artist. John Gielgud has described Edith Evans's approach as 'cutting away the dead wood until she has chosen the relevant emotion, cadence or nuance. Then it is played so that no one can miss it . . . Style – Congreve, Wilde, Chekhov, Hunter. It is to know what sort of play you're in.'[13] And to know what sort of actress you are. A great mannerist; a great soloist; a great technician; a great comedian; a great magician.

10 PEGGY ASHCROFT

The aim of an actor should not be the part, but the whole.

Peggy Ashcroft (1961)

IN HALF A CENTURY'S WORK, through many twists and turns of fashion, Peggy Ashcroft has remained at the top of her profession. On the verge of seventy, she is not only a classic actress but an incontrovertibly modern one. Like most great artists in maturity she is essentially ageless in performance. She has never seemed to strive in October for the look and sound of April but has assumed them effortlessly as required. Her age as a woman has been irrelevant. She has grown old, and then young again, to the right point of the imagined life in the theatre. Only the age of the character counts, the truth of the role.

When she was in her late twenties, the very incarnation of springtime love and poignant innocence, James Agate declared that 'her chief difficulty is to look old enough to play anything.' About that period she sometimes faced, like her friend John Gielgud, problems of communication with the audience: problems exacerbated by such wounding dicta as Agate's (he had more poisonous arrows in store). To a later enthusiast, J. C. Trewin, she then appeared something of a 'snow maiden'. It was largely, as so often in the making of an actress, 'a question of confidence' (as she describes it). Her beauty may have seemed an obstacle to artistic growth or, more accurately, to recognition of her developing powers. Her voice sounded, then, too light for the summits and profundities of tragedy. But in her steady progress towards the heights of her art Peggy Ashcroft learned to subsume her youthfulness, charm, delicacy and Englishness in the truths of the characters that she not only played but lived. In stretching her technique and toughening her experience she has disproved Hazlitt's adage that 'no actor becomes great by improvement.' What she has never learned is to accept the waste so conspicuous in the theatre of the past fifty years (her potboilers have been singularly few and far between) or to treat the stage as a part-time supplement to employment in other media – films and television have scarcely featured in her career; or to behave (on or off the stage) as a star. Dame Peggy has unostentatiously shown a theatrical team-spirit and a consistency of purpose unequalled by any other leading player of the century.

With passionate artistic integrity Peggy Ashcroft combines stubborn social conscience and liberal idealism. Although inveterately reticent about her private life she has made no secret of her political leanings to the left. In a public appearance of a kind unique in her career, during the general election of 1945 when her third husband Jeremy Hutchinson stood as a Labour candidate, she called at Number Ten to canvass Labour support from Mr Churchill's household. She has backed many libertarian causes and campaigns. She has worked hard to improve conditions for her fellow-players, on and off the Council of their trade union, Equity. She has served on the Arts Council (1962–5), and on the artistic committee of the English Stage Company since 1957. In 1943 she took the initiative in establishing the Apollo Society, which has done much to revive interest in the speaking of poetry. A founder-member of the Royal Shakespeare Company in 1960, she became one of its directors in 1968. 'Without Peggy Ashcroft', says Peter Hall, 'the RSC would never have survived and achieved what it has done.' She has been awarded many official and academic honours: CBE (1951) and DBE (1956); Hon. Litt. D., Oxford (1961) and Leicester (1964); Hon. D. Lit., London (1965); Hon. Litt. D., Cambridge (1972) and Warwick (1974). More significantly, perhaps, she is the first British actress to have had a theatre named after her: the Ashcroft in her birthplace of Croydon, in 1962.

In spite of her international theatrical fame and her public service off-stage, in spite of three marriages and divorces, Dame Peggy has managed to avoid personal publicity. She gave no press interviews for twenty years, and few indeed during the next twenty. She has not yet confided her experiences or opinions to the television cameras. She is not only the most private actress of our time but the least actressy of artists, living quietly in her Hampstead home between carefully selected, intensely studied roles in the theatre. How remarkably seldom, in the past half-century, she has put a foot wrong in her selection; how rarely she has compromised with West End kitsch; how persistently she has been praised by most of the critics; how little that incense seems to have clouded her self-critical search for perfection.

Edith Margaret Emily Ashcroft was born three days before Christmas in 1907 in the Surrey town of Croydon, on the fringe of south-west London suburbia. Like most leading British actresses of this century she came from a middle-class family with no professional theatre tradition. Her father, who was killed in the First World War, was an estate agent. But her mother (part Danish, part German-Jewish) had studied under Elsie Fogerty and was an enthusiastic amateur actress. Peggy's imagination was kindled in childhood by Mrs Ashcroft's interest in the theatre and by a poetry-loving grandfather who attended Shakespeare readings and gave her Palgrave's *Golden Treasury*; it blazed up in reading about Henry Irving and Ellen Terry; and it was kept steadily alight by her Croydon school, which enterprisingly permitted pupils to act Shakespeare as well as studying his plays as 'set books'. At twelve Peggy Ashcroft directed the ring scene from *The Merchant of Venice*, playing Portia for the first time; and she took the leading roles in the school's annual Shakespeare play, directed by the actress and pageant-mistress Gwen Lally. These were, however, male roles: Shylock and Cassius. She also played Marchbanks in *Candida*, but outside the school, where G.B.S. was taboo. She was deeply influenced by Shaw, not so much by his plays (she has appeared, briefly, in no more than two as by his reviews and prefaces, which stirred her socio-political awareness and opened her mind to a view of theatrical ends and means that differed from Irving's (and Mrs Ashcroft's).

Right from the start Peggy Ashcroft was sure that she wanted to be an actress. Shaw helped to reinforce that assurance. Her mother did her best to talk her out of it. Although Mrs Ashcroft finally agreed that Peggy should leave school at sixteen for the Central School of Speech Training, it must be, she said, to train as a teacher not an actress. But Elsie Fogerty, following her nose for talent, backed Peggy, who took the acting course without further opposition and picked up several prizes en route. Within two years, while still a student, she made her first appearance on a professional stage – in *Dear Brutus* at the Birmingham Rep for a week's run. This was an emergency operation, standing in for an actress who had suddenly fallen ill. It was not until the following year, at the age of nineteen, that Peggy Ashcroft started her professional career in London. Like most actresses in that period she started slowly, learning to endure long gaps between short engagements and other familiar disappointments of a theatrical novitiate. She had, moreover, to meet her difficulties alone, because her mother died before she left the Central School. But she did enjoy certain advantages of varying importance. The least important was, surely, luck. Peggy Ashcroft has always modestly insisted on its significance in her career, but the 'lucky' opportunities would have been useless had she not been endowed with un-usual talent, intelligence, presence and instinct. Even if these qualities had been overlooked (as, perhaps, they were in some girls by managers glancing over the widening pool of casual labour) it would have been hard to ignore the smouldering, fire-in-ice virginal beauty of this idealistic new recruit from Croydon.

Peggy Ashcroft's London debut was in an adaptation of Joseph Conrad at a new, short-lived fringe theatre, Playroom Six, in New Compton Street. This led immediately to a fellow actor's play at the Hampstead Everyman ('a poignantly emotional portrayal', said the *Stage,* already); and, shortly after, to work for the discriminating Nigel Playfair. He put her in a comedy at the Q; recommended her for a role at Birming-ham (Laurence Olivier, a Central contemporary, was in the same play); cast her in her first West End role, as a coffee-house girl and Edith Evans's second understudy in *The Way of the World* (1927); and took her to Hammersmith for the Quinteros' *A Hundred Years Old.* She appeared in several fringe produc-tions (Shaw, Yeats, Strindberg); toured in *The Silver Cord* and (for Playfair) *She Stoops to Conquer,* which introduced her to her first husband, Rupert Hart-Davis; and gained her first notice from a leading critic. Reviewing a play at the Everyman, W. A. Darlington wrote that her work 'bears all over it the stamp of an uncommon charm and ability'. A colleague, Austin Trevor, introduced her to the actor-manager Matheson Lang, for whom she read 'The Song of Solomon' as an audition. Five months later, in September 1929 – three years and fourteen parts after leaving drama school – Peggy Ashcroft achieved a signal personal success in Lang's latest West End hit, which ran for over two hundred performances. She played Naemi, the innocent and adoring daughter of *Jew Suss,* adapted from Feuchtwanger's best-selling novel. To this role she brought a quality of inner simplicity and integrity that was immediately recognized by many London critics and is still, after half a century, one of her distinctive assets. Harold Hobson, who saw the play in Manchester, has recalled her appearance in the fourth act of this religious sensation-drama, reading from the Old Testament with 'an immovable, sad peace'. It was, he said some forty years later, one of the seven times in his life that he had felt, on the strength of a single experience, that he was 'in the presence of greatness'. No critic said that at the time, but her performance, ending in a suicidal jump to escape a fate worse than death, 'took London by storm.'

Naemi led to Peggy Ashcroft's appearance as Desdemona to Paul Robeson's Othello (1930, Savoy). It was her first professional performance in Shakespeare, the first time she had seen the play, and the second time she was seen by John Gielgud, who had already spotted her talent in *The Silver Cord* and who was to play a key role in her life. When she made her first entrance in *Othello,* Gielgud wrote later, 'it was as if all the lights in the theatre had suddenly gone up.'[1] Her Desdemona won high praise from several critics not only for its sincerity, pathos and innocence, but for the quality of her speech ('her elocution is perfection') at a time when the habits of inaudibility and mumbling pseudo-naturalism had overlaid the old Shakespearian standards. During the next eighteen months Peggy Ashcroft played Judy in Maugham's *The Breadwinner,* followed by three unsuccessful adaptations of eminent Continental originals. In the last of these, a Spanish farce adapted by the Granville Barkers, she was directed by a key figure in the between-wars theatre, Theodore Komisarjevsky, the brilliant Russian whom she later married and by whose ideas she was influenced long after their brief marriage collapsed.

Early in 1932 Peggy Ashcroft worked for the first time with John Gielgud in his first production, *Romeo and Juliet* for the OUDS. With Edith Evans, the Motleys and George Devine she joined a combination of talents which was to have an invigorating impact on the London stage. Peggy's Juliet was, said *The Times* critic, not only the youngest and freshest of his experience, but one who was passionately in love. 'The high music of that love's despair sometimes tests her too far, but its melancholy is a rapture and its delights are delight itself.' What is more, her performance proved that 'in comedy Miss Ashcroft can go where she pleases.' Later that year she took a decisive leap forward by following Gielgud and Edith Evans to the Old Vic. It was the last season run by Harcourt Williams, who had tried to recruit her for the Waterloo Road in the previous year. In nine months she played ten parts: Miranda, Imogen, Rosalind, Juliet, Perdita and Portia, together with Drinkwater's Mary Stuart, Shaw's Cleopatra, Lady Teazle and Kate Hardcastle. 'It was a killing venture, quite beyond my scope at the time, and I knew it,' she said in 1970. During the season, moreover, she appeared for Komisarjevsky in a 'club' production of his Schnitzler adaptation *Fraulein Elsa*, a marathon part twice the length of Hamlet's. But she survived the Baylis ordeal and demonstrated her capacity in the classic repertoire: the fact that some of it was 'beyond her scope' was as for other Old Vic graduates) the point of going there. Harcourt Williams wrote of her later: 'her own particular technique, which demands absolute honesty in method and is free from any suspicion of false sentiment, was a joy to work with and observe. She does not know what it means to use a "trick" ... and as an artist instinctively rejects the commonplace.'[2] This integrity seemed to be widely recognized by reviewers.

What was Peggy Ashcroft to do next? After a gruelling stint at the Vic it was sometimes hard to reconnect with the majority theatre. From the historian's helicopter it looks as if she might briefly have lost her way. She appeared in Hauptmann, Pirandello and a mock Hindu musical at the Coliseum. She played in her first film, *The Wandering Jew*. (Fortunately for the theatre she was not believed to be 'photogenic', nor did she like studio acting. She has made only half a dozen films.) She toured for Cochran in a play about Mesmer directed by Komisarjevsky that never reached London. (About this time her first marriage ended in divorce.)

Within two years Peggy Ashcroft was back on course again, when Gielgud invited her to work with him at the New. First she played Juliet, with Gielgud and Olivier alternating as Romeo and Mercutio; then Nina in *The Seagull,* directed, translated and designed by Komisarjevsky (with whom she had now parted). Gielgud's invitation came at a critical point in her maturing. Nearly twenty-eight, she was given the chance to play Juliet for a third time, not among OUDS amateurs or in the pell-mell rush-and-stumble of the Old Vic, but under the aegis of London's leading manager (Bronson Albery) and directed by London's leading Shakespearian actor, working again with Edith Evans, Laurence Olivier, George Devine and the Motleys. 'For the first time she began to feel real confidence in her acting,' said Eric Keown in his study of her work.[3] It showed. Peter Fleming, who observed that both Edith Evans's Nurse and her Juliet were even better than in the OUDS production of 1932, wrote:

There is a triumphant beauty in Miss Peggy Ashcroft's Juliet, a passion not to be gainsaid; from the first we tremble for the child who challenges with such a love the inauspicious stars. Technically her performance is perfection; there is no one like her for conveying the sense of a difficult passage without, so to speak, being caught in the act ... She does more than make Shakespeare's expression of Juliet's thoughts seem natural; she makes it seem inevitable.

W. A. Darlington called her 'the finest as well as the sweetest Juliet of our time.' Her performance was an indispensable contribution to the brilliant teamwork that kept *Romeo and Juliet* running for 189 performances, breaking all records. Some years later Gielgud wrote:

Her lightness and spontaneity were a continual joy and inspiration, and she won all hearts with her flower-like, passionate Juliet. She had already developed considerably in power and endurance since her first performance at Oxford. To me, acting with her, she seemed utterly natural and sincere – it would have been impossible to use a false tone or play in an artificial or declamatory manner in acting a scene with this Juliet. . . .[4]

James Agate – who had dismissed her Old Vic Rosalind as 'a nice little girl in a wood' – was in the unimpressed minority. And when the following May she played Nina, Agate objected that although she was 'heartrending' in the earlier part (she began in pigtails) she lacked the power required for the end. Others were enthusiastic about her progress 'from dewy innocence to pale, storm-pelted desperation'. Alan Dent, among others, extolled the 'most harrowing effectiveness' of the final scene: 'Miss Ashcroft has never done anything quite so poignant as this.' In learning to understand Chekhov with the help of Komisarjevsky (whose sister Vera was the very first Nina), Peggy Ashcroft not only established herself as a major artist of the younger generation, but she saw more clearly than ever before the rewards of ensemble playing on which Chekhov's plays – more, perhaps, than those of any other master – depend for their successful realization.

This ensemble experience was extended in the following year when she returned to classical harness at the Queen's with John Gielgud in his first venture as an actor-manager. Gielgud was strongly influenced not only by Granville Barker and Komisarjevsky but, more immediately, by Michel St Denis, nephew of Jacques Copeau and leader of the *Compagnie des Quinze*. On its visits to England in the early 1930s this French troupe had impressed audiences and actors (including Peggy Ashcroft) by the unity of its acting, simplicity of design, totality of effect and rightness of style. With the French director's help Gielgud tried to create an ensemble in the West End outside the long-run system, setting up a 'permanent' company in a nine-month repertoire of four plays – *Richard II, The School for Scandal, The Three Sisters* and *The Merchant of Venice*. For Peggy Ashcroft this was a happy, exhilarating and enlightening period – not so much because of the roles she was playing (the Queen in *Richard II*, Lady Teazle, Irina and Portia) or their reception by the critics, but rather because of the backstage conditions and attitudes to the theatre. In *The Three Sisters*, particularly, she learned a great deal from St Denis, who became a major influence in her work, giving her the confidence in herself that Komis had, somehow, assumed to be there. For the first time in her career she was able to rehearse for as long as seven weeks.

Although the Queen's venture was unsubsidized, Gielgud made a small profit, an economic achievement soon to be unrepeatable in West End conditions. After the season ended in June 1938, however, the company was never reassembled. Gielgud was already 'tired' of management, and accepted an offer from H. M. Tennents to co-star with Dame Marie Tempest in a Dodie Smith comedy *Dear Octopus*. It was under the banner of Tennents, run by Hugh Beaumont, that Gielgud later renewed his attempts to establish a classical repertory in London. Meanwhile, Peggy Ashcroft was among the members of the Queen's team who reunited under St Denis's leadership in an ambitious bid to found a more permanent company. St Denis and Albery took a lease of the Phoenix with a programme that initially included Chekhov, Ibsen, Molière and Shakespeare, and a team led by Peggy Ashcroft, Michael Redgrave, Glen Byam Shaw, Stephen Haggard and George Devine. Support was promised by Edith Evans, Ralph Richardson and Laurence Olivier, who were cast to appear in *Twelfth Night*. But that production had to be staged earlier than planned because the Munich crisis had helped to kill off the opening play – Mikhail Bulgakov's *The White Guard*, in which Peggy Ashcroft and Redgrave shared the acting honours. They shared them again in *Twelfth Night,* for which Evans, Richardson and Olivier were not available. The production gained glowing reviews but not a paying audience. Within a few weeks the Phoenix venture collapsed. Even more powerfully than before, the economic forces at work in the British theatre were ranged against the application of ensemble playing to a repertoire of new and old work, performed in one West End theatre with a resident group of actors. From then onwards Peggy Ashcroft was an actress in search of a company. There were, inevitably, diversions and interruptions, not least by the responsibilities of motherhood. In 1940 she married Jeremy Hutchinson, then in the RNVR, who became a barrister and later a leading Q.C. after his wartime naval service. Their children Eliza and

Nicholas remained at the cherished centre of the private experience that Peggy Ashcroft has guarded carefully from public exposure, and in their early years she took long absences from the stage to be with them. But in the theatre the search went on. It took over twenty years to find what she was looking for, in the Royal Shakespeare Company.

To survey in chronological order all Dame Peggy's performances is a task that must be left to her biographer. Here we may take no more than a panoramic view, backwards and forwards. But before we do so, one fact should be observed: that since 1934, when she appeared in *The Golden Toy*, she has appeared on the London stage in no more than seven productions that could be reasonably classed as 'commercial' (see p. 173). These include some of her finest performances – notably in *The Heiress* (1949), *The Deep Blue Sea* (1952) and *The Chalk Garden* (1956), to which we shall return. Moreover, some of her work in the classics has been done under 'commercial' auspices: as in Gielgud's 1944–5 season at the Haymarket, which was managed by Hugh Beaumont. But both the infrequency and the quality of her 'commercial' work seem in notable contrast with that of many other top performers caught up in the entertainment industry. From 1938 until she joined the RSC, Peggy Ashcroft worked mostly in 'art' theatre productions, frequently at Stratford and the Old Vic, with such colleagues of the pre-war Queen's and Phoenix as Gielgud, Devine, St Denis and Byam Shaw.

Outside Shakespeare, Peggy Ashcroft has left the realms of pure comedy unexplored, to date, in spite of the wit, humour and comic warmth that have veined so many of her performances. Her main non-Shakespearian comic role was as Cecily Cardew in *The Importance of Being Earnest,* and the success of her elegant contribution to that Gielgud ensemble depended upon featherweight solemnity combined with technical precision. Since her first Old Vic season she has appeared in only two other plays between Shakespeare and Ibsen: *The School for Scandal* (1938) and *The Duchess of Malfi* (1944 and 1960). To the latter role (from which Agate boorishly disqualified her in 1945 as a 'teeny weeny': 'nothing but the grand manner will do') she brought in 1960 a union of authority and sensibility, poignancy and magnificence that lit up both the humanity and the poetry in Webster's Jacobean shocker. 'More than any other actress on the stage,' said Penelope Gilliatt, 'she has the moral alertness which separates the tragic from the merely melodramatic or pathetic.' At this point in her career Dame Peggy had, indeed, demonstrated – by her Old Vic Electra (1951) under St Denis's direction – that she could climb the heights of tragedy and get as near to the peaks as any actress of her generation might do – nearer, perhaps. 'These Greek parts were written for men to play, and only men can play them satisfactorily,' said W. A. Darlington; yet with one reservation (her lack of physical power) he praised Peggy Ashcroft's Electra as a 'wonderfully complete performance'. She seemed to have acquired a new hardness and a vocal variety and strength that were, to some critics, astonishing. This was acting on the grand scale, not merely in the grand manner.

Outside Shakespeare, Electra remains Peggy Ashcroft's only exploration of a major role in pre-Ibsen tragedy during her maturity, but she has frequently played tragic or near-tragic parts in the Shakespearian repertoire. To her Juliet, Desdemona and Ophelia she added in 1950, working again with Gielgud, a youthful and definitive Cordelia that seemed 'perfection' to several critics, including Philip Hope-Wallace. He could not imagine, he said, 'No cause, no cause' spoken more movingly, even by Ellen Terry; and T. C. Worsley described these words as 'marvellously dropped like two reassuring tears of forgiveness.' As Queen Katharine (1969) she fought regally, suffered poignantly and died beautifully in the great tradition, reinforcing the surface effects with that sense of vulnerable inner experience, shared with the audience, that has distinguished so much of her later work. As one young critic wrote: she 'endows each moment . . . with an emotional truth which is the crown of great technical achievement; there is, in each line, a lifetime's work.'

This queen came to the stage sixteen years after Peggy Ashcroft had met and overcome her greatest challenge in Shakespeare – Cleopatra to Redgrave's Antony. In a red pony-tail wig and bright orange and purple robes, playing against the grain of her personality, she took most of the critics by surprise. They had expected imagination, sensibility, authority and mastery of the language. But Cleopatra's sexual sluttishness, feline cruelty and Oriental abandon were thought to be beyond the range of an actress who had so often imbued the theatre with an atmosphere of nobility, idealism and moral discipline. This magnificent performance shook most preconceptions about the actress, if not about the part. She was said, variously, to be not altogether big enough or bitchy enough, insufficiently earthy and sexually replete. Some critics, including such veterans as Ivor Brown and Darlington, believed that Dame Peggy had not quite brought off the impossible, while recording amazed admiration that she had come so near to doing it. But Hope-Wallace and Worsley asserted that, in the end, she had transcended all limitations and achieved the role. She had now proved, said Alan Dent, that she was a great actress; and with extreme circumspection, like all serious critics, he used that word of no more than a handful of artists. Other circumspect colleagues still held the term in check; but in 1953–4 Cleopatra was, indeed, a landmark in Peggy Ashcroft's work and in mid-century Shakespearian acting.

Elsewhere in Shakespeare during the past twenty-five years she has returned to earlier roles, enriching them with her experience of life and the theatre accumulated in the intervening time. Her second Viola (1951, Old Vic) seemed simplicity itself, distilled emotional truth, sensitive to countless subtleties both in music and in meaning. Peggy Ashcroft's third Portia (1953, Stratford), reminding older critics once again of Ellen Terry, gave an enchanted emotional reality to the fairy-tale love in Belmont, and brought her newly-acquired steel to the trial scene. Kenneth Tynan, not one of Dame Peggy's most consistent admirers, said that 'the lines flow out new-minted' and that the last act 'bloomed golden at her touch.' Four years later her second Rosalind (1957, Stratford) appeared miraculously youthful, light and eager. At forty-nine she made nonsense of arithmetic, said Darlington. In spite of a Little-Lord-Fauntleroyish costume that might have crippled a vainer talent, Peggy Ashcroft achieved a similar triumph in *Cymbeline* some months later, winning acclamations as 'a rapturous creature', 'a spirit of beauty and truth' and 'Nature's Imogen'. Her ecstatic cry of 'Oh, for a horse with wings!' still hovers, for some of her auditors, in the Stratford air. This was her first experience of working under the direction of Peter Hall, who became a close friend and counsellor and, by setting up the RSC, the man who made her theatrical dreams come true.

Peggy Ashcroft also explored many new Shakespearian roles. Her Stratford Beatrice, with Gielgud as Benedick (1950, 1955) was, perhaps, her finest performance in comedy to date. She lacked the malice and astringency that some people had come to expect of 'My Lady Disdain'; nor was she the great lady of Victorian tradition. But the character she presented shone with wit, grace and humour, a relish of language and a quintessentially feminine warmth, that left one in no doubt that it was the authentic Beatrice. Playing opposite Gielgud, Dame Peggy has said, was 'like having a marvellous partner in a dance':[5] they were certainly marvellous to watch and to hear. As T. C. Worsley wrote, they played so beautifully together because 'they set off each other's best points, call out in each other the highest art' and 'double the value of their individual performances.' Mastery of technique was shared in perfect collaboration that made the play a celebration.

From 1950 onwards Peggy Ashcroft continually disproved pre-performance Jeremiads that she was 'too old' for roles. One of her bigger surprises was her Stratford Shrew in 1960. 'She confounds prophecy by demonstrating herself ideal for the part,' Tynan wrote. There was no sign, in this portrait of a woman in love, of that desperation with which autumnal actresses wriggle back into spring parts. It seems incredible, as Harold Hobson said, that in such a role she should actually increase her reputation. 'But this is the miracle that Dame Peggy performs. From her first entrance there is a radiance hidden behind Katharine's sullenness, waiting to be released, and at the end Dame Peggy is a woman liberated, not a woman cowed.' This was a captivatingly funny, touching performance, whose apparent innovations in emphasis all seemed (as is usual with Dame Peggy) warrantable by the text. In the same Stratford season her superb Paulina, displaying iron strength of presence and queenly control of phrasing, assumed old age in the final scene with a grandeur that almost made one forget the absurdity of Paulina's sixteen-year camouflage of her supposedly dead mistress, and prefigured the grey-haired matriarchs, ancient and modern, she was soon to play.

Among Shakespearian roles Peggy Ashcroft's Queen Margaret (1963, Stratford) belongs in a special category. As a minor part in the repertoire, usually cut by the leading actor or the director, 'Mad Margaret' in *Richard III* had been played by many of her predecessors; but none had combined this (as Dame Peggy did) with Margaret's earlier appearances in the *Henry VI* cycle. With remarkable skill, scholarship and audacity Peter Hall and John Barton telescoped four plays into the three-part *Wars of the Roses*, filling gaps and forging links with pastiche-lines that seemed to the lay ear (and, retrospectively, to the not-so-lay eye) indistinguishable from an original text whose complete Shakespearian authenticity has frequently been contested. Had any doubts lingered about Peggy Ashcroft's ability as a *comedienne* to remake her image they must have been stilled for ever by this monumental three-play performance. Spanning some thirty-five years, she grew convincingly from an incredibly youthful princess to an implacably cruel, towering soldier-queen and then, in the end, to a ruined, regal crone, with straying wits and grey hair straggling about her wrinkled face, suppurating with hatred and despair. This 'balefully persuasive' queen (as Tynan called her) was not only a far bigger part but a far bigger person than Margaret of Anjou had ever seemed before. Yet this was (despite the textual changes) not the invention of the actress and her directors but, in every sense, a truly Shakespearian creation. Among the most memorable moments of *The Wars of the Roses* were those in which Queen Margaret appeared, carrying with her a midden of vengeful and appalled experience, rallying her followers for a last stand or wiping the face of the doomed Duke of York with a cloth stained in the blood of his dead son. This astonishing performance helped to make *The Wars of the Roses* one of the major theatrical events of the 1960s and, indeed, of the past thirty years.

Outside Shakespeare, Peggy Ashcroft has won an especial reputation in Chekhov and Ibsen. Since her 1937 Nina, however, she has appeared in only two Chekhov roles. Her Arkadina (Queen's, 1964) was widely praised for its sensitivity, humanity and subtlety; but many critics were disappointed by her Madame Ranevsky, in St Denis's 1961 *Cherry Orchard*. To them it seemed as if St Denis had 'ironed out' the pathos they had come to expect, leaving 'a merely shallow woman with an easy gear-shift from tears to laughter', with 'scarcely a hint of the Madame Ranevsky who finds life and its transience a tragic affliction.' But that Madame they missed was not, in the view of Dame Peggy and her director, Chekhov's Madame.

It was in Ibsen, three years after *Electra*, that Peggy Ashcroft broke decisively away from the Shakespeare-Chekhov associations of her earlier career. In praising her 'flinty, marvellously impartial' *Hedda Gabler* (1954, Hammersmith) Kenneth Tynan wrote: 'How many temptations this actress resists! She makes no play for sympathy; nor does she imply that she despises the woman she is impersonating.' This icy, disgusted, savagely bored egotist had little in common with the 'flowery, bosomy romantic' of Mrs Patrick Campbell.

Peggy Ashcroft removed all the glamour from Hedda, pitilessly. She made her a vixen neurotic, detestable and ridiculous ... This element of satire tore away at one sweep the pretence that Hedda is a tragic heroine ... Once again she showed that although often cast as a romantic actress she was able to discard completely the trappings of romance and sink the charm of her personality in a rigorously honest dissection of an unromantic character.[6]

This dazzling performance – which was, among other things, sometimes intensely funny – was welcomed in Britain as one of Peggy Ashcroft's greatest artistic successes. In Ibsen's homeland it was hailed as exemplary acting, demonstrating to the Norwegian theatre just how Hedda should be played, and this recognition was sealed by King Haakon's award to her of the King's Gold Medal.

Five years later George Devine, who had played Tesman (admirably) with Peggy Ashcroft in *Hedda Gabler*, directed her in *Rosmersholm* (1959, Royal Court). Her Rebecca West was not greeted with such unanimous enthusiasm. Some critics complained that she was too naturalistic and could not communicate that 'pitch of exaltation' which carries Rebecca and Rosmer to their death in the mill-race. Yet *The Times,* taking the opposite view, declared that in going from strength to strength she was at her strongest in the final scene: 'it is Dame Peggy Ashcroft's triumph to make us believe completely in the courage and honesty which make the sacrifice possible.' And for W. A. Darlington it was one of the best performances of her career. When Dame Peggy played Mrs Alving eight years later at the Aldwych, it seemed to Harold Hobson an even greater achievement: 'one of the finest performances of our time.'

Between 1938 and 1976 Dame Peggy's work in contemporary plays may be divided into two main phrases: roles under commercial auspices on the West End stage (and Broadway); and roles for the subsidized London organizations – the English Stage, the Royal Shakespeare and the National Theatre Companies. It was a commercial role which provided her first big opportunity to break away from the realm of ingenues: in *Edward My Son* (1947, His Majesty's) she submerged her beauty, charm and youthfulness in the part of a near-alcoholic who seeks refuge from disillusion in drink. This performance was followed by other memorably poignant studies of suffering, frustrated and embittered women, victims of society, family life and their own temperaments. In *The Heiress* (1949, Haymarket) Dame Peggy masked her beauty even more emphatically as the shy, plain, over-fathered Catherine Sloper (adapted from Henry James's *Washington Square*) who learns through parental tyranny and sham romance to be cruel. 'Cruel? Of course I am cruel. I have been taught by masters.' In Rattigan's *The Deep Blue Sea* (1952, Duchess) Peggy Ashcroft – persuaded by Hugh Beaumont – grasped the opportunity to mine the truth of an emotional role on a scale that no dramatist since Pinero (said Tynan) had created for an English actress. She gave what Tynan described as 'a scorchingly realistic portrait of a woman in love beyond her means'. Four years later Dame Peggy returned to the West End in Enid Bagnold's *The Chalk Garden* (1956, Haymarket), collaborating once again with John Gielgud and Edith Evans. As a mysterious green-fingered 'companion', Miss Madrigal, nursing the secret of a life sentence from which she has learned the secret of life, she added largely to her laurels both official and unofficial (she was voted best actress of the year in the annual *Evening Standard* awards).

The second phase of Peggy Ashcroft's career in contemporary drama opened in the same year. It was the year that the English Stage Company was established at the Royal Court under George Devine's leadership, and under his direction

Dame Peggy made her debut in Brecht. In *The Good Woman of Setzuan* she brought off a brilliant double: as Shen Te (a tart with a golden heart) and Shui Ta, the ruthless male cousin whom Shen Te invents – with the aid of a half-mask, a black wig, a felt hat and a nasal voice – to protect her from the consequences of her own goodness. Two years later she played a more explicitly political role as Julia Raik, a revolutionary betrayed and a wife bereaved, in Robert Ardrey's stirring semi-documentary about the background to the Hungarian debacle of 1956, *Shadow of Heroes* (1958, Piccadilly) – a play that came before its time (presented and directed by Peter Hall). It was not until 1966 that Dame Peggy appeared in another contemporary play, with a very different social milieu – Marguerite Duras's *Days in the Trees* (Aldwych), to which she contributed a riveting study of a rich, possessive, ancient French matriarch with a colonial past. This introduction to Marguerite Duras led to an invitation from the Royal Court in 1971 to play in *The Lovers of Viorne*. Claire Lannes, the French housewife inexplicably driven to chop up her deaf and dumb cousin, proved to be one of her favourite roles, in which she gave a virtuoso display of (as Ronald Bryden described it) 'the gentle, stubborn apathy of an animal hiding from herself the volcanic rejection of her own existence which erupted in her crime.' About this time Dame Peggy gave two notable performances as rich American matriarchs in plays by Edward Albee. As Agnes in *A Delicate Balance* (1969, Aldwych) she played a weary wife trying to hold her family together and to master her own inner bitterness, displaying a remarkable felicity of adjustment to the baroque rhetoric of Albee's prose. And as the white-haired, waspish Wife in *All Over* (1972, Aldwych), waiting stiffly by the death-bed of the Great Man to whom she was linked in an apparently loveless marriage, she asserted an icy control over herself, the characters and the text, until at the very end the depths of the Wife's misery were revealed in the fourfold repetition of 'Because I'm unhappy', a howl of despair. 'As she delivers it, from the guts, it is comparable to Lear's nevers,' wrote Irving Wardle.

Moving into yet another dimension of theatre and language, Peggy Ashcroft appeared in 1969 in Harold Pinter's *Landscape* (Aldwych). Sitting dreamily in a kitchen chair, thinking aloud about her past, Beth conducts a reminiscent monologue in parallel with her stolid husband, islanded in lost experience. This entranced and entrancing soliloquy, ending in a last rapt cry of 'O my true love', was initially received by some reviewers with glum incomprehension. Yet Pinter's theatrical poem or duet, as realized at the Aldwych, was an achievement of unusual beauty and extreme simplicity; and when it was brought back to the repertoire in 1973 (with *A Slight Ache*, in which Dame Peggy played Flora) its performance achieved an even greater degree of both economy and ripeness (with a wider acceptance and understanding). From Pinter it seems a natural leap to Beckett. Dame Peggy's performance as Winnie in *Happy Days* (1975, Old Vic) may be compared in its virtuosity (if in nothing else) with her Queen Margaret, gaining the maximum effects from minimal theatre, sublimely expressive though buried to the neck in slag. Looking on the bright side over a wasteland of life everlasting, ageing a generation between the acts, this battered, garrulous survivor gives a poetic demonstration – deeply sad and also deeply funny – of courage in the face of loneliness and pain : a note of affirmation that has rung through many of Peggy Ashcroft's finest performances.

Here one stops short, looking forward to Dame Peggy's next decade. It would be premature to attempt a summary of her work at this point in the career of so resilient and unpredictable an artist. Yet it may be said that in her steady progression from a romantic ingenue to a tragic queen, from exquisite miniaturism to acting on the grand scale, Peggy Ashcroft has persistently shown the truth of Ellen Terry's prescription of 'intelligence, imagination and industry'. In John Gielgud's words, she has displayed 'an extraordinary theatrical instinct – where to be, how to move, how to pervade a scene' (but not how to steal one). A pillar of her achievement has been her feeling for the sense *and* the sound, the idea *and* the character, her alertness to psychological, theatrical and musical values. Like all virtuosos, she has been able to present revelations in silence, speaking volumes without saying a word. Yet it is in her understanding of language and respect for words that she has excelled : not only in the clarity of her diction, and the passionate imagination and sharp intelligence behind it, but the freshness with which she so often speaks her lines, as if they were being spoken for the very first time, as if she had just thought of them. How can one describe the voice of Peggy Ashcroft? One may only attempt to do so justly in the role she is playing. It may be lyrically tender or regally harsh; there is sadness in its gaiety, and its melancholy holds a fearful joy. It keeps words in the air like burning brands, or fills the mind with flowers. It can be like a trumpet or a violin, a sword or a magic wand. It seems the voice of truth as well as the voice of experience.

Time after time, through her wide range of roles, Peggy Ashcroft has served the author and the company. 'She gives as much as she takes in her acting,' says Gielgud. Over and over again, with determination and hard work, she has disproved the superstitions that a major artist cannot work in an ensemble, that only a *monstre sacrée* can be a great actress, that a social democrat cannot be a player queen. On the stage Dame Peggy Ashcroft exudes an inner serenity and strength, a queenlike authority, an emotional honesty, an absolute genuineness and spontaneity, communicated through a mastery of technique that is also a mastery of self. At the heart of her mystery there is, it seems, as profound a simplicity and humility as any professional actress can afford and sustain.

POSTSCRIPT

MANY AUTHORS AND REVIEWERS, dead and alive, have helped in the making and remaking of *The Player Queens*. The Book-list contains the principal contributors, and most of the direct quotations are credited in the Notes. I am indebted to the twentieth-century critics whose opinions I have quoted in the last four chapters; to Christopher Fry, Philip Hope-Wallace, Laurence Irving, John Perry and Sir Michael Redgrave, who were kind enough to read sections of the book in typescript; and to Dame Peggy Ashcroft and Sir John Gielgud for reading sections of the proofs. I am deeply grateful to them and to all those who helped me in my research. Without the aid of the British Library, the London Library, the Shakespeare Library at Stratford-on-Avon, the Enthoven Collection at the Victoria and Albert Museum, the library of the Vic-Wells Association and the library of the Garrick Club, this book could never have been completed.

For permission to quote from copyright material my thanks are due to Barrie & Jenkins (*Edith Evans* and *Sybil Thorndike* by J. C. Trewin, and *Peggy Ashcroft* by Eric Keown, originally published by Rockliff); Jonathan Cape (*The Second Sex*, by Simone de Beauvoir); William Collins Sons & Co. (*Lewis and Sybil*, by John Casson); George G. Harrap & Co. (*6001 Nights*, by W. A. Darlington); William Heinemann (*Sarah Siddons* and *Ellen Terry* by Roger Manvell); Heinemann Educational Books (*Early Stages* by John Gielgud); Hutchinson Publishing Group (*Ellen Terry and her Secret Self* by Gordon Craig); and the Society of Authors on behalf of the Bernard Shaw Estate.

NOTES

FOREWORD

1 Rosamond Gilder, *Enter the Actress*, p. 46.
2 Christopher Hill, *The World Turned Upside Down* (1972), p. 249.
3 Simone de Beauvoir, *The Second Sex*, p. 537.
4 Ibid., p. 711.

1 THE NEW WOMEN

1 Sheila Rowbotham, *Women, Resistance and Revolution*, p.28–9.
2 William Prynne, *Histriomastix* (1633).
3 Juliet Dusinberre, *Shakespeare and the Nature of Women*, p. 252.
4 Ibid., p. 233.
5 Ibid., p. 5.
6 E. Gegen, *The New Woman*, p. 9.
7 John Wilson Bowyer, *The Celebrated Mrs Centlivre* (Durham, N.C., 1952), p. 42.
8 E. Gegen, p. 165.
9 Allardyce Nicoll, *History of English Drama* (1952 edn.), vol. 1, p. 221.
10 Glynne Wickham, *Early English Stages*, vol. 1, p. 272.
11 Allardyce Nicoll, p. 12.
12 J. H. Wilson, *All the King's Ladies*, p. 20.
13 Ibid., p. 73.
14 Ibid.
15 Hugh Hunt, 'Restoration and Acting', in *Restoration Theatre*, p. 182.
16 J. Sutherland, *Oxford History of English Literature*, p. 36.
17 Tom Brown, quoted J. H. Wilson, p. 26.
18 Hugh Hunt, p. 184

2 FOUR PIONEERS

1 Thomas Davies, *Dramatic Miscellanies*, vol. 3, p. 397.

2 Charles Gildon, *The Life of Mr Thomas Betterton*, p. 7.
3 J. H. Wilson, *Nell Gwyn, Royal Mistress*, p. 319.
4 Graham Greene, *Lord Rochester's Monkey*, p. 125.
5 J. H. Wilson, *Nell Gwyn*, p. 2.
6 R. G. Ham, *Otway and Lee* (1931), p. 86.
7 Graham Greene, p. 173.
8 *A Comparison Between Two Stages*, ed. Staring B. Wells, p. 13.
9 Harold Love, *Congreve* (1974), p. 9.
10 Colley Cibber, *Apology*, vol. 1, p. 230–1.
11 p. 106.
12 Kathleen M. Lynch, *A Congreve Gallery*, p. 10.

3 MOSTLY GEORGIAN

1 Alison Adburgham, *Women in Print* (1972), p. 33.
2 Robert Gore-Browne, *Gay Was the Pit*, p. 45.
3 Ibid., p. 83.
4 W. R. Chetwood, *A General History of the Stage*, p. 202.
5 J. Oldmixon, *Arthur Maynwaring. The Life and Posthumous Works* (1715), p. 43.
6 J. Doran, *Their Majesties' Servants* (1897 edn.), p. 152.
7 John Fyvie, *Tragedy Queens of the Georgian Era*, p. 34.
8 Dr Burney, *A History of Music*, vol. 1, p. 654.
9 Tate Wilkinson, *Memoirs*, vol. 2, p. 175.
10 William Cookes, *Memoirs of Samuel Foote* (1805), vol. 1, p. 23–4.
11 Percy Fitzgerald, *The Life of Mrs Catherine Clive*, p. 13.
12 Ibid., p. 75.
13 Ibid., p. 44.
14 Tate Wilkinson, *The Wandering Patentee*, vol. 2, p. 31.
15 *Works* (1966), vol. 1, p. 451.
16 *Thraliana*, vol. 2, p. 715.
17 John Hill, *The Actor*, p. 195.
18 Theophilus Cibber, quoted by Bertram Joseph, *The Tragic Actor*, p. 160.
19 Quoted by Carola Oman, *David Garrick* (1958), p. 158.
20 John Hill, p. 60.
21 Quoted by Dennis Bartholomeusz, *Macbeth and the Players*, p. 49.
22 Thomas Gray, quoted by Bertram Joseph, p. 161.
23 John Genest, *Some Account of the English Stage*, vol. 5, p. 173.
24 Edward Gibbon, *Journal* (New York, 1929), p. 186.
25 J. Doran, p. 243.
26 Quoted by Bertram Joseph, p. 160.
27 Thomas Davies, *David Garrick*, vol. 2, p. 148.
28 Thomas Davies, *Dramatic Miscellanies*, vol. 2, p. 183.

29 J. Doran, p. 245.
30 *The Letters of David Garrick*, vol. 2, p. 557.
31 *Thraliana*, p. 726.
32 Charles Dibdin, *A Complete History of the English Stage*, vol. 5, p. 353.
33 *An Account of the Life of Susannah Maria Cibber* (1887), p. 5.
34 P. H. Baker, *Mr Cibber of Drury Lane* (1939).
35 *A History of Music*, vol. 4, p. 526.
36 Quoted by Cecil Price, *Theatre in the Age of Garrick* (1973), p. 39.
37 Richard Cumberland, *Memoirs* (1806), vol. 1, p. 80–1.
38 Mrs Clement Parsons, *Garrick and his Circle* (1906), p. 118.
39 Thomas Davies, *David Garrick*, vol. 2, p. 108.
40 *The Actor*, p. 107.
41 Benjamin Victor, *The History of the Theatres of London* (1771), p. 82.
42 Charles Dibdin, vol. 5, p. 207.
43 Quoted by Mrs Clement Parsons, p. 118.
44 *Memoires*, p. 7.
45 Augustin Daly, *Woffington* (1888), p. 15.
46 Janet Camden Lucey, *Lovely Peggy*, p. 78.
47 Ibid., p. 132.
48 Tate Wilkinson, *Memoirs*, vol. 1, p. 117–20.
49 Thomas Davies, *David Garrick*, vol. 1, p. 347.
50 Quoted Janet Dunbar, *Peg Woffington and her World*, p. 210.
51 Janet Camden Lucey, p. 223–5.
52 *The Actor*, p. 105–6.
53 Charles Dibdin, vol. 5, p. 208.

4 SARAH SIDDONS

1 Tate Wilkinson, *The Wondering Patentee*, vol. 4, p. 23.
2 Thomas Campbell, *Life of Mrs Siddons*, vol. 1, p. 190.
3 Quoted Roger Manvell, *Sarah Siddons,* p. 299.
4 *Collected Works* (1903), vol. 8, p. 312.
5 *The Autobiography of Benjamin Robert Haydon* (1936), pp. 244, 400.
6 *The Old Playgoer* (1846), p. 18.
7 Thomas Campbell, vol. 1, p. 201.
8 James Boaden, *Memoirs of Mrs Siddons*, vol. 2, p. 116.
9 Quoted Roger Manvell, p. 342.
10 Mrs Clement Parsons, *The Incomparable Siddons*, p. 12.
11 *Diary and Letters of Madame D'Arblay*, vol. 3, p. 401.
12 *The Beauties of Mrs Siddons* (1786), p. 4.
13 *The Wandering Patentee,* vol. 1, p. 254.

14   James Boaden, vol. 1, p. 287–9.
15   Ibid., vol. 1, p. 171.
16   Thomas Campbell, vol. 1, p. 210.
17   Ibid., vol. 2, p. 145.
18   James Boaden, vol. 1, p. 171.
19   Thomas Davies, *Dramatic Miscellanies*, vol. 3, p. 249.
20   Thomas Campbell, vol. 1, p. 210.
21   Ibid., vol. 2, p. 157–8.
22   *Macready's Reminiscences*, p. 42–3.
23   *Dramatic Essays*, p. 13.
24   *Macready's Reminiscences*, p. 152–3.
25   For sources of this summary of Mrs Siddons's Lady Macbeth, see:
     Dennis Bartholomeusz; Mrs Clement Parsons; A. C. Sprague;
     Bertram Joseph; James Boaden; H. C. Fleming Jenkin; Brander
     Mathews.
26   Thomas Campbell, vol. 1, p. 36.
27   Roger Manvell, p. 10.
28   Mrs A. Kennard, *Mrs Siddons*, p. 16.
29   Thomas Campbell, vol. 1, p. 6.
30   Roger Manvell, p. 20.
31   *Reminiscences of Sarah Siddons*, p. 6.
32   Thomas Campbell, vol. 1, p. 82.
33   Percy Fitzgerald, *The Kembles* (1871), vol. 1, p. 32–3.
34   *Reminiscences of Sarah Siddons*, p. 13.
35   James Boaden, vol. 1, p. 178.
36   *Reminiscences of Sarah Siddons*, p. 12.
37   Quoted Thomas Campbell, vol. 2, p. 110.
38   John Galt, *The Lives of the Players* (1831), vol. 2, p. 304.
39   Quoted Roger Manvell, p. 114.
40   *Thraliana*, p. 738.
41   Ibid., p. 176.
42   Roger Manvell, p. 243.
43   *Thraliana*, p. 769.
44   Quoted Yvonne ffrench, *Mrs Siddons, Tragic Actress*, p. 216.
45   Oswald G. Knapp (ed.), *An Artist's Love Story*, p. 82.
46. Ibid., p. 132.
47   Roger Manvell, p. 265.
48   Thomas Campbell, vol. 2, p. 315–6.
49   T. S. Whalley, *Journals and Correspondence*, vol. 2, p. 100.
50   Quoted Roger Manvell, p. 360, from letter in Harvard Theatre
     Collection.
51   Thomas Campbell, vol. 2, p. 198.
52   Quoted Roger Manvell, p. 298.
53   Revd G. Croly, quoted Mrs Clement Parsons, p. 63.

54 Mrs Williams Wynn, quoted Mrs Clement Parsons, p. 65.
55 Quoted Mrs Clement Parsons, p. 74–5.
56 Oswald G. Knapp, p. 82.
57 Roger Manvell, p. 125.
58 P. W. Clayden, *Rogers and his Contemporaries* (1889), vol. 1, p. 354.
59 Roger Manvell, p. 122.
60 Thomas Moore, *Memoirs*, vol. 5, p. 297.
61 Mrs Clement Parsons, p. 167.
62 Thomas Campbell, vol. 2, p. 122.
63 James Boaden, vol. 2, p. 322.
64 William Robson, p. 19.
65 *The Beauties of Mrs Siddons*, p. 5.
66 Fanny Kemble, *Records of a Girlhood*, p. 190.
67 Thomas Campbell, vol. 2, p. 3.
68 *Stanislavsky on the Art of the Stage* (1950), p. 82.
69 Thomas Campbell, vol. 2, p. 14.
70 James Boaden, vol. 2, p. 180.
71 *Dramatic Essays*, p. 13.
72 Quoted Thomas Campbell, vol. 2, p. 382.
73 Macready, *Reminiscences*, p. 42.
74 Charles Mayne Young, quoted Thomas Campbell, vol. 2, p. 383.
75 Yvonne ffrench, p. 242.
76 Mrs Clement Parsons, p. 83.
77 *Collected Works*, vol. 2, p. 382.

5 VICTORIAN LADIES

1 See Ray Strachey, *The Cause* (1928), p. 407.
2 Mrs Kendal, *Dramatic Opinions* (1890), p. 79.
3 Ray Strachey, *Careers and Openings for Women* (1934), quoted Virginia Woolf, *Three Guineas* (1938), p. 81.
4 Sir Theodore Martin, *Helena Faucit (Lady Martin)* (1890), p. 404–5.
5 Fanny Kemble, *Journal* (1835), vol. 1, p. 149.
6 St John Ervine, *The Theatre in my Time* (1933), p. 83.
7 *The Life of Charles James Mathews* (1879), vol. 2, p. 76.
8 Quoted Lynton Hudson, *The English Stage 1850–1950* (1952), p. 40.
9 Herbert Swears, *When All's Said and Done* (1937), p. 177.
10 *Dame Madge Kendal By Herself* (1933), p. 70–2.
11 G. B. Shaw, *Our Theatres in the Nineties* (1932), vol. 1, p. 279.

6 ELLEN TERRY

1 Laurence Irving, *Henry Irving* (1951), p. 309.

2   G.B.S., quoted *Ellen Terry's Memoirs*, p. vii.
3   Lady Lucy Duff Gordon, *Discretions and Indiscretions* (1932), p. 33.
4   Gordon Craig, *Index to the Story of My Days* (1957), p. 131.
5   Henry James, *The Scenic Art* (1949), p. 143.
6   Hesketh Pearson, *Beerbohm Tree* (1956), p. 11.
7   Graham Robertson, *Time Was* (1931), p. 287.
8   John Gielgud, *Distinguished Company* (1972), p. 14.
9   *Edy*, p. 77.
10 Interviewed in *Madame* (6 December 1902).
11 Naomi Royde-Smith, *The Private Life of Mrs Siddons* (1934), p. 44.
12 *Ellen Terry's Memoirs* (1933), p. 80.
13 T. Edgar Pemberton, *Ellen Terry and her Sisters* (1902), p. 265-6.
14 Gordon Craig, *Ellen Terry and her Secret Self* (1931), p. 158.
15 Quoted by Roger Manvell, *Ellen Terry* (1968), p. 200.
16 Walter Calvert, *Souvenir of Miss Ellen Terry* (1897).
17 William Archer, *Theatrical World for 1896* (1897), p. 275.
18 Max Beerbohm, quoted in *The Ibsen Heritage* (1972), p. 418.
19 *Henry Irving*, p. 316.
20 She believed she was born in 1848: that date is on her tomb in St Paul's, Covent Garden, and in several books.
21 Max Beerbohm, *Lost Theatres* (1970), p. 243-4.
22 *Ellen Terry's Memoirs*, p. 44.
23 Ibid., p. 11.
24 G. B. Shaw, *Our Theatres in the Nineties* (1932), vol. 3, p. 193.
25 Dutton Cook, *The Theatre* (1 June 1880).
26 *Ellen Terry's Memoirs*, p. 31.
27 Ibid., p. 35.
28 T. Edgar Pemberton, p. 64-5.
29 *Ellen Terry's Memoirs*, p. 37.
30 Ibid., p. 38.
31 Ibid., p. 40.
32 Ibid., p. 40.
33 *Ellen Terry and Bernard Shaw: A Correspondence* (1931), p. 122.
34 David Loshak in *Burlington Magazine* (November 1963). Quoted by Roger Manvell, p. 52.
35 *Letters from Graham Robertson* (1953), p. 409.
36 Quoted by Roger Manvell, p. 47 (abridged in *Shaw–Terry Correspondence*).
37 *Ellen Terry's Memoirs*, p. 46.
38 Ibid., p. 48.
39 Ibid., p. 48.
40 Ibid., p. 62.
41 Ibid., p. 66.

42 Ibid., p. 91.
43 Ibid., p. 86–7.
44 *Letters from Graham Robertson*, p. 260.
45 *Ellen Terry's Memoirs*, p. 116.
46 Gordon Craig, *Ellen Terry and her Secret Self*, p. 66.
47 *Shaw–Terry Correspondence*, p. xxxii.
48 G. B. Shaw, *Our Theatres in the Nineties*, vol. 1, p. 282.
49 Clement Scott, *Ellen Terry*, p. 112.
50 *Shaw–Terry Correspondence*, p. xxxii.
51 *Our Theatres in the Nineties*, vol. 1, p. 17.
52 *Ellen Terry's Memoirs*, p. 39.
53 Marguerite Steen, *A Pride of Terrys* (1962).
54 Quoted in *We Saw Him Act* (1939), p. 310.
55 *Ellen Terry's Memoirs*, p. 124.
56 Ibid., p. 128.
57 Ibid., p. 271–2.
58 *Shaw–Terry Correspondence*, p. xv.
59 Roger Manvell, p. 8.
60 *Ellen Terry's Memoirs*, p. 67.
61 Ibid., p. 66.
62 G. B. Shaw, *Pen Portraits and Reviews*, p. 67.
63 *Time Was*, p. 55.
64 *Ellen Terry and her Secret Self*, p. 165.
65 Ibid., p. 166.
66 John Gielgud, *Distinguished Company*, p. 14.
67 Virginia Woolf, *New Statesman and Nation* (8 February 1941).
68 Gordon Craig, p. 20.
69 *Ellen Terry's Memoirs*, p. 276.
70 *Shaw–Terry Correspondence*, p. 74.

7 EDWARDIANS AND AFTER

1 Lynton Hudson, *The English Stage 1850–1950* (1951) p. 92.
2 G. B. Shaw, *Collected Letters 1898–1910*, p. 439.
3 Ibid., p. 301.
4 G. B. Shaw, *Our Theatres in the Nineties* (1932), vol. 3, p. 79.
5 William Archer, *The Theatrical World for 1893* (1894), p. 80.
6 G. B. Shaw, *Our Theatres in the Nineties*, vol. 1, 232.
7 Ibid., vol. 3, p. 139.
8 G. B. Shaw, *Collected Letters 1898–1910*, p. 223.
9 Ibid., p. 332.
10 Ibid., p. 771.
11 Ibid., p. 308.
12 *Letters from Graham Robertson* (1953), p. 98.

13 Alan Dent, *Mrs Patrick Campbell* (1961), p. 182.
14 Ibid., p. 254.
15 Ibid., p. 68.

8 SYBIL THORNDIKE

1 John Casson, *Lewis & Sybil*, p. 45.
2 Ibid., p. 205.
2 *Great Acting*, p. 49.
4 Elizabeth Sprigge, *Sybil Thorndike Casson* (1971), p. 41.
5 Ibid., p. 51.
6 Ibid., p. 71.
7 J. C. Trewin, *Sybil Thorndike* (1955), p. 23.
8 *Great Acting*, p. 50.
9 John Casson, p. 202.
10 W. A. Darlington, *6001 Nights* (1960), p. 89.
11 Russell Thorndike, *Sybil Thorndike* (1950 edn.), p. 289.
12 John Casson, p. 118.
13 *Sybil Thorndike Casson*, p. 170.
14 John Casson, p. 170.
15 Ibid., p. 249.
16 Ibid., p. 250.
17 *Theatre Programme* (1954), p. 123.
18 J. C. Trewin, p. 64.
19 Sybil and Russell Thorndike, *Lilian Baylis*, p. 35.
20 Gordon Crosse, *Shakespeare Playgoing 1890–1952* (1953), p. 51–3.
21 Elizabeth Sprigge, p. 56.
22 J. C. Trewin, p. 15.
23 Micheál MacLiammóir, *All for Hecuba* (1946), p. 334–5.

9 EDITH EVANS

1 Janet Watts, *Guardian* (18 April 1974).
2 To the author.
3 Robert Speaight, *William Poel and the Elizabethan Revival* (1954), p. 199.
4 Joseph Hone, *George Moore* (1936), p. 302.
5 Nigel Playfair, *Hammersmith Hoy* (1930), p. 245.
6 J. C. Trewin, *Edith Evans* (1954), p. 49.
7 Ibid., p. 61.
8 Laurence Kitchin, *Mid-Century Drama* (1969), p. 44.
9 Tyrone Guthrie, *A Life in the Theatre* (1960), p. 166.
10 John Gielgud, *Early Stages*, p. 236.
11 In a letter to the author.

12 Lena Ashwell, *Myself a Player* (1936), p. 114.
13 John Gielgud, *The Times* (31 July 1959).

10 PEGGY ASHCROFT

1 John Gielgud, *Early Stages*, p. 174.
2 Harcourt Williams, *Four Years at the Old Vic*, p. 227.
3 Eric Keown, *Peggy Ashcroft* (1955), p. 56.
4 John Gielgud, p. 232.
5 Ronald Hayman, *John Gielgud*, p. 171–2.
6 Eric Keown, p. 85.

BOOKLIST

Adlard, Eleanor (ed.), *Edy. Recollections of Edith Craig* (1949).
Agate, James, *The Amazing Theatre* (1939).
Agate, James, *The Contemporary Theatre 1923, 1924, 1925, 1926* (1924, 1925, 1926, 1927).
Agate, James, *First Nights* (1934).
Agate, James, *More First Nights* (1937).
Archer, William, *The Theatrical World for 1893, 1894, 1895, 1896, 1897* (1894, 1895, 1896, 1897, 1898).
Ashwell, Lena, *Myself a Player* (1936).
Aston, Anthony, *A Brief Supplement to Colley Cibber, Esq.* (1747), *see* Colley Cibber.
Baker, P. H., *Mr Cibber of Drury Lane* (1939).
Bancroft, Squire and Marie, *Mr and Mrs Bancroft on and off the Stage* (1888).
Bartholomeusz, Dennis, *Macbeth and the Players* (1969).
Bax, Clifford, *Pretty Witty Nell* (1932).
Beauvoir, Simone de, *The Second Sex* (1953).
Beerbohm, Max, *Around Theatres* (1953).
Beerbohm, Max, *More Theatres* (1969).
Beerbohm, Max, *Last Theatres* (1970).
Bellamy, George Anne, *An Apology for the Life of George Anne Bellamy* (1785).
Billington, Michael, *The Modern Actor* (1973).
Bleakley, Horace, *Ladies Fair and Frail* (1925).
Boaden, James, *Memoirs of Mrs Siddons* (1827).
Burton, Hal (ed.), *Great Acting* (1965).
Calvert, Walter, *Souvenir of Miss Ellen Terry* (1897).
Campbell, Thomas, *Life of Mrs Campbell* (1834).
Casson, John, *Lewis and Sybil* (1972).
Chetwood, W. R., *A General History of the Stage* (1749).

Churchill, Charles, *The Rosciad* (1767).

Cibber, Colley, *An Apology for the Life of Mr Colley Cibber* (1740), ed. Robert W. Lowe, 'Beaux and Belles' edn. (including Anthony Aston) 2 vols.

Cibber, Susannah, *An Account of the Life of Susannah Maria Cibber* (1887).

Craig, Edward, *Gordon Craig* (1968).

Craig, Gordon, *Ellen Terry and her Secret Self* (1931).

Craig, Gordon, *Index to the Story of My Days* (1957).

Crosse, Gordon, *Shakespeare Playgoing 1890–1952* (1953).

Cunningham, Peter, *The Story of Nell Gwyn*, ed. Gordon Goodwin (1903).

Daly, Augustin, *Woffington: A Tribute* (privately printed, 1888).

Darlington, W. A., *The Actor and his Audience* (1949).

Darlington, W. A., *6001 Nights* (1960).

Davies, Thomas, *Dramatic Miscellanies* (1784).

Davies, Thomas, *Memoirs of the Life of David Garrick* (1808 edn.).

Dent, Alan (ed.), *Bernard Shaw and Mrs Patrick Campbell. Their Correspondence* (1952).

Dent, Alan, *Mrs Patrick Campbell* (1961).

Dibdin, Charles, *A Complete History of the English Stage* (1797–1800).

Dobree, Bonamy, *Restoration Comedy* (1924).

Dobree, Bonamy, *Restoration Tragedy* (1929).

Doran, John, *Their Majesties' Servants* (1897 edn.).

Dunbar, Janet, *Peg Woffington and her World* (1968).

Dusinberre, Juliet, *Shakespeare and the Nature of Women* (1975).

Ervine, St John, *The Theatre in My Time* (1933).

Etherege, Sir George, *Poems of Sir George Etherege*, ed. James Thorpe, (Princeton, N.J., 1963).

Farjeon, Herbert, *The Shakespearean Scene*.

Faucit, Helena, *On Some of Shakespeare's Female Characters* (1897 edn.).

ffrench, Yvonne, *Mrs Siddons, Tragic Actress* (1954 edn.).

Fitzgerald, Percy, *The Life of Mrs Catherine Clive* (1888).

Fitzgerald, Percy, *The Kembles* (1871).

Fyvie, John, *Comedy Queens of the Georgian Era* (1906).

Fyvie, John, *Tragedy Queens of the Georgian Era* (1909).

Galindo, C., *Mrs Galindo's Letter to Mrs Siddons* (1809).

Garrick, David, *The Letters of David Garrick,* ed. David M. Little and George M. Kahrl (1963).

Gegen, Eleanor, *The New Woman. Her Emergence in English Drama 1600–1730* (New York, 1954).

Genest, Revd John, *Some Account of the English Stage* (1832).

Gielgud, John, *Early Stages* (1948 edn.).

Gielgud, John, *Distinguished Company* (1972).

Gilder, Rosamund, *Enter the Actress* (1931).

Gildon, Charles, *The Life of Mr Thomas Betterton* (1710).

Gore-Browne, Robert, *Gay Was the Pit* (1957).

Greene, Graham, *Lord Rochester's Monkey* (1974).

Guthrie, Tyrone, *A Life in the Theatre* (1960).

Ham, R. G., *Otway and Lee* (1931).

Hayman, Ronald, *John Gielgud* (1971).

Hazlitt, William, *Collected Works,* ed. A. C. Waller and Arnold Glover (1903).

Hill, Aaron, with William Popple, *The Prompter,* sel. and ed. William A. Appleton and Kalman A. Burnim (1966).

Hill, John, The Actor (1750).

Hudson, Lynton, *The English Stage 1850–1950* (1951).

Hunt, Hugh, 'Restoration Acting', in *Restoration Theatre* (1965).

Hunt, Leigh, *Dramatic Essays* ed. William Archer and Robert W. Lowe (1894).

Irving, Laurence, *Henry Irving* (1951).

Irving, Laurence, *The Successors* (1967).

Irving, Laurence, *The Precarious Crust* (1971).

James, Henry, *The Scenic Art,* ed. Allan Wade (1949).

Jameson, Anna, *Shakespeare's Heroines. Characteristics of Women, Moral, Poetical and Historical* (1891).

Jenkin, Henry C. F., *Papers Literary, Scientific, etc* (1887).

Jenkin, Henry C. F., *Mrs Siddons as Lady Macbeth and as Mrs Siddons* (1915).

Johns, Eric, *Dames of the Theatre* (1974).

Joseph, Bertram, *The Tragic Actor* (1950).

Kemble, Fanny, *Journal* (1835).

Kemble, Fanny, *Records of a Girlhood* (1879).

Kendal, Madge, *Dramatic Opinions* (1890).

Kendal, Madge, *Dame Madge Kendal. By Herself* (1933).

Kennard, Mrs A., *Mrs Siddons* (1887).

Keown, Eric, *Peggy Ashcroft* (1955).

Knapp, Oswald G., (ed.) *An Artist's Love Story. Told in the Letters of Sir Thomas Lawrence, Mrs Siddons and her Daughters* (1904).

Love, Harold, *Congreve* (1974).

Lucey, Janet Camden, *Lovely Peggy* (1952).

Lynch, Kathleen, *A Congreve Gallery* (Harvard, 1951).

MacQueen-Pope, W., *Ladies First* (1952).

Macready, W. S., *Macready's Reminiscences and Selections from his Diaries and Letters.* ed. Sir Frederick Pollock. (1876 edn.).

Manvell, Roger, *Ellen Terry* (1968).

Manvell, Roger, *Sarah Siddons* (1970).

Martin, Sir Theodore, *Helena Faucit (Lady Martin)* (1890).

Mathews, Brander, (ed.) *Papers on Acting* (1958).

Mathews, Charles James, *The Life of Charles James Mathews,* (1879).

Maynwaring, Arthur, *The Life and Posthumous Works* ed. J. Oldmixon (1715).

Maynwaring, Arthur, *Memoires of the Celebrated Mrs Woffington* (1760).

Nicoll, Allardyce, *A History of the English Drama 1660–1900* (1952 edn.).

Parsons, Mrs Clement, *The Incomparable Siddons* (1909).

Pemberton, T. Edgar, *The Kendals* (1900).

Pemberton, T. Edgar, *Ellen Terry and her Sisters* (1902).

Piozzi, Hester, *The Intimate Letters of Hester Piozzi and Penelope Pennington 1788–1822* ed. Oswald G. Knapp (1914).

Piozzi, Hester, *Thraliana: the Diary of Hester Lynch Thrale* ed. Kathleen Balderston (1951).

Playfair, Nigel, *Hammersmith Hoy* (1930).

Preston, Kerrison, (ed.) *Letters from Graham Robertson* (1953).

Reynolds, Myra, *The Learned Lady in England* (1920).

Robertson, Graham, *Time Was* (1931). *see* Kerrison Preston.

Robins, Elizabeth, *Both Sides of the Curtain* (1940).

Robson, William, *The Old Playgoer* (1846).

Royde-Smith, Naomi, *The Private Life of Mrs Siddons* (1933).

Rowbotham, Sheila, *Women, Resistance and Revolution* (1972).

Russell, Clark, *Representative Actors* (1872).

Shaw, Bernard, *Collected Letters 1898–1910* ed. Dan. H. Laurence (1972).

Shaw, Bernard, *Our Theatre in the Nineties* (1932 edn.).

Shaw, Bernard, *The Quintessence of Ibsenism* (1891).

Shaw, Bernard, *see* Alan Dent and Christopher St John.

St John, Christopher, (ed.) *Ellen Terry and Bernard Shaw. A Correspondence* (1933).

Siddons, Sarah, *The Reminiscences of Sarah Siddons* ed. by William Van Lennep (Cambridge, Mass., 1942).

Speaight, Robert, *Shakespeare on the Stage* (1973).

Speaight, Robert, *William Poel and the Elizabethan Revival* (1954).

Sprigge, Elizabeth, *Sybil Thorndike Casson* (1971).

Steen, Marguerite, *A Pride of Terrys* (1962).

Swears, Herbert, *When All's Said and Done* (1937).

Terry, Ellen, *Ellen Terry's Memoirs* (With Preface, Notes and Additional Autobiographical Chapters by Edith Craig and Christopher St John), (1933).

Terry, Ellen, *Ellen Terry and Bernard Shaw. A Correspondence* ed. by Christopher St John (1931).

Terry, Ellen, *Four Lectures on Shakespeare* (1932).

Thorndike, Russell, *Sybil Thorndike* (1950 edn.).

Trewin, J. C., *Edith Evans* (1954).

Trewin, J. C., *Sybil Thorndike* (1955).

Trewin, J. C., *The Theatre Since 1900* (1951).

Victor, Benjamin, *The History of the Theatres of London and Dublin* (1761).

Victor, Benjamin, *The History of the Theatres of London from 1760 to the Present Time* (1771).

Walkley, A. B., *Frames of Mind* (1899).

Wells, Staring B., (ed.) *A Comparison Between Two Stages* (1942).

Whalley, T. S. *Journals and Correspondence* (1863).

Wickham, Glynne, *Early English Stages* vol. 1 (1959).

Wilkinson, Tate, *Memoirs of his Own Life* (1790).

Wilkinson, Tate, *The Wandering Patentee* (1795).

Williams, Clifford John, *Madame Vestris* (1973).